ANALYTICAL GEOMETRY

For

BA, B.Com., B.Sc., and BSW

By
Vimal Kumar Sharma

Useful For

Delhi University (DU), IGNOU, Berhampur University (Odisha), University of Kashmir, Sambalpur University (Odisha), University of Kalyani (West Bengal), Gurukula Kangri Vishwavidyalaya (Uttarakhand), Himachal Pradesh University, Cooch Behar Panchanan Barma University (West Bengal), Ranchi University, University of Culcutta, Pune University, University of Mumbai, Andhra University, School of Open Learning (DU), Gondwana University (Maharashra), Babasaheb Bhimrao Ambedkar University (Lucknow), Dr. Babasaheb Ambedkar Marathwada University (Aurangabad), University of Madras, Netaji Subhas Open University (Kolkata), Odisha State Open University, all other Indian Universities.

GULLYBABA PUBLISHING HOUSE PVT. LTD.
ISO 9001 & ISO 14001 CERTIFIED CO.

Published by:
GullyBaba Publishing House Pvt. Ltd.

Regd. Office:
2525/193, 1st Floor, Onkar Nagar-A,
Tri Nagar, Delhi-110035
(From Kanhaiya Nagar Metro Station Towards Old Bus Stand)
Ph. 011-27387998, 27384836, 27385249

Branch Office:
1A/2A, 20, Hari Sadan,
Ansari Road, Daryaganj,
New Delhi-110002
Ph. 011-23289034
011-45794768

E-mail: hello@gullybaba.com, Website: GullyBaba.com

New Edition

Price:
Author: GullyBaba.Com Panel
ISBN: 978-81-89086-84-8

Preface

This book is mainly targeted for the exam of Analytical Geometry for all Universities. It has been introduced in market after seeing the huge demand of ready to grasp material for exams with high level of quality, and its un-availability in market. We the GullyBaba Publishing House took a step ahead to publish the quality material focusing on exams at the same time giving you indepth knowledge about the subject.

GPH Book is the pioneer effort that provides a unique methodology so as to perform better in exams. If your goal is to attain higher grade use this powerful study tool independently or along with your text.

On the Web : ***www.gullybaba.com*** *is the vital resource for your exams acting as catalyst to boost up your preparation. Now you can access us on the net through* ***www.doeacconline.com,*** ***www.ignouonline.com,*** ***and*** ***www.astrologyeverywhere.com.***

Feedback about the book can be sent at **mte05writers@gullybaba.com.**

Acknowledgments :

We appreciate the staff and facility support provided by GullyBaba Publishing House. In particular, we appreciate the encouragement and professional advises received from Dr. A. K. Saini, Mr. Maman Kumar Singh, Mrs. Seema Bhatia and many more.

Also we would like to thank Gullybaba team Mrs. Bhawna Verma, Mr. Bal Kishan, Mr. Mohit Garg, Mr. Shravan, Ms. Seema, Mr. Jyoti, Ms. Manorama, Mr. Mukesh, and Mr. Vijay.

We gratefully acknowledges the significant contributions of Mr. Mahesh Chand, Mrs. Bimla Devi, Mrs. Bhawna Verma and our experts in bringing out this publication.

Constructive criticism is always welcome as it will add to our knowledge. You can email at feedback@gullybaba.com.

New Delhi

Topics Covered

Contents

Question Papers

Section A

Analytical Geometry (2D)

Chapter-1

Introduction of coordinate geometry and study of Straight Line

Plane Geometry (Co-ordinate Geometry) : The branch of mathematics in which geometrical problems are solved through algebra by using co-ordinate system, called co-ordinate geometry or analytical geometry or plane geometry.

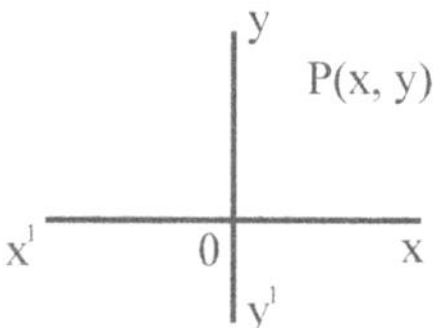

Two perpendicular lines if meets at a point, called co-ordinate axis or rectangular axis and their meeting point is called origin(o). Line xox' is called x-axis and yoy' called y-axis. If a point P(x, y) located in this plane this (x, y) is called co-ordinates of point P where x is called abscissa and y is called ordinate of point P

Sign conventions in plane :

(-, +) (+, +)

(-, -) (+, -)

Distance between two points :

$$d=(PQ)=\sqrt{(x_2-x_1)^2+(y_2-y_1)^2}$$

$P(x_1, y_1)$ $Q(x_2, y_2)$

d

OR

$$d = \sqrt{(x_1 - x_2)^2 + (y_1 - y_2)^2}$$

Division of a line by a point :

Internal Division :

Let R(x,y) divides PQ in m:n ratio

R

m n

P (x, y) Q

(x_1, y_1) (x_2, y_2)

$$R = \left\{ \frac{mx_2 + nx_1}{m+n}, \frac{my_2 + ny_1}{m+n} \right\}$$

External Division:

$$R = \left\{ \frac{mx_2 - nx_1}{m-n}, \frac{my_2 - ny_1}{m-n} \right\}$$

m n

(x, y)

P Q R

(x_1, y_1) (x_2, y_2)

Mid point of a straight line PQ :

$$R = \left(\frac{x_1 + x_2}{2}, \frac{y_1 + y_2}{2} \right)$$

P 1 : 1 Q

(x_1, y_1) (x, y) (x_2, y_2)

Centroid of the Δ ABC :

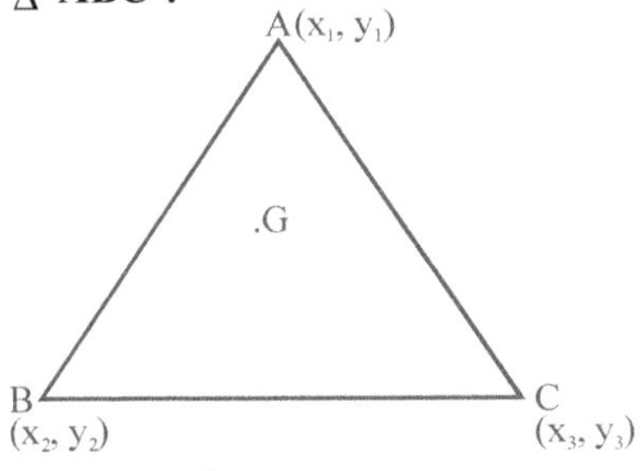

$$G = \left\{ \frac{x_1 + x_2 + x_3}{3}, \frac{y_1 + y_2 + y_3}{3} \right\}$$

Area of triangle : Let A, B, C are vertices of a triangle such that

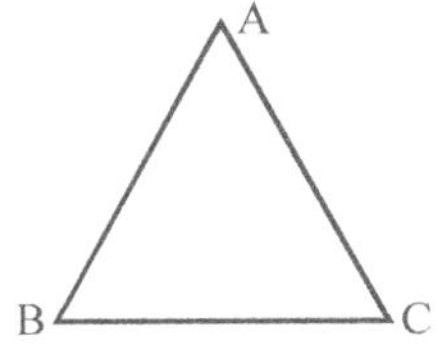

$A = (x_1, y_1), B = (x_2, y_2), C = (x_3, y_3)$
then area (A or Δ) of triangle given by :

$$\Delta = \frac{1}{2}\{x_1(y_2 - y_3) + x_2(y_3 - y_1) + x_3(y_1 - y_2)\}$$

OR

$$\Delta = \frac{1}{2}\{x_1y_2 - x_2y_1 + (x_2y_3 - x_3y_2) + x_3y_1 - x_1y_3)\}$$

OR

$$\Delta = \frac{1}{2}\begin{pmatrix} x_1 & y_1 & 1 \\ x_2 & y_2 & 1 \\ x_3 & y_3 & 1 \end{pmatrix}$$

Special Notes :

1. If 3 points are colliner then $\Delta = 0$ OR Sum of distances between 2 pairs is equal to the distance between the third pair.

2. For a square, four sides and two diagonals are equal.

3. For Rhombus, four sides are equal and two diagonals are not equal.

4. For Rectangle, opposite sides and two diagonals are equal.

5. For parallelogram, opposite sides are equal and diagonals are not equal.

Straight line : Any linear equation may represent a straight line such as : $ax + by + c = 0$ where a,b,c are constant straight line parallel to x-axis is y = a.

Straight line parallel to y axis is x=b.

Slope of a straight line : This is denoted by m.

Let $P = (x_1, y_1)$ and $Q = (x_2, y_2)$

then $m = \dfrac{y_2 - y_1}{x_2 - x_1}$,

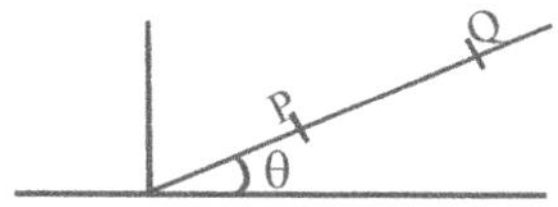

if θ is the inclination of PQ with x-axis then

$m = \tan\theta$

Various forms of straight lines :

(i) In terms of intercepts $\dfrac{x}{a} + \dfrac{y}{b} = 1$

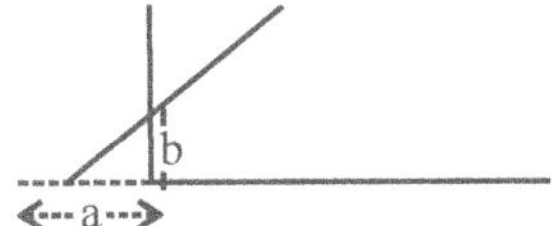

(ii) In terms of slope : $y = mx + c$

(iii) When line passes through two point $P(x_1, y_1)$ and $Q(x_2, y_2)$ then equation to the line PQ is :

$$(y - y_1) = \frac{y_2 - y_1}{x_2 - x_1}(x - x_1)$$

If line passes only one point (x_1, y_1) and has slope m then equation to the straight line is :

$$y - y_1 = m(x - x_1)$$

(iv) In terms of normal form : $x \cos\alpha + y \sin\alpha = p$ where p is the length of perpendicular from origin and α is the inclination of perpendicular with x-axis.

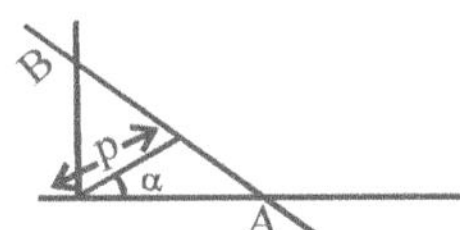

(v) Angle between two straight lines :

$y = m_1 x + c_1$ ... (1)

$y = m_2 x + c_2$ ... (2)

where m_1 and m_2 are slopes of lines and θ_1, θ_2 are angles of line with x-axis. Let φ be the angle between them.

Then, $\tan\varphi = \frac{m_1 \sim m_2}{1 + m_1 m_2}$ where $m_1 = \tan\theta$, $m_2 = \tan\theta_2$

lines are perpendicular if $m_1 m_2 = -1$ and lines are parallel if $m_1 = m_2$

Point of intersection of two straight lines : Let lines are :

$a_1x + b_1y + c_1 = 0$ and

$a_2x + b_2y + c_2 = 0$

then point of intersection is obtained as :

$$\left(\frac{b_1c_2 - b_2c_1}{a_1b_2 - a_2b_1}, \frac{c_1a_2 - a_1c_2}{a_1b_2 - a_2b_1}\right)$$

If lines are parallel then, $a_1b_1 - a_2b_1 = 0$ i.e. $\frac{a_1}{b_2} = \frac{a_2}{b_1}$

Equation of the line through point of intersection of two lines : Let two lines are :

$P \equiv a_1 x + b_1 y + c_1 = 0$ ... (i)

and

$Q \equiv a_2 x + b_2 y + c_2 = 0$ ... (ii)

the equation of line through intersection of above equations is :

$P + \lambda Q = 0$ ... (iii)

Let point of intersection of lines P and Q is (x' , y'). The value of λ will be obtained by passing (iii) through (x',y') and thus will be obtained. The length of perpendicular p from $P(x_1,y_1)$ on a straight line.

Let line is ax + by +c = 0

$$\therefore p = \frac{ax_1 + by_1 + c}{\sqrt{a^2 + b^2}}$$

If p = (0, 0) i.e. origin, then $p = \frac{c}{\sqrt{a^2 + b^2}}$

The equation of the bisector of the angles between two lines : Let lines are :

$a_1x + b_1y + c_1 = 0$
$a_2x + b_2y + c_2 = 0$

Equation of bisectors are given by :

$$\frac{a_1 x + b_1 y + c_1}{\sqrt{a_1^2 + b_1^2}} = \pm \frac{a_2 x + b_2 y + c_2}{\sqrt{a_2^2 + b_2^2}}$$

Condition for concurrency of three lines :

Let lines are :

$a_1x + b_1y + c_1 = 0$
$a_2x + b_2y + c_2 = 0$
$a_3x + b_3y + c_3 = 0$

Condition is :

$$\begin{vmatrix} a_1 & b_1 & c_1 \\ a_2 & b_2 & c_2 \\ a_3 & b_3 & c_3 \end{vmatrix} = 0$$

General Equation of Second degree :

$ax^2 + 2hxy + by^2 + 2gx + 2fy + c = 0$

This will represent pair of straight lines if g = 0 = f

i.e. $\therefore ax^2 + 2hy + by^2 + c = 0$ will represent equation to the pair of straight line.

Let pair of straight line passes through origin, then c = 0

$\therefore ax^2 + 2hxy + by^2 = 0$

angle between lines is given by : $\tan \theta = \frac{2\sqrt{h^2 - ab}}{a + b}$

lines are perpendicular if a+b = 0 and are parallel if $h^2 = ab$

Equation of bisector of angle between pair of straight lines is given by :

$$\frac{x^2 - y^2}{a - b} = \frac{xy}{h}$$

Co-ordinate axis: When two mutually perpendicular lines meets at a point, called areas. The horizontal line referred as x-axis and vertical line as y-axis. Their meeting point is termed as origin.

Sign conventions

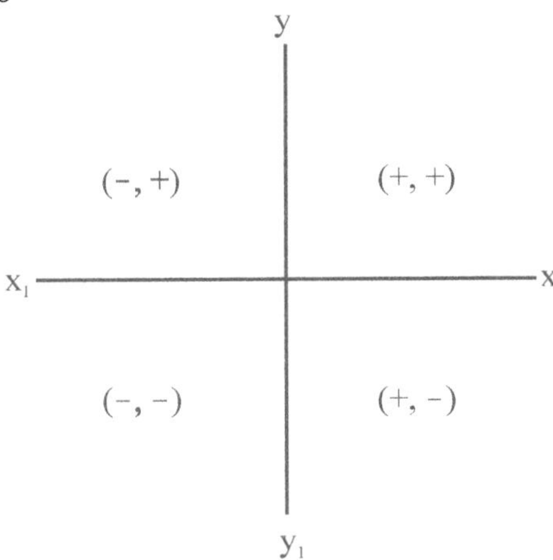

General Equation of Straight line

$ax + by + c = 0$ ... (1)

Line parallel to it is written as

$ax + by + \lambda = 0$ ... (2)

and line perpendicular to (1) is written as

$bx - ay + \lambda = 0$ ... (3)

the value of λ is obtained by passing (2) or (3) through given point.

Transformation of Axis

Transformation of axis may be done by 3 ways

(i) By change of origin

(ii) By rotation of axes

(iii) By shifting origin to another place and rotating axis by some angle.

Transformation of axis by change of origin

Let ox, oy are original axis. At (h, k), o^1x, o^1y are new axes parallel to old axes. Co-ordinate of any point P are P(x, y) and P(X, Y) in old and new axis respectively.

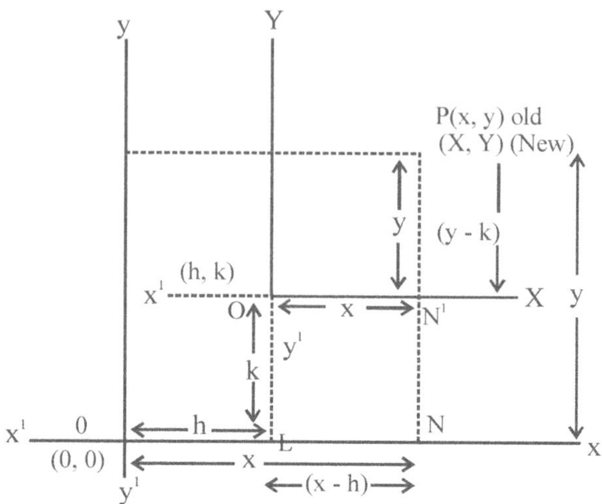

From figure we see that

$$\boxed{\begin{array}{l} X = x - h \\ Y = y - k \end{array}}$$

Both are equations of transformed axis

Rotation of axis

In this situation axis rotates by some angle (let θ) but origin remains fix x See figure

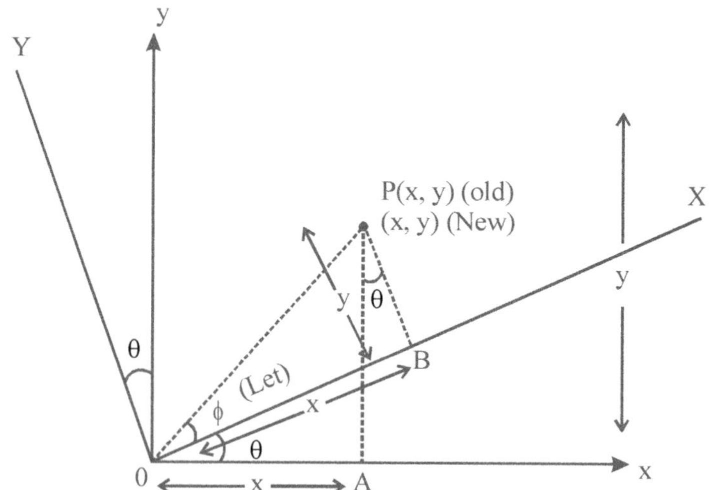

ox, oy old axis.
OX, OY new axis.
Rotation angle $= \theta$

In ΔOAP, $\cos(\theta + f) = \dfrac{OA}{OP}$

$\therefore OA = OP\cos(\theta + f)$

$OP = x = OP\cos(\theta + f) = OP\cos\theta\cos f - OP\sin\theta\sin f$ ... (1)

$\sin(\theta + f) = \dfrac{AP}{OP}$,

$AP = y = OP\sin(\theta + f)$

$y = OP\sin\theta\cos f + OP\cos\theta\sin f$ ... (2)

In ΔOPB,

$\cos f = \dfrac{OB}{OP}$ $\quad \therefore OB = OP\cos f = X$

$\therefore\ x = OP\cos f$ put in (1) and (2)

$\sin f = \dfrac{PB}{OP}$ $\quad PB = y = OP\sin f$

We get, $x = X\cos\theta - y\sin\theta$
$y = X\sin\sigma + Y\cos\sigma$
or

$X = x\cos\sigma + y\sin\sigma$ $Y = -x\sin\sigma + y\cos\sigma$	Equations of transformed axes.

Shifting of origin and rotation of axis

If both changes occurs simultaneously then we put $h + X\cos\theta - Y\sin\theta$ and $h + X\sin\theta + Y\cos\theta$ in place of x and y respectively.

Polar co-ordinate

Co-ordinate of a point in (r, θ) is referred as polar co-ordinate.

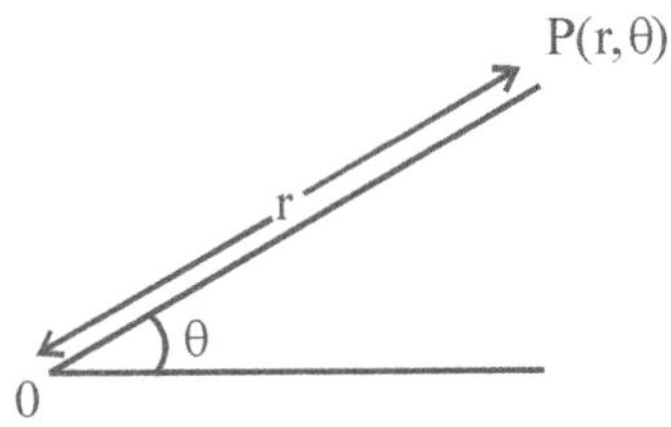

SOLVED EXAMPLES

Q1. What are the equation of the coordinate axes?
Ans. The x and y-axis are y = 0 and x = 0, respectively.

Q2. Check if the triangle PQR, where P, Q and R are represented by (1, 0), (–2, 3) and (1, 3), is an equilateral triangle.

Ans. PQ = $\sqrt{\{1-(-2)\}^2+(0-3)^2}=\sqrt{18}$

QR = $\sqrt{(-2-1)^2+(3-3)^2}=3$

PR = $\sqrt{(1-1)^2+(0-3)^2}=3$

Thus, the sides of the triangle are not equal in length.
Hence, Δ PQR is not equilateral.

Q3. What is the distance of
(a) y = mx + c from (0, 0)?
(b) x cos α + y sin α = p from (cos α, sin α a) ?

Ans. (a) $d=\left|\frac{m.0 - 0 + c}{\sqrt{m^2+1}}\right|=\frac{c}{\sqrt{m^2+1}}$

(b) $d=\frac{\cos^2\alpha+\sin^2\alpha-p}{\sqrt{\cos^2\alpha+\sin^2\alpha}}$

$=\frac{1-p}{\sqrt{1}}$

$=\frac{1-p}{1}$

$=1-p$

Q4. Find the equation of the line parallel to y + x + 1 = 0 and passing through (0, 0).
Ans. Any line parallel to y + x + 1 = 0 is of the form y + x + λ = 0, Since (0, 0) lies on it, 0 + 0 + λ = 0, that is, λ = 0.
Thus, the required line is y + x = 0.

Q5. Which axis is the curve $y^2 = 2x$ symmetric about? Is it symmetric about the origin?

Ans. If we replace y by (–y) in the given equation, it remains unchanged. Thus, the curve is symmetric about the x-axis. If we replace x by (–x), the curve changes to $y^2 = -2x$. Thus, it is not symmetric about the y-axis.

If we replace x by (–x) and y by (–y), in the equation, it changes to $y^2 = -2x$. Thus, it is not symmetric about the origin.

Q6. Discuss the symmetries of the line y = 2.

Ans. It is not symmetric about either axis or the origin.

Q7. Transform the quadratic equation $5x^2 + 3y^2 + 20x - 12y + 17 = 0$ to parallel axes

(a) through the point (–2, 2), and

(b) through the point (1, 1).

Ans. (a) If the new coordinates are x' and y', then $x = x' - 2$, $y = y' + 2$.

Thus, the equation becomes

$5(x'-2)^2 + 3(y'+2)^2 + 20(x'-2) - 12(y'+2) + 17 = 0$

$= 5x'^2 + 3y'^2 - 15 = 0$

$= \frac{x'^2}{3} + \frac{y'^2}{5} = 1.$

(b) The equation becomes

$5(x'+1)^2 + 3(y'+1)^2 + 20(x'+1) - 12(y'+1) + 17 = 0$

$= 5x'^2 + 3y'^2 + 30x' - 6y' + 33 = 0.$

Q8. Suppose the origin is shifted to (–2, 1) and the rectangular Cartesian axes are rotated through 45°. Find the resultant transformation of the equation $x^2 + y^2 + 4x - 2y + 4 = 0$.

Ans. By shifting the origin, the new coordinates x' and y' are related to x and y by

$x = x' - 2$, $y = y' + 1$.

Thus, the equation becomes

$(x' - 2)^2 + (y' + 1)^2 + 4(x' - 2) - 2(y' + 1) + 4 = 0$

$= x'^2 + y'^2 = 1$ ... (1)

Now, rotating the axes through 45°, we get new coordinates x and y given by,

$x' = \frac{X - Y}{\sqrt{2}}$ and $y' = \frac{X + Y}{\sqrt{2}}$

Thus, (1) becomes

$$\left(\frac{X - Y}{\sqrt{2}}\right)^2 + \left(\frac{X + Y}{\sqrt{2}}\right)^2 = 1$$

$= X^2 - 2XY + Y^2 + X^2 + 2XY + Y^2 = 2.$

$= X^2 + Y^2 = 1$

Q9. Show that the polar equation of the line AB in Fig. is r cos $(\theta - \alpha) =$ p.

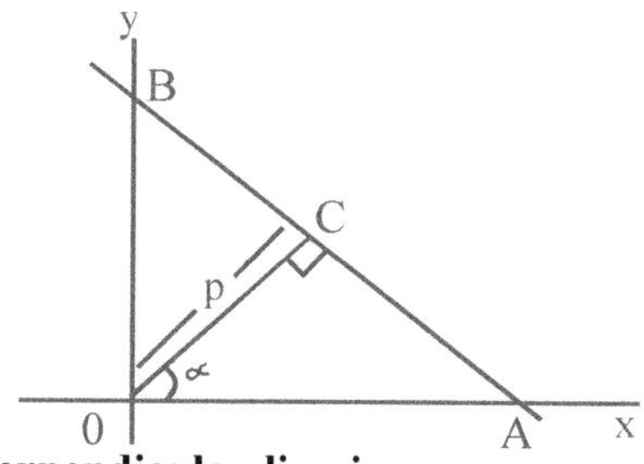

Ans. Equation of perpendicular line is:

$x \cos \alpha + y \sin \alpha = p$ ... (1)

Let x = r cos θ put in (i)

y = r sin θ

So r = $\sqrt{x^2 + y^2}$

$\theta = \tan^{-1} \frac{y}{x}$

r cos θ cos α + r sin θ sin α = p

r (cos θ cos α – sin θ sin α) = p

$$\boxed{r \cos(\theta - \alpha) = p}$$

Q10. Find the condition that the point (x, y) may lie on the line joining points (3, 4) and (–5, –6).

Ans. A = (x, y) B = (3, 4), C = (–5, –6) and point A, B and C lies on a straight line, the Δ =0

$$\Rightarrow \frac{1}{2}\left[x(4+6) + 3(-6-y) + (-5)(y-4)\right] = 0$$

$\frac{1}{2} \neq 0, 10x - 8y + 2 = 0$

$\Rightarrow 5x - 4y + 1 = 0$ which is required condition.

Q11. If p be the length of the perpendicular from origin to the line whose intercepts on the x and y axis are a and b respectively, then show that $\mathbf{\frac{1}{p^2} = \frac{1}{a^2} + \frac{1}{b^2}}$

Ans. Let equation to straight line in term of intercepts is :

$$\frac{x}{a} + \frac{y}{b} = 1 \text{ or } \frac{1}{a}x + \frac{1}{b}y - 1 = 0$$

$$P = (0, 0)$$

$$\therefore p = \frac{\frac{1}{a} \times o + \frac{1}{b} \times o - 1}{\sqrt{\frac{1}{a^2} + \frac{1}{b^2}}} = \frac{-1}{\sqrt{\frac{1}{a^2} + \frac{1}{b^2}}}$$

$$\therefore p^2 = \frac{1}{\frac{1}{a^2} + \frac{1}{b^2}} = \frac{a^2 b^2}{a^2 + b^2}$$

$$\therefore \frac{1}{p^2} = \frac{a^2 + b^2}{a^2 b^2} = \frac{a^2}{a^2 b^2} + \frac{b^2}{a^2 b^2} = \frac{1}{a^2} + \frac{1}{b^2}$$

$$\therefore \frac{1}{p^2} = \frac{1}{a^2} + \frac{1}{b^2} \text{ Showed}$$

Q12. If lines $\mathbf{y = m_1 x + a_1}$, $\mathbf{y = m_2 x + a_2}$ and $\mathbf{y = m_3 x + a_3}$ meet in a point, then prove that $\mathbf{m_1(a_2 - a_3) + m_2(a_3 - a_1) + m_3(a_1 - a_2) = 0}$

Ans. : Lines are :

$y = m_1 x + a_1$ ... (i)

$y = m_2 x + a_2$ ... (ii)

$y = m_3 x + a_3$ ... (iii)

from (i) and (ii)

$m_1 x + a_1 = m_2 x + a_2$

$(m_1 - m_2)\, x = a_2 - a_1$

$x = \frac{a_2 - a_1}{m_1 - m_2}$ put in (i)

$$y = \left(\frac{a_2 - a_1}{m_1 - m_2}\right)m_1 + a_1 = \frac{m_1 a_2 - m_2 a_1}{m_1 - m_2}$$

$\therefore$ point of intersection of lines (i) and (ii) is :

$$\left(\frac{a_2 - a_1}{m_1 - m_2}, \frac{m_1 a_2 - m_2 a_1}{m_1 - m_2}\right)$$

If three lines are concurrent, then above point will satisfy equation (iii), from (iii)

$$\left(\frac{m_1 a_2 - m_2 a_1}{m_1 - m_2}\right) = m_3\left(\frac{a_2 - a_1}{m_1 - m_2}\right) + a_3$$

$$m_3(a_2 - a_1) - (m_1 a_2 - m_2 a_1) + a_3(m_1 - m_2) = 0$$

$$-m_1(a_2 - a_3) - m_2(a_3 - a_1) - m_3(a_2 - a_1) = 0$$

or

$m_1(a_2 - a_3) + m_2(a_3 - a_1) + m_3(a_2 - a_1) = 0$, hence proved.

Q13. Find the area of the Δ formed by the lines y-x = 0, x+y = 0 and x-k = 0 ?

Ans.

$y - x = 0$ ... (i)

$x + y = 0$ ... (ii)

$x - k = 0$ ... (iii)

on solving lines (i)(ii), (ii)(iii) and (iii)(i) pair-wise we will find pointsA (k, -k), B(k, k), C(0, 0) .

$\therefore$ Area of Δ ABC $= \frac{1}{2}\left[\left(k^2 + k^2\right) + (0-0) + (0-0)\right]$

$= k^2$ Square units

Q14. Which of the following statements are true. Justify your answer with a valid reason. **[June98, Q1(a)]**

(a) The equation

$7x^2 + 60xy + 32y^2 - 14x - 60y + 7 = 0$

represents a pair of straight lines.

Ans. True

The given equation is

$7x^2 + 60xy + 32y^2 - 14x - 60y + 7 = 0$

Here

$a = 7$, $h = 30$, $b = 32$, $g = -7$, $f = -30$, $c = 7$

Now

$$\begin{vmatrix} a & h & g \\ h & b & f \\ g & f & c \end{vmatrix} = \begin{vmatrix} 7 & 30 & -7 \\ 30 & 32 & -30 \\ -7 & -30 & 7 \end{vmatrix}$$

$$= \begin{vmatrix} 0 & 30 & -7 \\ 0 & 32 & -30 \\ 0 & 30 & 7 \end{vmatrix} \quad C_1 \leftarrow C_1 + C_3$$

= 0 Thus it represent pair of straight lines.

(b) A pair of straight lines is a conic section. **[Dec98, Q1(a)]**
Ans. True,
The general second degree equation $ax^2 + 2hxy + by^2 + 2gx + 2fy + c = 0$, represents a conic. It is a pair of straight line if

$$\begin{vmatrix} a & h & g \\ h & b & f \\ g & f & c \end{vmatrix} = 0$$

If the condition is satisfied, then the angle between the lines is

$$\tan^{-1}\left(\frac{2\sqrt{h^2 - ab}}{a + b}\right)$$

(c) Under a rotation of the axes, a curve which is symmetric about the x-axis does not remain symmetric about the new x-axis. [June99, Q1(iv)]
Ans. True
The rotation of axes is a rigid body motion. Thus shape of curve does not change. If curve is symmetric about the x-axis does not symmetric about the new axis.

(d) 2x + 3y = 9 represents a line in 3-dimensional space.[Dec99, Q1(c)]
Ans. False,
The given equation $2x + 3y = 9$ represents two dimensional space because it covers only x-axis and y-axis.

(e) The eccentricity of a pair of straight lines is less than 1.
[Dec99, Q1(e)]

Ans. False

Because when eccentricity e = 1 it is parabola.

(f) The equation $x^2 + 3xy + y^2 = 0$ represents a pair of real straight lines. [Dec01, Q1(b)]

Ans. False,

Here

a = 1, b = 1, h = 3/2

$$ab - h^2 = 1.1 - \left(\frac{3}{2}\right)^2$$

$$= 1 - \frac{9}{4}$$

$$= \frac{-5}{4} < 0$$

It represents a hyperbola.

(g) Under a rotation of the coordinate axes through 30°, the slope of the line y = x – 1 does not change. [June03, Q1(a)]

Ans. False,

The given equation is

Y = X – 1, Slope = 1

Now $X = X' \cos\theta - Y' \sin\theta$

$= X' \cos 30° - Y' \sin 30°$

$$= \frac{\sqrt{3}X'}{2} - \frac{Y'}{2}$$

$Y = X' \sin\theta - Y' \cos\theta$

$= X' \sin 30 + Y' \cos 30$

$$= \frac{X'}{2} + \frac{\sqrt{3}Y'}{2}$$

Now given equation is

$$\frac{X'}{2} + \frac{\sqrt{3}Y'}{2} = \frac{\sqrt{3}X'}{2} - \frac{Y'}{2} - 1$$

$$\Rightarrow \frac{\sqrt{3}Y'}{2} + \frac{Y'}{2} = \frac{\sqrt{3}X'}{2} - \frac{X'}{2} - 1$$

$$\Rightarrow Y'\left(\frac{\sqrt{3}}{2}+\frac{1}{2}\right)=\left(\frac{\sqrt{3}}{2}+\frac{1}{2}\right)X'-1$$

$$\Rightarrow \left(\frac{\sqrt{3}+1}{2}\right)Y'=\frac{\sqrt{3}-1}{2}X'-1$$

After rotation slope of equation $=\frac{\sqrt{3}-1}{2}$

Q15. Find the equation of a line perpendicular to the line $2y + x + 1 = 0$ and passing through (2, –1). **[June04, Q1(a)]**

Ans. Given line is $2y + x + 1 = 0$ or $x + 2y + 1 = 0$ ... (1)

Equation of line perpendicular to (1) is

$2x - y + \lambda = 0$ ... (2)

which passes through (2, -1)

$2\times 2 - (-1) + \lambda = 0$

$4 + 1 + d = 0$ $\quad\because \lambda = -5$ put in (2)

$2x - y - 5 = 0$ required line

Q16. Give an example, with justification, of a curve which is symmetric with respect to the line y = x but not symmetric with respect to either of the coordinate axes. **[June03, Q4(b)]**

Ans. The line in Fig given below is symmetric about the origin but not symmetric about any other axis.

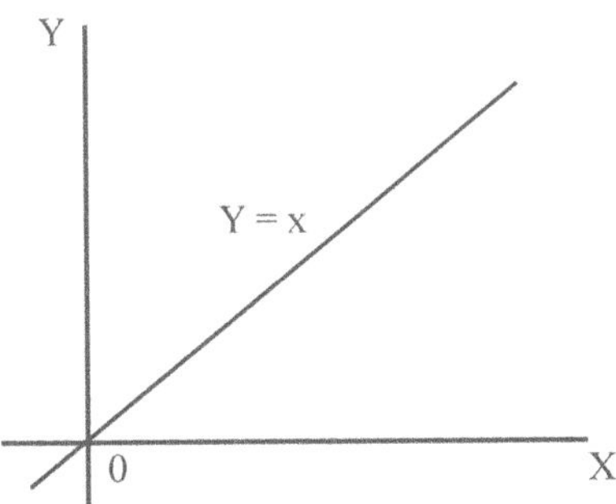

Geometrically, if a curve is symmetric about the x-axis, it means that portion of the curve below the x-axis is the mirror image of the portion above the x-axis. A similar visual interpretation is true for symmetry about the y-axis. And what does symmetry about the origin mean geometrically. It means that the mirror of the portion of the curve in the first quadrant is the position in the third quadrant and the mirror image of the portion in the seconquadrant is the portion in the fourth quadrant.

Q17. Find the transformed equation of the curve $x^2 + y^2 - 6x + 2y + 1 = 0$ after shifting the origin to (3, -1) and rotating the axes through 30°. [June00, Q4(b)]

Ans. The given equation is

$x^2 + y^2 - 6x + 2y + 1 = 0$ ... (1)

By shifting the origin, the new coordinates x' and y' are related to x and y by

$x = x' + 3, y = y' - 1$

Thus equation becomes

$(x' + 3)^2 + (y' - 1)^2 - 6(x' + 3) + 2(y' - 1) + 1 = 0$

$\Rightarrow x'^2 + 6x' + 9 + y'^2 - 2y' + 1 - 6x' - 18 + 2y' - 2 + 1 = 0$

$\Rightarrow x'^2 + y'^2 - 9 = 0$ ... (2)

Now, rotating the axis through 30° we get new coordinates

$x' = x \cos\theta + y \sin\theta$

$= x \cos 30° + y \sin 30°$

$$= \frac{\sqrt{3}x}{2} + \frac{y}{2}$$

$y' = x \sin 30° + y \cos 30°$

$$= \frac{-x}{2} + \frac{\sqrt{3}}{2}y$$

Thus (2) becomes

$$\left(\frac{\sqrt{3}x + y}{2}\right)^2 + \left(\frac{-x + \sqrt{3}y}{2}\right)^2 - 9 = 0$$

$\Rightarrow 3x^2 + xy\, 2\sqrt{3} + y^2 + x^2 - 2\sqrt{3}\, xy + 3y^2 - 18 = 0$

$\Rightarrow 4x^2 + 4y^2 - 18 = 0$

$\Rightarrow 2x^2 + 2y^2 - 9 = 0$

$\Rightarrow x^2 + y^2 = 9/2$

Q18. Write the equation of the pair of straight lines through the points of intersection of $4x^2 + 9y^2 = 36$ and $4xy = 9 + 2x$. [June00, Q4(b)]

Ans. The given lines are

$4x^2 + 9y^2 = 36$ ... (i)

$4xy = 9 + 2x$ ... (ii)

Hence $4x^2 + 9y^2 - 36 = 0$

$2x + 9 - 4xy = 0$

Equation of pair of straight line is

$(4x^2 + 9y^2 - 36)(2x + 9 - 4xy) = 0$

Q19. Find the new equation obtained from $x^2 + y^2 + 4y - 2y + 4 = 0$ after shifting the origin to (–2, 1) and then rotating the axes through 45°.

[June00, Q2(b)]

Ans. By shifting the origin, the new coordinates x' and y' are related to x and y by

$x = x' - 2; \qquad y = y' + 1$

Thus the equation becomes,

$(x' - 2)^2 + (y' + 1)^2 + 4(x' - 2) - 2(y' + 1) + 4 = 0$

$x'^2 - 4x' + 4 + y'^2 + 2y' + 1 + 4x' - 8 - 2y' - 2 + 4 = 0$

$\Rightarrow x'^2 + y'^2 - 1 = 0$

$\Rightarrow x'^2 + y'^2 = 1$ ... (1)

Now, rotating the axes through 45°, we get new coordinates x and y given by,

$x' = \dfrac{x - y}{\sqrt{2}}$ and $y' = \dfrac{x + y}{\sqrt{2}}$

Thus equation (1), becomes

$\Rightarrow x'^2 + 2xy + y^2 + x^2 + 2xy + y^2 = 2$

$\Rightarrow x^2 + y^2 = 1$

Q20. Find the value of k, such that [Dec99, Q3(a)]

(i) $4x^2 - 15xy + ky^2 = 0$ represents a pair of perpendicular lines.

(ii) $3x^2 - 4kxy + 5y^2 = 0$ represents a pair of coincident lines.

Ans. If θ the angle between the lines then

$$\tan\theta = \frac{\pm 2\sqrt{h^2 - ab}}{a + b} \qquad \text{... (1)}$$

If the lines are perpendicular then

$\theta = 90°$

$\therefore a + b = 0$

$\Rightarrow a + b = 0$

(i) The given equation is

$4x^2 - 15xy + ky^2 = 0$

$\therefore a = 4,\ h = \dfrac{15}{2}$, and $b = k$

$\therefore 4 + k = 0$

$\Rightarrow k = -4$

(ii) The given equation is

$3x^2 - 4kxy + 5y^2 = 0$

$\therefore\ a = 3,\ h = -2k,\ b = 5$

If line is parallel (or coincident)

then $\theta = 0$ $\quad\quad \therefore\ \tan\theta = 0$ $\quad\quad \therefore\ h^2 = ab$

$\therefore (-2k)^2 = 3$

$\Rightarrow 4k^2 = 15$

$$\Rightarrow k = \frac{\sqrt{15}}{4} = \frac{\sqrt{15}}{2}$$

Q21. If at one origin, co-ordinate of a point are (x, y) and (x^1, y^1). And if ux + vy is a relation and its transform form is $u^1x + v^1y$ then prove that $u'^1 + v'^2 = u^2 + v^2$ where u and v are in dependent variables.

Ans. Let angle between original and transformed axes is θ .

Then $x = x^1 \cos\theta - y^1 \sin\theta$

$y = x^1 \sin\theta + y^1 \cos\theta$

then $ux + vy = u\,(x^1 \cos\theta - y^1 \sin\theta) + v\,(x^1 \sin\theta + y^1 \cos\theta)$

$ux + vy = x^1 (u \cos\theta + v \sin\theta) + y^1 (v \cos\theta - u \sin\theta)$

$\because ux + vy$ is transformed to $ux^1 + vy^1$

$\because\ ux + vy = u^1x^1 + v^1y^1$

$\because\ u' = u \cos\theta + v \sin\theta$

$\because v' = v \cos\theta - u \sin\theta$

On Squaring and adding we get

$u'^2 + v'^2 = u^2 \cos^2\theta + v^2 \sin^2\theta + 2uv \sin\theta \cos\theta + v^2 \cos^2\theta + u^2 \sin^2\theta - 2uv$
$\sin\theta\ \cos\theta$

$= (u^2 + v^2) \cos^2\theta + (u^2 + v^2) \sin^2\theta$

$= (u^2 + v^2) (\cos^2\theta + \sin^2\theta)$

$= u^2 + v^2$

Chapter-2

Standard Conics

(General Theory of Conics and Standard Conics)

General Equation to the conic is given by :

$F(x,y) \equiv ax^2 + 2hxy + by^2 + 2gx + 2fy + c = 0$............(1)

Equation (1) represents different conics on different conditions :

(i) $\Delta \neq 0, a = b, h = 0$ *then* (1) *will be a circle i.e.* $ax^2 + ay^2 + 2gx + 2fy + c = 0$

$\Rightarrow x^2 + y^2 + \left(\frac{2g}{a}\right)x + \frac{2f}{b}y + \frac{c}{a} = 0$

(ii) $\Delta \neq 0$, $h^2 = ab$ then (1) will be a parabola.

(iii) $\Delta \neq 0$, $h^2 < ab$ then (1) will be an ellipse

(iv) $\Delta \neq 0$, $h^2 > ab$ then (1) will be a hyperbola

(v) $\Delta \neq 0$, $h^2 > ab$ and $a+b=0$ then (1) will be a rectangular hyperbola

(vi) $\Delta = 0$, $ab - h^2 \neq 0$ then (1) will be pair of intersecting lines.

(vii) $\Delta = 0$, $ab - h^2 = 0$ then (1) will be pair of parallel lines.

(viii) $\Delta = 0$, $a+b=0$, then (1) will be pair of perpendicular lines.

where $\Delta = \begin{vmatrix} a & h & g \\ h & b & f \\ g & f & c \end{vmatrix} = abc + 2fgh - af^2 - bg^2 - ch^2$

Equation of tangent to the conic (1) is :

$T \equiv axx_1 + h(xy_1 + yx_1) + g(x + x_1) + f(y + y_1) + c = 0$, where (x_1, y_1) be the point of contact.

Condition of tangency for conic (1) :

$F(x, y) \equiv ax^2 + by^2 + 2hxy + 2gx + 2fy + c = 0$ ... (1)

$T \equiv axx_1 + h(xy_1 + yx_1) + g(x + x_1) + f(y + y_1) + c = 0$ ... (2)

and $lx+my+n = 0$ ....(3) be any line then required condition is :

$$\begin{vmatrix} a & h & g & l \\ h & b & f & m \\ g & f & c & n \\ l & m & n & 0 \end{vmatrix} = 0$$

CONIC : A conic with eccentricty (e) is called :

(i) a parabola if $e = 1$

(ii) an ellipse if $e < 1$

(iii) a hyperbola if $e > 1$

where e is a positive real number, which is always greater than zero i.e. $e > 0$.

Parabola : Let '' be a fixed line and F be a fixed point (not on). Let P be any point in the plane of line and the point F. Let M be the foot of perpendicular from P on the line 'l'. Then the set of all points P such that PF = PM, is called Parabola.

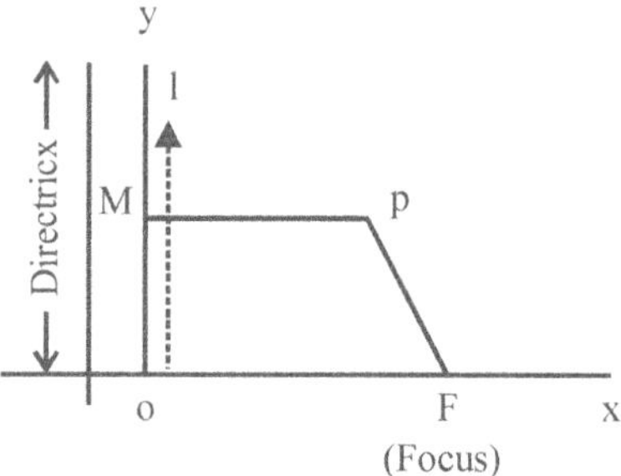

Standard Equation of Parabola : $y^2 = 4ax$ where 4a is called Latus Rectum.

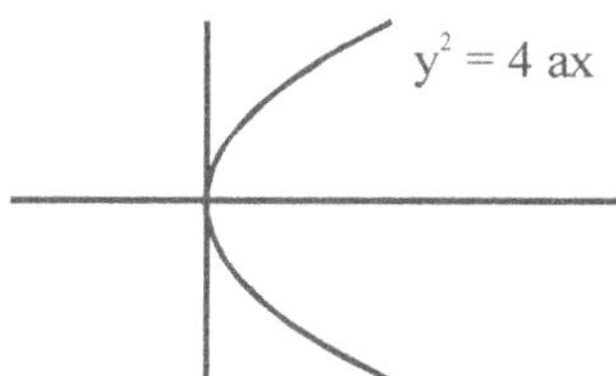

Other forms of parabola : $x^2=4ay$, $y^2 = -4ax$ and $x^2 = -4ay$

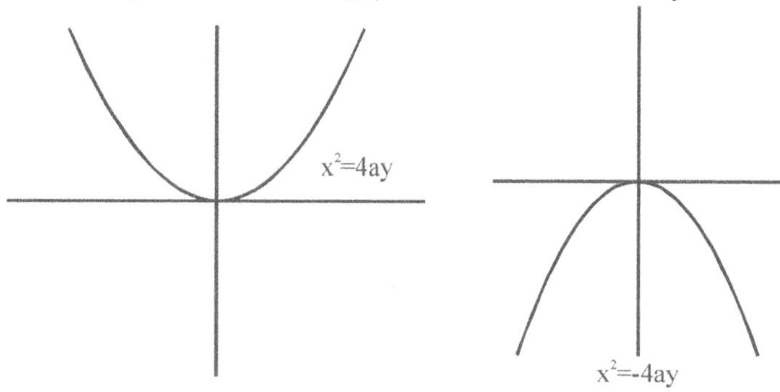

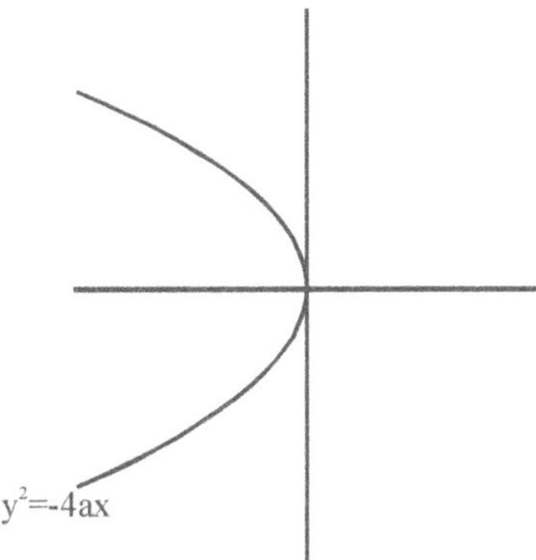

Table for all types of parabola :

Equation	$y^2 = 4ax$ (a>0)	$y^2 = -4ax$ (a>0)	$x^2 = 4ay$ (a>0)	$x^2 = -4ay$ (a>0)
Vertex	(0, 0)	(0, 0)	(0, 0)	(0, 0)
Focus	(a, 0)	(-a, 0)	(0, a)	(0, - a)
Directrix	x + a = 0	x - a = 0	y + a = 0	y - a = 0
Axis	y =0	y =0	x = 0	x = 0
Latus Rectum	4a	4a	4a	4a

General Equation of parabola or Mathematical definition of parabola

Let P(x, y) be a variable point and lx + my + n = 0 is a fixed line, and S(h, k) be fixed point.

$$PS = \sqrt{(x-h)^2 + (y-k)^2}$$

$$PM = \frac{\ell x + my + m}{\sqrt{\ell^2 + m^2}}$$

$$\because \frac{PS}{PM} = e = 1$$

$$\therefore PS = PM$$

$$\sqrt{(x-h)^2 + (y-k)^2} = \frac{\ell m + my + n}{\sqrt{\ell^2 + m^2}}$$

Squraring on both sides

$$(x-y)^2+(y-k)^2=\frac{(\ell x+my+n)^2}{\ell^2+m^2}$$

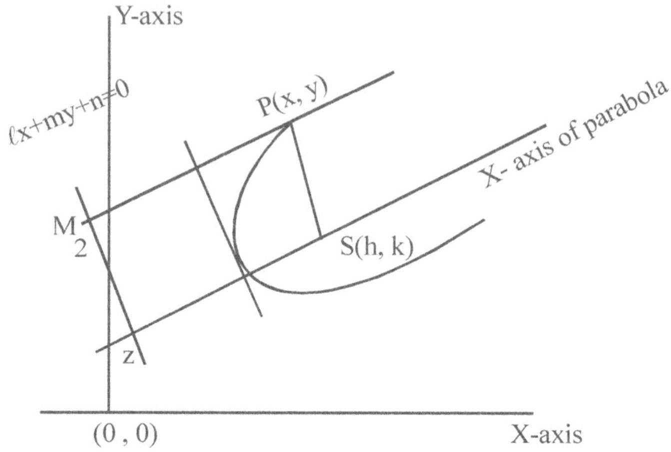

$$\therefore\ (\ell^2+m^2)\left\{(x-y)^2+(y-k)^2\right\}=(\ell x+my+n)^2$$

On solving we get

$(mx-\ell y)^2=-2(gx+fy)-c$ which is standard equation to the parabola where

$$g=2\left\{h(\ell^2+m^2)+\ell m\right\},\ f=-k\left\{(\ell^2+m^2)+mn\right\}$$

$$\&\ \ c=(\ell^2+m^2)(h^2+k^2)-n^2$$

Ellipse

Ellipse is a locus of that point which moves such that ratio of distances of from a fixed point to the fixed line is always remains constt which is smaller than 1, this constt is called eccentricity and denoted by e.

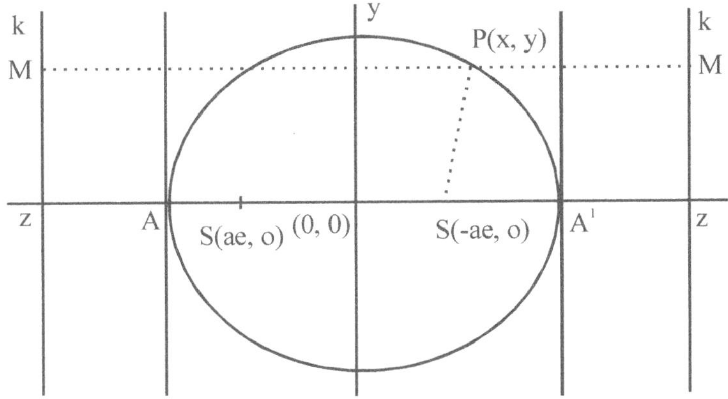

Equation of Ellipse

$$\frac{x^2}{d^2}+\frac{y^2}{b^2}=1$$

Table for Ellipse :

Equation	$\frac{x^2}{a^2}+\frac{y^2}{b^2}=1$	$\frac{x^2}{b^2}+\frac{y^2}{a^2}=1$
Centre	(0, 0)	(0, 0)
Equation of major axis	y = 0	x = 0
Equation of minor axis	x = 0	y=0
Length of major axis	2a	2b
Length of minor axis	2b	2a
Focii	$(\pm$ ae, 0)	(0, $\pm$ae)
Vertices	$(\pm$ a, 0)	(0, $\pm$a)
Directrices	x = $\pm$a/e	y = $\pm$a/e
Length of Latus Rectum	$\frac{2b^2}{a}$	$\frac{2b^2}{a}$

General Equation of Ellipse:

Let focus (fixed point) be S(h, k) and equation of directix is lx + my + n = 0 and e be the eccentricity.

Then $PS^2 = (x - h)^2 + (y - k)^2$

$$PM_1 = \frac{lx + my + n}{\sqrt{l^2 + m^2}}$$

$$PM^2 = \frac{(lx + my + n)^2}{l^2 + m^2}$$

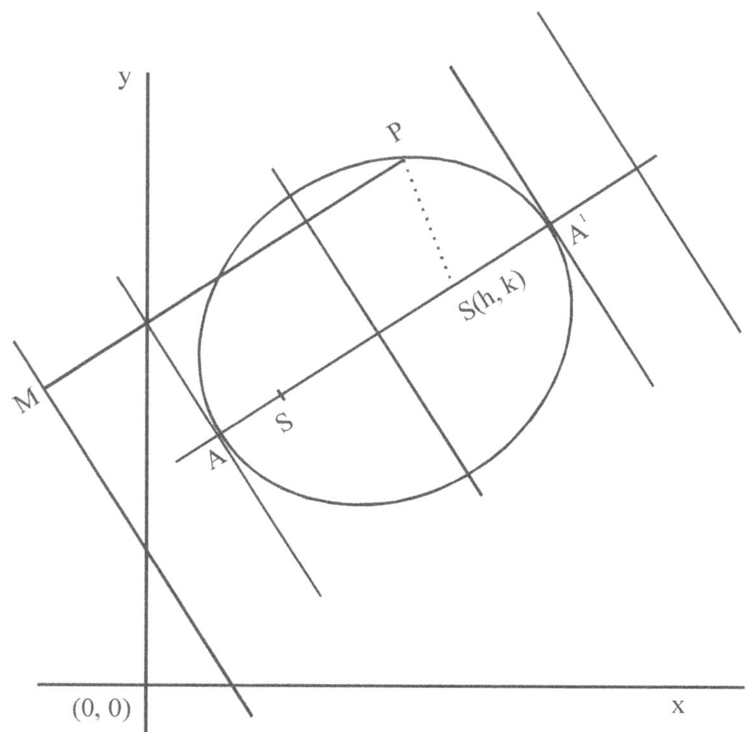

$$\because \frac{PS}{PM} = e$$

$$\therefore \frac{(PS)^2}{(PM)^2} = e^2$$

$$\therefore (PS)^2 = e^2 (PM)^2$$

$$\boxed{(x-h)^2 + (y-k)^2 = e^2 \frac{(lx + my + n)^2}{l^2 + m^2}}$$

Which is general equation of ellipse

Hyperbola

Definition : It is a locus of a point which moves such a way that ratio of distances from a fixed point and to the fixed to line, is always a constt (e) and e > 1.

Equation of Hyperbola

$$\frac{x^2}{a^2} - \frac{y^2}{b^2} = 1$$

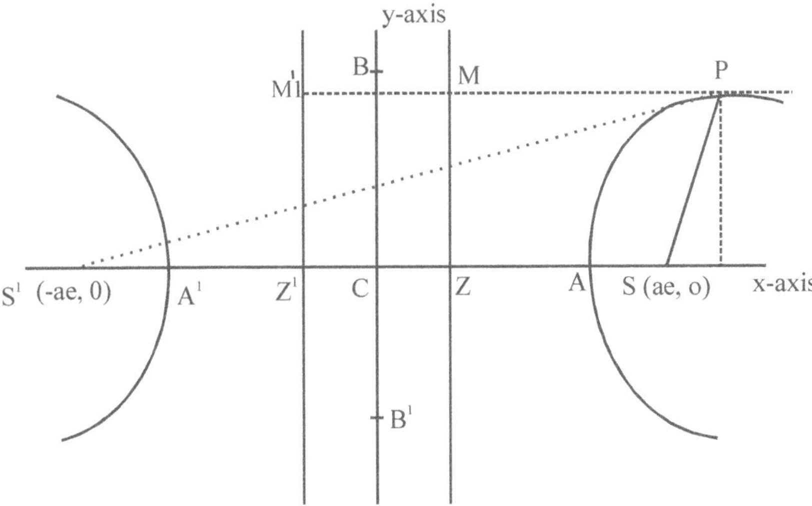

General Equation of Hyperbola

$$(x-h)^2 + (y-k)^2 = e^2 \frac{(lx+my+n)^2}{l^2+m^2}$$

Students may drive general equation with the help of derivation of general equation of ellipse

Table for both Hyperbolas

Equation	$\frac{x^2}{a^2}-\frac{y^2}{b^2}=1$	$\frac{x^2}{b^2}-\frac{y^2}{a^2}=1$
Centre	(0, 0)	(0, 0)
Equation of tranverse axis	y = 0	x = 0
Equation of conjugate axis	x = 0	y=0
Length of tranverse axis	2a	2a
Length of conjugate axis	2b	2b
Focii	($\pm$ ae, 0)	(0, $\pm$ae)
Vertices	($\pm$ a, 0)	(0, $\pm$a)
Equation of Directries	x = $\pm$a/e	y =$\pm$a/e
Length of Latus Rectum	$\frac{2b^2}{a}$	$\frac{2b^2}{a}$

Tangent and Normal Equations of Conics :

1. For Parabola :

$y^2 = 4ax$

(i) Equation of tangent at P (x_1, y_1)

$yy_1 = 2a(x+x_1)$

(ii) Equation of tanent in terms of slope : $y = mx + \frac{a}{m}$, $P\left(\frac{a}{m^2}, \frac{2a}{m}\right)$

(iii) Equation of normal at $P(x_1, y_1)$

$$y-y_1 = -\frac{y_1}{2a}(x-x_1)$$

(iv) Equation of normal in terms of slope

$y = mx - 2am - am^3$, $P(am^2, -2am)$

2. For Ellipse :

$$\frac{x^2}{a^2}+\frac{y^2}{b^2}=1$$

(i) Equation of tangent at $P(x_1, y_1)$

$$\frac{xx_1}{a^2}+\frac{yy_1}{b^2}=1$$

(ii) Equation of tangent in terms of slope :

$$y = mx \pm\sqrt{a^2m^2+b^2}, \quad c=\pm\sqrt{a^2m^2+b^2}$$

(iii) Equation of normal

at P (x_1, y_1)

$$\frac{x-x_1}{\left(\frac{x_1}{a^2}\right)}=\frac{y-y_1}{\left(\frac{y_1}{b^2}\right)}$$

3. For Hyperbola :

$$\frac{x^2}{a^2}-\frac{y^2}{b^2}=1$$

(i) Tangent at P (x_1, y_1)

$$\frac{xx_1}{a^2}-\frac{yy_1}{b^2}=1$$

(ii) Tangent in terms of slope :

$y = mx \pm\sqrt{a^2m^2-b^2}$, $c=\pm\sqrt{a^2m^2-b^2}$

(iii) Equation of normal at $P(x_1, y_1)$

$$\frac{x-x_1}{\left(\frac{x_1}{a^2}\right)}=\frac{y-y_1}{\left(\frac{y_1}{b^2}\right)}$$

Parametric Equations:

For parabola

Point is P = $(at^2, 2at)$

$\therefore x = at^2$, $y = at^2$, at t.

For ellipse

Point P = (a cos f , b sin f)

x = a cos f

y = b sin f

For Hyperbola

Point P = (a sec f , b tan f)

x = a sec f , y = b tan f

where f be any parameter.

Reflecting property of Parabola:

A tangent to a parabola has several properties, one of them is reflecting property which states that, if L is a line parallel to the axis of parabola, meets the parabola at a point P. This tangent to these parabola at P makes equal angle with L and with the focal radius PS i.e. $\alpha = \beta$

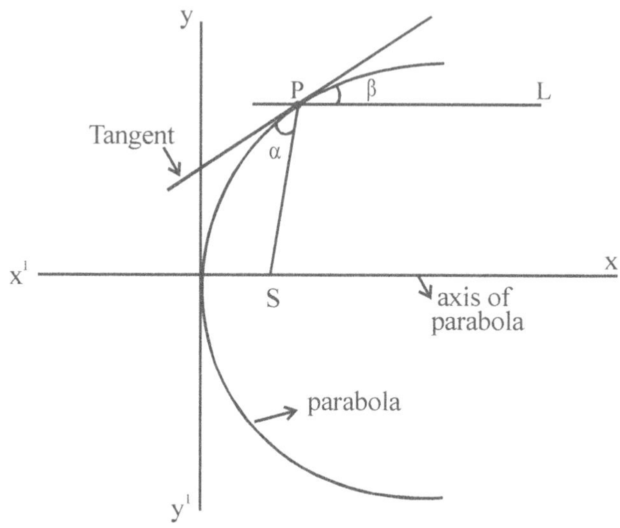

Application of Reflecting property

If light falls parallel on axis of parabola at parabolic mirror, the reflected ray will pass through the focus of the parabola.

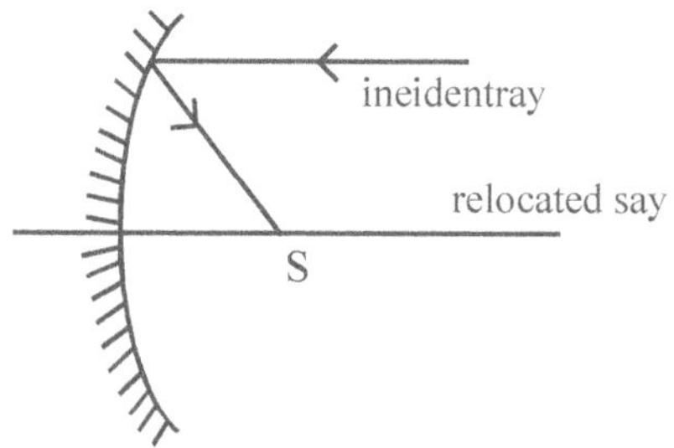

String property of ellipse

The sum of the focal distances of any point on an ellipse is the length at the mirror axis of ellipse.

Conversely, the set of all points P in a plane such that the sum of distances of P from two fixed points S and S' in the plane is a constant, is an ellipse.

String property of Hyperbola

The difference of the focal distances of any point on a hyperbola is equal to the length of its transverse axis.

Conversely, the set of points P such that $|P S_1 - P S_2| = 2a$ where S_1 and S_2 are two fixed points a is a constant and $S_1S_2 > 2a$ is a hyperbola.

Polar Equations of Conics

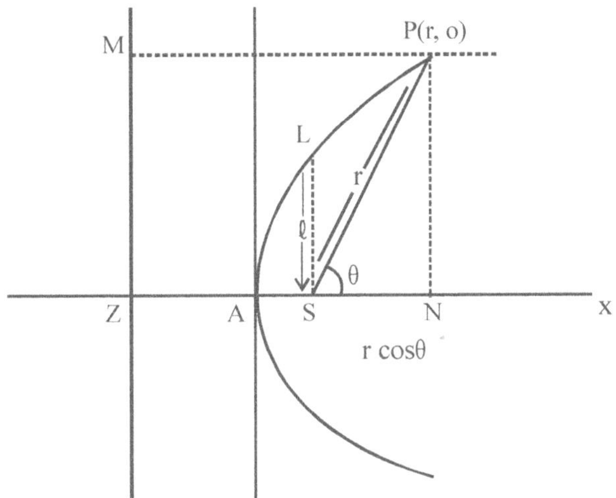

We have that focus of parabola supposed as pole.
Let focus (pole) be S ZM, the directix Ax the initial line. P (r, θ) be point on parabola. Such that PS = r, $\angle PSX = \theta$ LS be the semitatus rectum $= \ell$

directrix $SZ = \dfrac{\ell}{e}$

$\dfrac{PS}{PM} = e$ (definition of conic)

$PS = ePM = e\, ZN = (SZ + SN)e \quad (\because PM = ZN)$

$PS = r$ ZN

$r = e\left(\dfrac{1}{e} + SP\cos\theta\right)$ In Δ PSN

$r = 1 + er\cos\theta$ $\cos\theta = \dfrac{SN}{PS}$

$l = r - er\cos\theta$ SN = PS $\cos\theta$

$l = r(1 - e\cos\theta)$ $= r\cos\theta$

$$\boxed{\frac{l}{r} = 1 - e\cos\theta} \quad \ldots (1)$$

If direction SZ of the initial line is taken to be negative the equation would be

$$\boxed{\frac{l}{r} = 1 + e\cos\theta} \quad \ldots (2)$$

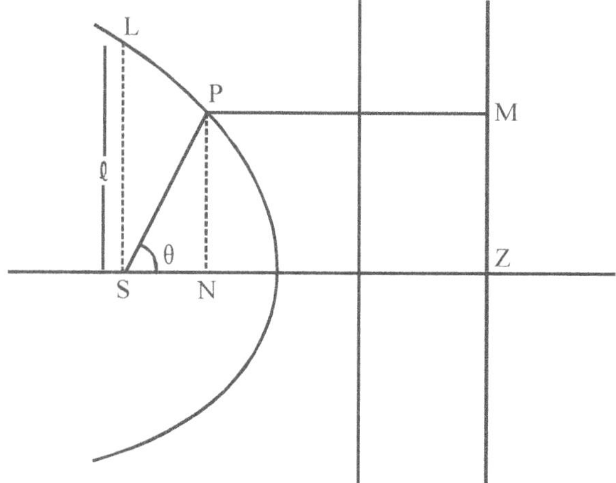

Put e = 1, in equation (1) and (2) we get

$$\boxed{\frac{l}{r} = 1 - \cos\theta} = 2\sin^2\frac{\theta}{2}$$

$$\boxed{\frac{l}{r} = 2\sin^2\frac{\theta}{2}}$$

And $\boxed{\frac{l}{r} = 1 + \cos\theta} = 2\cos^2\frac{\theta}{2}$

$$\boxed{\frac{l}{r} = 2\cos^2\frac{\theta}{2}}$$

Equation (1) and (2) represents ellipse or hyperbola depends on the fact that e < 1 or e > 1.

Solved Examples

Q1. Find the equation of the conic section with
(a) eccentricity 1, (2, 0) as its focus and x = y as its directrix,
(b) eccentricity 1/2, 2x + y = 1 as its directrix and (0, 1) as its focus.

Ans. (a) The required equation is $(x-2)^2 + y^2 = 1^2 \frac{(x-y)^2}{2}$

$\Leftrightarrow x^2 + y^2 + 2xy - 8x + 8 = 0.$

(b) The required equation is $x^2 + (y-1)^2 = \frac{1}{4}\,\frac{(2x+y-1)^2}{5}$

$\Leftrightarrow 16x^2 - 4xy + 19y^2 + 4x - 38y + 19 = 0.$

Q2. Find the equation of the tangent to
(a) $x^2 + 2y = 0$ at its vertex, and
(b) $y^2 + 4x = 0$ at the ends of its latus rectum.

Ans. (a) The equation is $xx_1 + 2\left(\frac{y+y_1}{2}\right) = 0$ where $x_1 = y_1 = 0$, that is, y = 0.

(b) The ends of the lactus rectum are (-1, 2) and (-1, -2). The tangents at these points are $x + y - 1 = 0$ and $x - y - 1 = 0$.

Q3. Under what conditions on m and c, will y = mx + c be a tangent to x^2 = 4ay?

Ans. The first point to note is that no tangent line can be parallel to the axis of the parabola. For any other m, the line will be a tangent at (x_1, y_1) if $x_1^2 = 4ay_1$, $y_1 = mx_1 + c$, and $x_1^2 = 4a(mx_1 + c)$ has coincident roots. Thus, y = mx + c will be a tangent if $m \neq \tan \pi/2$ and $c = -am^2$.

Q4. A parabolic mirror for a searchlight is to be constructed with width 1 metre and depth 0.2 metres. Where should the light source be placed? In Fig, we have given a cross section of the mirror.

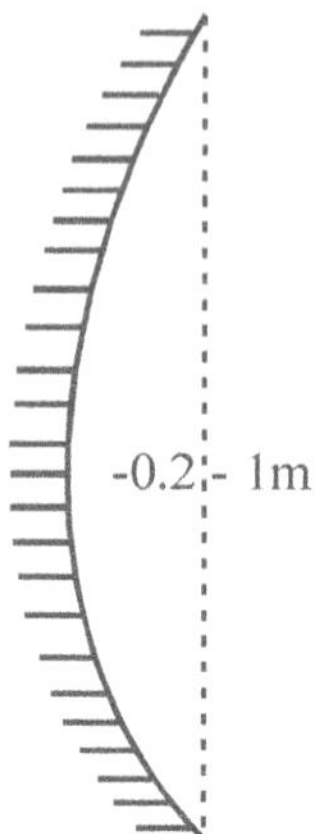

Ans. We have to find the focus of the parabola. We know that (0.2, 0.5 lies on it. Therefore,

$0.25 = 4a(0.2) = 0.8a \Rightarrow a = 0.3125.$

Q5. Find the equation of the tangent and normal at (1, 1) to the parabola $x^2 = 4y$.

Ans. The tangent is $x = 2(y + 1)$. Its slope is $\frac{1}{2}$.

and the normal is $y-1 = -2(x-1)$.

See formula from study material for more explanation.

Q6. What is the normal at the point of contact of the tangent $y = mx + \frac{a}{m}$ to the curve $y^2 = 4ax$?

Ans. The point of contact is $\left(\frac{a}{m^2}, \frac{2a}{m}\right)$.

The slope of the normal is $-\frac{1}{m}$.

Thus, its equation is

$$y - \frac{2a}{m} = -\frac{1}{m}\left(x - \frac{a}{m^2}\right)$$

$$\Leftrightarrow x + my = a\left(2 + \frac{1}{m^2}\right)$$

Q7. Sketch the ellipse $\frac{x^2}{9}+\frac{y^2}{25}=1$.

Ans This ellipse intersec ts the x-axis in $(\pm 3,0)$, and the y-axis in $(0,\pm 5)$. Its major axis lies along the y-axis, and the minor axis lies along the x- axis.

If e is the eccentricity of this ellipse, then $9 = 25(1-e^2)$. Therefore, $e = \frac{4}{5}$. Thus, the foci lie at (0, 4) and (0, -4). The directrices of this ellipse are $y = \pm \frac{25}{4}$. We sketch the ellipse in Fig.

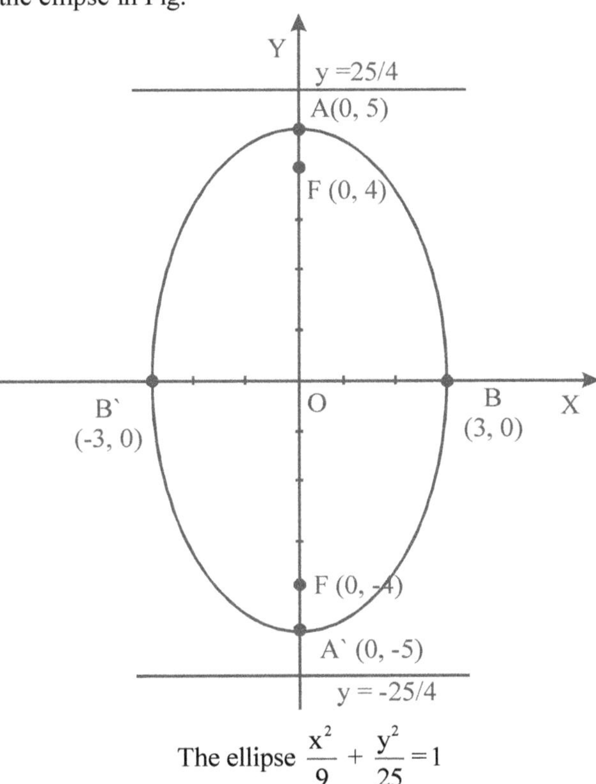

The ellipse $\frac{x^2}{9}+\frac{y^2}{25}=1$

Q8. Find the length of the major and minor axes, the eccentricity, the coordinates of the vertices and the foci of $3x^2 + 4y^2 = 12$. Hence sketch it.

Ans. The equation can be rewritten as $\frac{x^2}{4}+\frac{y^2}{3}=1$.

The major axis is of length 4 and lies along the x-axis.

The minor axis is of length $2\sqrt{3}$.

$\therefore \left(\sqrt{3}\right)^2 = 2^2\left(1-e^2\right)$, where e is the eccentricity.

$\Rightarrow e = \dfrac{1}{2}$.

The vertices are $(\pm 2, 0)$ and the foci are $(\pm 1, 0)$. We trace the curve in Fig.

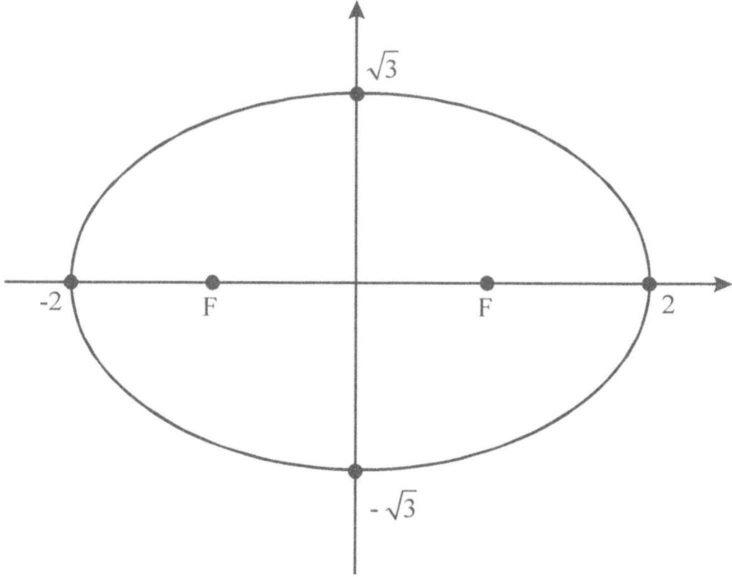

Q9. Find the equations of the tangents at the vertices and ends of the minor axis of the ellipse $\dfrac{x^2}{a^2}+\dfrac{y^2}{b^2}=1$.

Ans. The tangent at (a, 0) is $\dfrac{xa}{a^2}+\dfrac{y\,.\,0}{b^2}=1 \Rightarrow x = a$. Similarly, the tangents at (–a, 0), (0, b) and (0, –b) are x = –a, y = b and y = –b respectively.

Q10. Check whether y = x + 5 touches the ellipse $2x^2 + 3y^2 = 1$.

Ans. In this case $a^2 = \dfrac{1}{2}$, $b^2 = \dfrac{1}{3}$, c = 5 and m = 1.

$\therefore c^2 \neq a^2 m^2 + b^2$ .So the line is not a tangent to the given ellipse.

Q11. (a) Show that the equation of a conic with focus at (0, 0), directrix x +c = 0 and eccentricity e > 1 is

$$\left(x+\frac{ce^2}{e^2-1}\right)^2-\frac{y^2}{e^2-1}=\frac{e^2c^2}{\left(e^2-1\right)^2}.$$

(b) Shift the origin suitably so as to get the equation

$$\frac{x'^2}{a^2}-\frac{y'^2}{b^2}=1,$$

where $a=\frac{ec}{e^2-1}, b=a\sqrt{e^2-1}$.

(c) What are the coordinates of the focus and the equation of the directrix in the X'Y' – system?

Ans. (a) Put e = 1 in given we see that

$x^2 + y^2 = e^2 (x + c)^2$

$$\Rightarrow\left(x+\frac{ce^2}{e^2-1}\right)^2-\frac{y^2}{e^2-1}=\frac{e^2c^2}{\left(e^2-1\right)^2}$$

(b) Shifting the origin to $\left(-\frac{ce^2}{e^2-1},0\right)$, the equation in (a) becomes

$$x'^2-\frac{y'^2}{e^2-1}=\frac{e^2c^2}{\left(e^2-1\right)^2}$$

$$\Rightarrow\frac{x'^2}{a^2}-\frac{y'^2}{b^2}=1, \text{ where } a=\frac{ec}{e^2-1} \text{ and } b = a\sqrt{e^2-1}.$$

(c) In the X'Y' – system the focus is (-ae, 0) and directix is $x+\frac{a}{e}=0$.

Let P(x, y) be a point

$PS=\sqrt{x^2+y^2},\ PS^2=x^2+y^2$

$Pm=\frac{x+c}{\sqrt{1}},\ Pm^2=(x+c)^2$

$PS^2 = e^2Pm^2$
$x^2 + y^2 = e^2 (x + c)^2$
$x^2 + y^2 = e^2x^2 + e^2c^2 + 2xec$
$x^2 - e^2x^2 + y^2 = e^2c^2 + 2xec$
$(e^2 - 1)x^2 - y^2 = -e^2c^2 + 2xec$

$$x^2 - \frac{y^2}{e^2-1} = -\frac{e^2c^2 - 2xec}{e^2-1}$$

Q12. For the hyperbola $4x^2 - 9y^2 = 36$ find the vertices, eccentricity, foci and the axes.

Ans. Equation in standard form is $\frac{x^2}{9} - \frac{y^2}{4} = 1$.

$a = 3, b = 2.$

Therefore, the vertices are $(\pm 3, 0)$.

Now, since $b^2 = a^2 (e^2 - 1)$, $e^2 = \frac{13}{9}$. Thus, the eccentricity is $\frac{\sqrt{13}}{3}$. Then the foci are $(\pm ae, 0)$, that is, $(\pm\sqrt{13}, 0)$. The transverse axis is the line segment joining (3, 0) and (–3, 0), and the conjugate axis is the line segment joining (0, 2) and (0, –2).

Q13. Find the standard equation of the hyperbola with eccentricity $\sqrt{2}$.

Ans. The required equation is

$$\frac{x^2}{a^2} - \frac{y^2}{a^2(2-1)} = 1 \Leftrightarrow x^2 - y^2 = a^2$$

Which is an equation of rectangular hyperbola.

Q14. Find the tangent and normal to $\frac{x^2}{4} - \frac{y^2}{9} = 1$ at each of its vertices.

Ans. The vertices are (2, 0) and (–2, 0).
The tangents at these points are $x = 2$ and $x = -2$, respectively. The normals at both these points is the x-axis.

Q15. Find the asymptotes of the rectangular hyperbola $x^2 - y^2 = a^2$. Are they the same for any value of a?

Ans. $y = \pm x$, which are independent of a. Thus, these are the asymptotes of any rectangular hyperbola.

Q16. Find the slopes of the tangents drawn from (2, 2) to $4x^2 + y^2 = 4$. Hence give their equations.

Ans. The given equation is

$4x^2 + y^2 = 4$

$$\Rightarrow \frac{x^2}{1} + \frac{y^2}{4} = 1$$

$\therefore a^2 = 1,\ b^2 = 4$

Given point is (2, 2) (i.e. $x_1 = 2,\ y_1 = 2$)

Now equation of tangent is

$$\frac{xx_1}{a^2} + \frac{yy_1}{b^2} = 1$$

Putting the values of a^2 and b^2, and passing through (2, 2), we get

$$\Rightarrow 2x + \frac{2y}{4} = 1$$

$\Rightarrow 4x + y = 2$

$\therefore y = -4x + 2$

$\therefore m = -4$

$\therefore$ slope $= -4$

Q17. Find the equation of the tangents to the ellipse $x^2 + 3y^2 = 3$ which are parallel to the line $y = 4x + 7$. **[Dec99, Q2(a)]**

Ans. Given ellipse is $x^2 + 3y^2 = 3 \therefore \frac{x^2}{3} + \frac{y^2}{1} = 1 \therefore a^2 = 3\ b^2 = 1$

$\therefore$ tangent is parallel to line

$y = 4x + 7$

$\Rightarrow y = mx + c$

$m = 4$

$\therefore$ slope of the tangent, $m = 4$

Equation of the tangent to the ellipse

$$\frac{x^2}{a^2} + \frac{y^2}{b^2} = 1 \text{ is}$$

$y = mx \pm \sqrt{a^2m^2 + b^2}$

$y = 4x \pm \sqrt{3 \times 16 + 1}$

$= 4x \pm \sqrt{49}$

$y = 4x \pm 7$

Q18. Find the equation of the tangent to the parabola $y^2 = 7x$, which is perpendicular to the line $4x + y = 3$. [Dec99(2), Q2(a)]

Ans. The given equation of parabola

$y^2 = 7x$

$\Rightarrow y^2 = 4.\frac{7}{4}x$

$\therefore a = \frac{7}{4}$

We know that $y = mx + \frac{a}{m}$ is the equation of the tangent to the parabola $y^2 = 4ax$.

Since $4x + y = 3$ is perpendicular to the tangent let m_2, is slope of $4x + y = 3$

$\Rightarrow m_1 = -4$

$\therefore m_2 = (-4) = 4$

Hence equation of tangent

$y = \frac{mx}{2} + \frac{a}{m_2}$

$\Rightarrow y = 4x + \frac{\frac{7}{4}}{4}$

$y = 4x + \frac{7}{16}$

Q19. Let 2a be the length of the major axis of the ellipse

$r = \frac{ed}{1 + e\cos\theta}$ Show that $a = \frac{ed}{1 - e^2}$. [Dec99, Q3(b)]

Ans. We know that

$$FA = \frac{ed}{1-e} \text{ and } FA' = \frac{ed}{1+e}$$

Where A and A' are the vertices of the ellipse and F is a focus.

Then

$2a = AA'$

$2a = FA + FA'$

$$2a = \frac{ed}{1-e} + \frac{ed}{1+e} = \frac{ed(1+e)+ed(1-e)}{(1-e)-(1+e)}$$

$$2a = \frac{ed + e^2d + ed - e^2d}{(1 - e^2)}$$

$$\Rightarrow 2a = \frac{2ed}{1-e^2}$$

$$\Rightarrow a = \frac{ed}{1-e^2} \text{ Proved}$$

Q20. A bridge in the form of a semi-elliptical arc is 15 metres high and has a span of 40 metres. To construct the arc properly it is necessary to know the height at different points. Find the height of the bridge, upto one decimal point, at a point 8 metres from the centre. [Dec99, Q5(a)]

Ans.

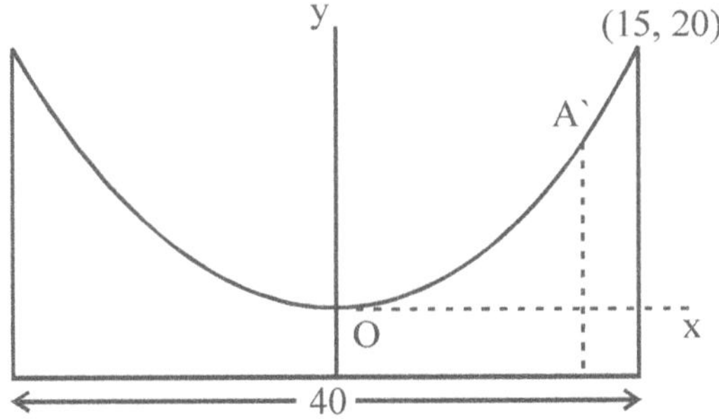

Let O be the centre of semi-elliptical path

$\therefore x^2 = 4ay$

$400 = 4a \times 15$

$$a = \frac{400}{4 \times 15} = \frac{20}{3}$$

$\therefore$ Let the co-ordinates of A'

$x^2 = 4ay$

$$x^2 = 4 \times \frac{20}{3} \times y$$

$$64 = \frac{80}{3} \times y$$

$$y = \frac{64 \times 3}{80}$$

$y = 2.4$ m

Q21. Prove that the portion of a tangent to a parabola cut off between the directrix and the parabola is the hypotenuse of a right-angled triangle, with the right-angle at the focus of the parabola. [June00, Q3(b)]

Ans. Let the parabola be $y^2 = 4ax$ ... (1)

Let P($at_1^2, 2at_1$) and Q ($at_2^2, 2at_2$) be the extremities of a focal chord.

Equation of chord CD is

$$y(t_1 + t_2) = 2(x + at_1.t_2) \qquad \text{... (2)}$$

Since line(2) passes through the point (a, 0)

$$\therefore 2a(1 + t_1.t_2) = 0$$

$$\therefore t_1.t_2 = -1 \qquad \text{... (3)}$$

The equation of the tangents at P and Q are respectively

$$t_1 y = x + at_1^2 \qquad \text{... (4)}$$

and $t_2 y = x + at_2^2$ ... (5)

Slope of line (4) is $1/t_1$ and slope of line (5) is $1/t_2$.

Product of the slopes

$$= \frac{1}{t_1} . \frac{1}{t_2}$$

$$= \frac{1}{t_1 t_2} . \frac{1}{-1} = -1$$

Solving (4) and (5) we get

$$x = at_1.t_2 = -a$$

Since abscissa of a point of intersection is –a, it lies on the line x = -a, i.e. on the directrix. Hence tangent to a parabola which cut off between the directrix and parabola is hypotenuse of a right angled triangle.

Q22. Reduce the following equations to standard form, and hence identify the conics or conicoids they represent: [Dec00, Q4(b)]

(i) $r \sin^2 \theta = 2a \cos$

(ii) $(x - y)^2 + (x - a)^2 = 0$

where $a \in R$ $a \neq 0$

Ans. (i) $r \sin^2 = 2a \cos\theta$

Changing to cartesian coordinates this equation is $y^2 = 2ax$, a parabola.

(ii) $(x - y)^2 + (x - a)^2 = 0$

$\Rightarrow 2x^2 - 2xy + y^2 - 2ax + a^2 = 0$

Here $a = 2$, $b = 1$, $h = -1$, $g = -a$,

$f = 0$, $c = a^2$

$\therefore ab - h^2 > 0$

Thus conic is an ellipse.

Q23. Find the equation of a parabola with focus F(3, –4) and directrix x + y = 2. [June01, Q2(a)]

Ans. Let P(x, y) be any point on the then the distance of P(x, y) from (3, –4) must be equal to its perpendicular distance from

$x + y - 2 = 0$

$$\therefore \sqrt{(x-3)^2 + (y+4)^2} = \frac{|x+y-2|}{\sqrt{(1)^2 + (1)^2}}$$

$$\text{or, } \sqrt{(x-3)^2 (y+4)^2} = \frac{(x+y-2)}{\sqrt{2}}$$

$$\text{or, } (x-3)^2 + (y+4)^2 = \frac{(x+y-2)^2}{2}$$

or, $2\,[x^2 - 6x + 9 + y^2 + 16 + 8y] = [x^2 - y^2 + 4 + 2xy - 4y - 4x]$

or, $2x^2 - 12x + 2y^2 + 16y + 50 - x^2 - y^2 - 4 - 2xy + 4y + 4x = 0$

$x^2 + y^2 - 2xy - 8x + 20y + 46 = 0$

This is required equation for parabola.

Q24. For the hyperbola $16x^2 - 25y^2 = 9$ find the vertices, eccentricity, foci, length of axes and the asymptotes. [Dec01, Q3(b)]

Ans. The given equation of hyperbola is

$16x^2 - 25y^2 = 9$

$$\Rightarrow \frac{16x^2}{9} - \frac{25y^2}{9} = 1$$

$$\Rightarrow \frac{\frac{x^2}{\frac{9}{16}}}{} - \frac{\frac{y^2}{\frac{9}{25}}}{} = 1$$

$$\Rightarrow \frac{x^2}{\left(\frac{3}{4}\right)^2} - \frac{y^2}{\left(\frac{3}{5}\right)^2} = 1$$

$$\therefore a = \frac{3}{4},\ b = \frac{3}{5}$$

$$\because a^2 = b^2\left(e^2 - 1\right)$$

$$\Rightarrow \frac{9}{16} = \frac{9}{25}\left(e^2 - 1\right)$$

$$\Rightarrow \frac{25}{16} = e^2 - 1$$

$$\Rightarrow e^2 = \frac{25}{16} + 1$$

$$= \frac{41}{16}$$

$$\therefore e = \sqrt{\frac{41}{16}}$$

$$= \frac{\sqrt{41}}{4}$$

Vertices are A (9, 0) and A (–9, 0)

$$\Rightarrow A\left(\frac{3}{4}, 0\right) \text{and } A'\left(\frac{-3}{4}, 0\right)$$

Foci F (ae, 0) and F’ (-ae, 0) that is F$\left(\frac{3\sqrt{41}}{4}, 0\right)$ and F’$\left(\frac{-3\sqrt{41}}{4}, 0\right)$ equation of directrix is

$$x = \pm\frac{a}{e}$$

$$= \pm \frac{\frac{3}{4}}{\frac{\sqrt{41}}{4}}$$

$$= \pm \frac{3}{\sqrt{41}}$$

Transverse axis = 2a

$$= 2 \times \frac{3}{4}$$

$$= \frac{3}{2}$$

Q25. Reduce the following equations to the cartesian form and hence identify the curves they represent: [Dec01, Q5(b)]

(i) $\mathbf{r \cos\left(\theta - \frac{\pi}{4}\right) = \sqrt{2}}$

(ii) $\mathbf{r^2 = 3r \sin\theta}$

Ans. (i) $r \cos\left(\theta - \frac{\pi}{4}\right) = \sqrt{2}$

$$\Rightarrow r\left(\cos\theta.\cos\frac{\pi}{4} + \sin\theta.\sin\frac{\pi}{4}\right) = \sqrt{2}$$

$$\Rightarrow r\cos\theta.\frac{1}{\sqrt{2}} + r.\sin\theta.\frac{1}{\sqrt{2}} = \sqrt{2}$$

$\Rightarrow r\cos\theta + r.\sin\theta = \sqrt{2}.\sqrt{2}$

$\Rightarrow x + y = 2$

Since, $x = r\cos\theta$, $y = r\sin\theta$

It represents a line.

(ii) $r^2 = 3r\sin\theta$

$\Rightarrow x^2 + y^2 = 3y$

Since $r^2 = x^2 + y^2$ and $y = r\sin\theta$

It represents a curve.

Q26. Obtain the equation of an ellipse whose eccentricity is ½, one focus is (–1, 1) and the corresponding directrix is x – y + 3 = 0.[June02, Q2(a)]

Ans. S = (–1, 1), $e = \frac{1}{2}$, Equation of directrix (ZM) $\equiv$ x – y + 3 = 0

We have

$$\frac{PS}{PM} = e \text{ (by definition of ellipse)}$$

where e < 1

$\therefore PS = ePM \quad \therefore PS^2 = e^2\ PM^2$ ... (1)

where P(x, y) be any variable point

$$\therefore PS = \sqrt{(x+1)^2 + (y-1)^2}$$

$$e = \frac{1}{2}$$

$$\therefore PS^2 = (x+1)^2 + (y-1)^2$$

given x – y + 3 = 0

PM = $\perp^r$ on ZM from P(x, y)

$\therefore \ell = 1, m = -1, n = 3$

$$= \frac{x - y + 3}{\sqrt{(1)^2 + (-1)^2}} = \frac{x - y + 3}{\sqrt{2}}$$

Hence equation of ellipse is

$$\therefore Pm^2 = \frac{(x - y + 3)^2}{2}$$

Putting the values of PS^2, e^2, PM^2 in (1) we get

$$(x+1)^2 + (y-1)^2 = \frac{\left(\frac{1}{2}\right)^2 (x - y + 3)^2}{2}$$

$$\Rightarrow x^2 + 2x + 1 + y^2 - 2y + 1 = \frac{(x - y + 3)^2}{4 \times 2} = x^2 + y^2 - 2xy + 9 + 6x - 6y$$

$$\Rightarrow 8x^2 + 16x + 16 + 8y^2 - 16y = x^2 + y^2 - 2xy + 6x - 6y + 9$$

$$\Rightarrow 7x^2 + 7y^2 + 10x - 10y + 7 = 0$$

which is required equation of ellipse.

Q27. Find the equations of the tangents to the ellipse

$4x^2 + 3y^2 = 24$ drawn parallel to $y = 2x$. **[June02, Q4(a)]**

Ans. The equation of ellipse is

$4x^2 + 3y^2 = 24$

$$\Rightarrow \frac{4x^2}{24} + \frac{3y^2}{24} = 1$$

$$\Rightarrow \frac{x^2}{6} + \frac{y^2}{8} = 1$$

$\therefore a^2 = 6, b^2 = 8$

Here $a = \left(\sqrt{6}\right), b = \sqrt{8}$

The equation of st. line is

$y = 2x$

$\therefore m = 2$

Hence tangent of ellipse parallel to $y = 2x$ is

$$y = mx \pm \sqrt{a^2m^2 + b^2}$$

$$\Rightarrow y = 2x \pm \sqrt{6 \times 4 + 8}$$

$$\Rightarrow y = 2x \pm \sqrt{32}$$

Hence tangent of equation as

$y = 2x + \sqrt{32}$ and $y = 2x - \sqrt{32}$

Q28. The difference between the focal distances of a hyperbola is 2 and its eccentricity is $\sqrt{2}$. Find its equation. **[June03, Q2(b)]**

Ans. Let the equation of the hyperbola be

$$\frac{x^2}{a^2} - \frac{y^2}{b^2} = 1$$

and eccentricity $e = \sqrt{2}$ (given)

but $b^2 = a^2 (e^2 - 1)$

$$b^2 = a^2\left(\left(\sqrt{2}\right)^2 - 1\right)$$

$b^2 = a^2 (2 - 1)$

$b^2 = a^2$

$b = a$

Distance between two focal = 2ae

$2ae = 2$

$$ae = \frac{2}{2}$$

$ae = 1$

$\therefore b^2 = a^2(e^2 - 1) = a^2e^2 - a^2 = 1 - a^2$

$b^2 + a^2 = 1$

$a^2 + a^2 = 1 \ (\because b = a)$

$2a^2 = 1$

$\therefore a^2 = 1/2$

$\therefore b^2 = \frac{1}{2}$

$\therefore \frac{x^2}{1/2} - \frac{y^2}{1/2} = 1$

Q29. The angle between the lines joining the foci of an ellipse to an extremely of the minor axis is 90°. If the major axis of the ellipse has length $2\sqrt{2}$, find the equation of the ellipse. [Dec03, Q1(a)]

Ans.

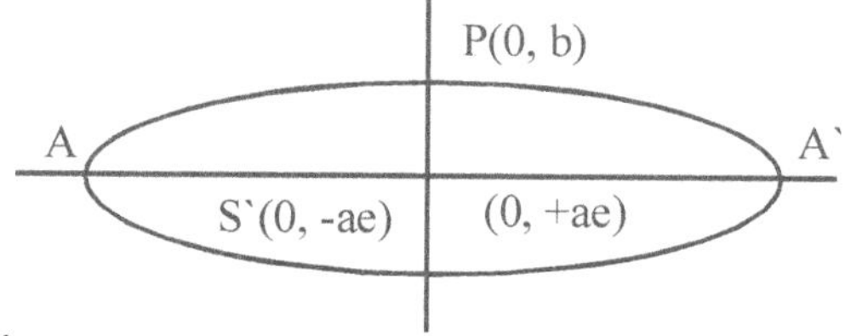

AA' = Major axis

$\because PS' \perp PS \ [\because \angle P = 90]$

$\therefore M_1 \times M_2 = -1$

$\therefore$ co-ordinate of (0, b)

co-ordinate of S' = (– ae, 0)

co-ordinate of S = (ae, 0)

$\therefore$ slope of PS' $(M_1) = \frac{b}{-ae}$

slope of PS $(M_2) = \frac{b}{ae}$

$\therefore \frac{b}{-ae} \times \frac{b}{ae} = -1$

$\frac{b^2}{2} = e^2$

$\therefore \frac{b}{a} = e$

But $2a = 2\sqrt{2}$

$\therefore a = \sqrt{2}$

$\frac{b^2}{2} = e^2$

$\therefore b^2 = 2e^2$

We know that

$e^2 = 1 - \frac{b^2}{a^2}$

$e^2 = 1 - e^2$

$2e^2 = 1$

$e^2 = \frac{1}{2}$

$\therefore b^2 = 2 \times \frac{1}{2} = b = \pm 1$

$\therefore$ The required equation of ellipse

$\frac{x^2}{2} + \frac{y^2}{1} = 1$

$x^2 + 2y^2 = 1$

Q30. Show that the line y = x + 2 is a tangent to $y^2 = 8x$. Also find the point of contact and the equation of the normal at this point.

[Dec03, Q2(a)]

Ans. Given equation of line $y = x + 2$ ... (i)

and equation of curve $y^2 = 8x$ ... (ii)

from (i) and (ii)

$(x + 2)^2 = 8x$

$x^2 + 4x + 4 = 8x$

$x^2 - 4x + 4 = 0$

$(x - 2)^2 = 0$

$\therefore y = 4$

$\therefore$ the line intercept only one point (2, 4) on the curve

$\therefore$ line is tangent to the curve.

∴ equation of normal

$$y - y_1 = \frac{-y}{2a}(x - x_1)$$

$$1\ y - 4 = \frac{4}{2.2}(x - 2)$$

$$y - 4 = x - 2$$

$x - y = 2.$

Q31. Show that the product of the distance from any point on a hyperbola to the asymptotes of the hyperbola is a constant. [June04, Q3(b)]

Ans. A hyperbola is the locus of a point which moves in such a way that the difference of its distance from two fixed points (foci) is always constant.

Let P(x, y) be any point on the hyperbola $\frac{x^2}{a^2} - \frac{y^2}{b^2} = 1$

SP = e PM and S'P = e PM'

Now

SP = e PM ⇒ SP = e(NK) = e(CN – CK) = e(x – a/e) = ex – a

and S'P = e PM' ⇒ S'P = e(NK') = e(CN + CK')

$$= e\left(x + \frac{a}{e}\right) = ex + a$$

∴ S'P – SP = (ex + a) – (ex – a) = 2a = transverse axis (constant)

hence, the difference of the focal distance of a point on the hyperbola is constant and is equal to the length of the transverse axis of the hyperbola.

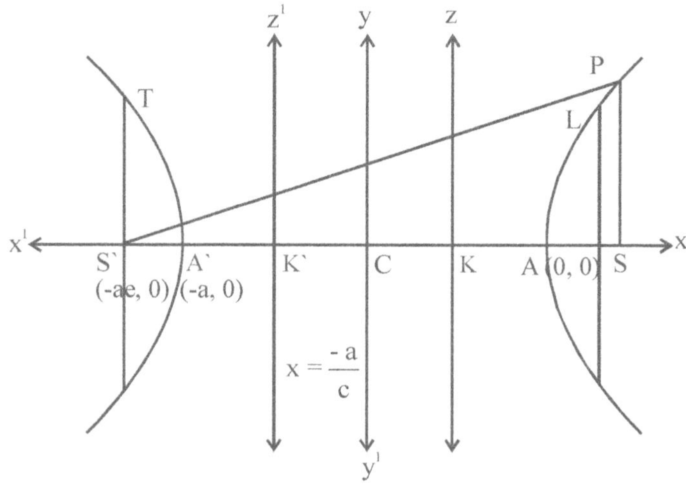

Q32. Reduce r = (4 + cot θ) cosec θ to Cartesian form. Identify the conic it represents *after reducing* it to standard form. [June04, Q4(a)]

Ans. $r = (4 + \cot\theta)\text{cosec}\,\theta$

$r = 4\,\text{cosec}\,\theta + \cot\theta.\text{cosec}\,\theta$

$$r = \frac{4}{\sin\theta} + \frac{\cos\theta}{\sin\theta}.\frac{1}{\sin\theta}$$

$$r = \frac{4\sin\theta + \cos\theta}{\sin^2\theta}$$

$$\left(r^2\sin^2\theta\right) = \left(4\ \sin\ \theta + \cos\theta\right)\times r$$

$$\left(r\sin\theta\right)^2 = 4r\sin\theta + r\cos\theta$$

Here $x = r\cos\theta$ and $y = r\sin\theta$

$y^2 = 4y + x$

$y^2 = x + 4y$

which is a standard form of $r = (4 + \cot\theta)\ \text{cosec}\,\theta$.

Q33. Find the area of the triangle formed by the lines joining the vertex of the parabola $x^2=12y$ to the ends of its latus rectum.

Ans.

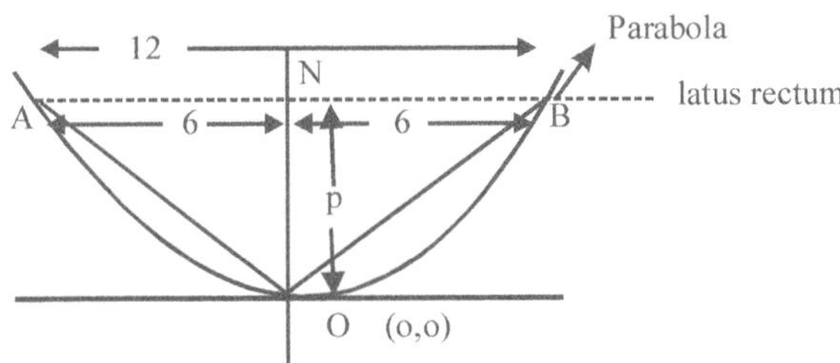

Compare with $x^2 = 4a\,y$

$x^2 = 12\,y$

Latus Rectum $4a = 12$ (AB)

$\therefore AB = 12$

$p = ON$

$12p = 6^2 = 36\ \therefore p = 3$

$$\therefore \text{Area of } \triangle OAB = \frac{1}{2}\times AB\times P = \frac{1}{2}\times 12\times 3 = 18\,Sq.Units$$

Q34. Find eccentricity, major axis, minor axis Focii, vertices. Equation of directrices for ellipse $x^2+16y^2=16$?

Ans. $\frac{x^2}{16}+\frac{y^2}{1}=1$

on comparing with $\frac{x^2}{a^2}+\frac{y^2}{b^2}=1$

$a^2 = 16, b^2 = 1 \quad \therefore a = 4, b = 1$

We have

$b^2 = a^2 (1-e^2)$

$1 = 16 (1-e^2)$

$1-e^2 = \frac{1}{16}, \quad e^2 = 1 - \frac{1}{16} = \frac{15}{16}$

$e = \frac{\sqrt{15}}{4} < 1$

Major axis = 2a = 2 × 4 = 8

Minor axis = 2b = 2 × 1 = 2

Focii = $(\pm a e, 0) = (\pm \sqrt{15}, 0)$

Vertices = $(\pm a, 0) = (\pm 4, 0)$

Directrices $\Rightarrow x=\pm\frac{a}{e}=\frac{\pm 16}{\sqrt{15}}$

Q35. Trace the equation $4x^2–12xy + 9y^2 – 4x + 6y – 5=0$?

Ans. Compare the given equation with (1)

a=4, 2h=–12, h=–6, b=9, 2g=–4, g=–2, 2f=6 ∴ f=3, c=–5

$\Delta = abc + 2fgh – af^2 – bg^2 – ch^2$

$= –180 + 72 – 36 – 36 + 180$

$\Delta = 0$

$h^2 – ab = (–6)^2 – 4 \times 9 = 0$

Therefore, given equation represents pair of parallel lines and these may be obtained as separating IInd degree terms and I degree terms i.e. $4x^2 – 12xy + 9y^2 – 2(2x – 3y) = 5$

$(2x-3y)^2 – 2(2x – 3y) = 5$

the given line is $2x – 3y = 1 \pm\sqrt{6}$ for tracing, put x =0, point is $\left[0,\frac{1+\sqrt{6}}{3}\right]$ and now put y = 0, point is $\left[\frac{1+\sqrt{6}}{3},0\right]$

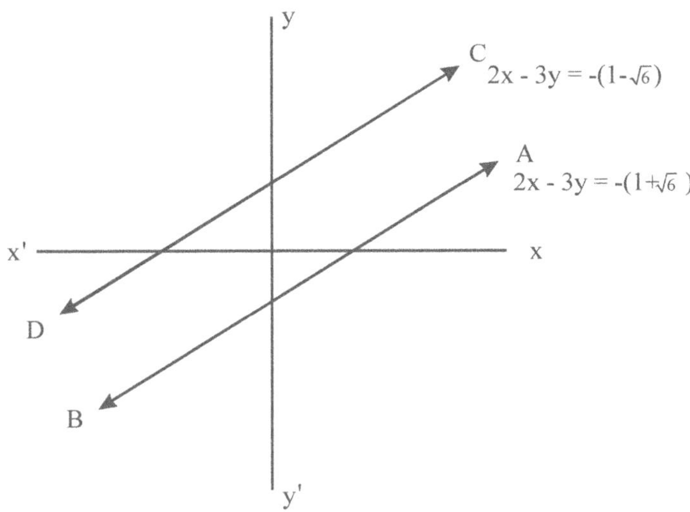

Q36. Prove that the given equation : $9x^2 + 6xy + y^2 + 60x + 20y + 75 = 0$ will represent a parabola of parallel line ?

Ans. Compare the given equation with general equation.

a=9, h=3, b=1, g=30, f=10, c=75

$\Delta = abc + 2fgh - af^2 - bg^2 - ch^2$

$= 9 \times 1 \times 75 + 2 \times 10 \times 30 \times 3 - 9(10)^2 - 1(30)^2 - 75(3)^2$

$= 675 + 1800 - 900 - 900 - 675$

$= 0$

$h^2\text{-}ab=(3)2 - 9 \times 1 = 0$

Hence given equation will represent pair of straight lines.

Q37. Find the eccentricity, the foci and the length of the latus rectum of $5x^2 + 4y^2 = 2$ Dec 2005 Q2 (a)

Ans. Try to your self.

Q38. A point P moves so that the sum of its distances from two fixed points S, S' is constant and equal to 2a. Show the P lies on the conic.

$\frac{a(1-e^2)}{r} = 1 - e\cos\theta$, referred to S as the pole and SS' as the initial line.

SS' being equal to 2ae.

Ans.

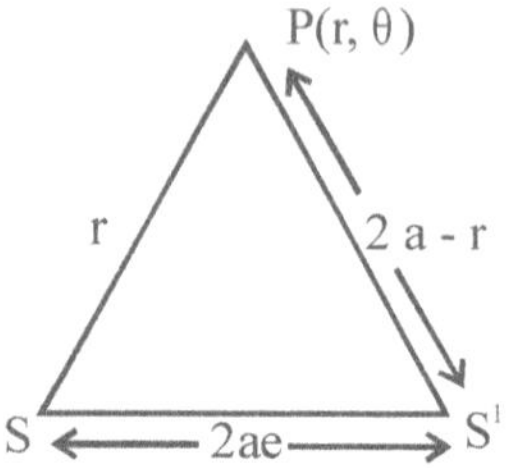

Let P be the point (r, θ) referred to S as pole and SS' as initial line so that,

SP = r and, $\angle PSS' = \theta$

Now SP is perpendicular to S'P = 2a (given)

So that S' P = 2a – SP = 2a – r

Hence from $\Delta PSS'$, we have

$S'P^2 = SP^2 + SS'^2 - 2SP.SS' \cos\theta$

$(2a - r)^2 = r^2 + (2ae)^2 - 2r.2ae \cos\theta$

$4a^2 + r^2 - 4ar = r^2 + 4a^2 e^2 - 4aer \cos\theta$

$a(1 - e^2) = r(1 - e \cos\theta)$

or $\frac{a(1 - e^2)}{r} = 1 - e\cos\theta$

Chapter-3

General Equation of Second Degree

General equation of second degree is

$ax^2 + 2hxy + by^2 + 2gx + 2fy + c = 0$ ... (1)

This equation represent various conic on various conditions

Straight line:

(i) IF $\Delta = abc + 2fgh - af^2 - bg^2 - ch^2 = 0$ ... (2)

Then (1) represents pair of st. lines and the point of intersection of line are

$$x_1 = \frac{hf - bg}{ab - h^2}, y_1 = \frac{gh - af}{ab - g^2}$$

(ii) Angle between lines is given as

$$\theta = \tan^{-1}\left\{\frac{\pm 2\sqrt{h^2 - ab}}{a + b}\right\}$$

Circle

Equation (1) represents Equation of circle. If a = b, or a = b = 1, and h = 0 which have radius $= \sqrt{g^2 + f^2 - c}$ and centre = (-g, -f)

Parabola

If $ab = h^2$, (1) represents parabola.

Ellipse

If $ab > h^2$, (1) represents an ellipse.

Hyperbola : If $ab < h^2$, (1) represents hyperbola.

Note: Equation (2) may be easily solved by

$$\Delta \equiv \begin{vmatrix} a & h & g \\ h & b & f \\ g & f & c \end{vmatrix}$$

Here is a table showing all conditions that given general equation (1) what represent at what condition, let us see

Conditions	Types of conics
I Case When $\Delta \equiv 0$	I Degenerate conics
(i) $ab - h^2 = 0$	(ii) two parallel lines; lines are coincident or single line or empty set
(ii) $ab - h^2 \neq 0$	(iii) intersecting lines
(a) $ab < h^2$	(a) point if intersecting lines.
(b) $ab > h^2$	(b) point or empty set
(iii) $ab - h^2 \neq 0$ $a + b = 0$	lines are perpendicular
II Case $\Delta \neq 0$	(II) Non degenerate conic
(i) $h = 0, a = b$	(i) circle
(ii) $ab - h^2 = 0$	(ii) Parabola
(iii) $ab - h^2 > 0$ (When $\Delta \neq 0$, not satisfied)	(iii) Ellipse
(iv) $ab - h^2 < 0$	(iv) Hyperbola
(v) $ab - h^2 > 0$ $a + b = 0$	(v) Rectangular Hyperbola
III Case	
$ab \neq h^2$	conic central
$ab = h^2$	non central conic.

Central conic

A conic that has a centre is called a central conic. E.g. ellipse, hyperbola. A centre is a unique in conic.

If we have general equation of second degree, representing Ellipse or Hyperbola.

$$ax^2 + 2hxy + by^2 + 2gx + 2fy + c = 0$$

Non central conic: The conics which do not have centre, called non central conic.

Note: We will learn Tracing of conic by solved examples.

SOLVED EXAMPLES

Q1. Show that $x^2 - 5xy + 6y^2 = 0$ represents a pair of straight lines. Find the angle between these lines.

Ans. On comparing with

$ax^2 + 2hxy + by^2 + 2gx + 2fy = 0$

$a = 1, h = -\frac{5}{2}, b = 6, g = 0 = f = c.$

$$\Delta \equiv \begin{vmatrix} 1 & -\frac{5}{2} & 0 \\ -\frac{5}{2} & 6 & 0 \\ 0 & 0 & 0 \end{vmatrix}, = 1(O-0) - \frac{5}{2}(0) + 0$$

$= 0$

Thus, the given equation represents a pair of lines.

The angle between them is $\tan^{-1}\left(\frac{2}{7}\sqrt{\frac{25}{4}} - 6\right) = \tan^{-1}\frac{1}{7}$.

Q2. Check whether $3x^2 + 7xy + 2y^2 + 5x + 5y + 2 = 0$ represents a pair of lines.

Ans. In this case $a = 3, b = 2, c = 2, f = \frac{5}{2} = g, h = \frac{7}{2}$.

$$\Delta \equiv \begin{vmatrix} a & h & g \\ h & b & f \\ g & f & c \end{vmatrix} = \begin{vmatrix} 3 & \frac{7}{2} & \frac{5}{2} \\ \frac{7}{2} & 2 & \frac{5}{2} \\ \frac{5}{2} & \frac{5}{2} & 2 \end{vmatrix} = 0$$

Hence the given equation represents a pair of lines.

Q3. Identify the conic $x^{2s} - 3xy + y^2 + 10x - 10y + 21 = 0$. If it is central, find its centre.

Ans. In this case $a = 1 = b, h = -\frac{3}{2}$.

$\therefore ab - h^2 = -\frac{5}{4} < 0$. (Hyperbola)

So the given equation is central, and can be a hyperbola or a pair of intersecting lines.

Since $\begin{vmatrix} 1 & -\frac{3}{2} & 5 \\ -\frac{3}{2} & 1 & -5 \\ 5 & -5 & 21 \end{vmatrix} \neq 0$,

We can say that the equation represents a hyperbola. Its centre is the intersection of

$x - \frac{3}{2}y + 5 = 0$ and $-\frac{3}{2}x + y - 5 = 0$, that is, (-2, 2).

Q4. Find the conic represented by
$9x^2 - 24xy + 16y^2 - 124x + 132y + 324 = 0$.

Ans. The given equation is of the form (1), where a = 9, b = 16, h = -12. Now let us rotate the axes through an angle θ, where

$\tan 2\theta = \frac{2h}{a - b} = \frac{24}{7}$, that is, $\frac{2\tan\theta}{1-\tan^2\theta} = \frac{24}{7}$, that is,

$12\tan^2\theta + 7\tan\theta - 12 = 0 \cdot$

So we can take $\tan\theta = \frac{3}{4}$, and then $\sin\theta = \frac{3}{5}$ and $\cos\theta = \frac{4}{5}$.

Then, in the new coordinate system the given equation becomes

$25y'^2 - \frac{124}{5}(4x' - 3y') + \frac{132}{5}(3x' + 4y') + 324 = 0$, that is,

$\left(y' + \frac{18}{5}\right)^2 = \frac{4}{5}x$.

Now let us shift the origin to $\left(0, -\frac{18}{5}\right)$. Then the equation becomes

$Y^2 = \frac{4}{5}X$,

where X and Y are the current coordinates.

This is a parabola. Since the transformations we have applied do not alter the curve, the original equation also represents a parabola.

Q5. Show that the conic $x^2 + 2xy + y^2 - 2x - 1 = 0$ is a parabola. Find its axis and trace it.

Ans. Here a = 1, b = 1, h = 1. $\therefore ab - h^2 = 0$.

Further, the discriminant of the conic is $\begin{vmatrix} 1 & 1 & -1 \\ 1 & 1 & 0 \\ -1 & 0 & -1 \end{vmatrix} = -1 \neq 0$.

Thus, the given conic is a parabola.

We can write the given equation as $(x + y)^2 = 2x + 1$.

Now we let a constant c so that we can write the equation in the form

$$\left(\frac{Ax + By + c}{\sqrt{A^2 + B^2}}\right)^2$$

$$= k\frac{(A'x + B'y + c)}{\sqrt{A'^2 + B'^2}}$$

So,

$(x + y + c)^2 = 2x + 1 + 2cx + 2cy + c^2$, that is,

$(x + y + c)^2 = 2(1 + c)x + 2cy + c^2 + 1$ ... (1)

We will choose c in such a way that the lines $x + y + c = 0$ and $2(1 + c)x + 2cy + c^2 + 1 = 0$ are perpendicular.

$$(-1)\left[\frac{-2(1+c)}{2c}\right] = -1 \Rightarrow c = -\frac{1}{2}.$$

Then (1) becomes

$$\left(x + y - \frac{1}{2}\right)^2 = x - y + \frac{5}{4}, \text{ that is,}$$

$$\left(\frac{x + y - \frac{1}{2}}{\sqrt{2}}\right)^2 = \frac{1}{\sqrt{2}}\left(\frac{x - y + \frac{5}{4}}{\sqrt{2}}\right).$$

This is in the form of parabola.

Thus, the axis of the parabola is $x + y - \frac{1}{2} = 0$, and the tangent at the vertex is $x - y + \frac{5}{4} = 0$.

The vertex is the intersection of these two lines, that is, $\left(-\frac{3}{8},\frac{7}{8}\right)$.

The length of the latus rectum of the parabola is $\frac{1}{\sqrt{2}}$.

Thus the focus is at $\left(-\frac{3}{8}+\frac{1}{4\sqrt{2}}\cos\theta,\frac{7}{8}+\frac{1}{4\sqrt{2}}\sin\theta\right)$, where θ is the angle that the axis makes with the x-axis, that is, $\theta=\tan^{-1}(-1)$.

$\therefore \sin\theta=-\frac{1}{\sqrt{2}},\cos\theta=\frac{1}{\sqrt{2}}$.

Therefore, the focus is $F\left(-\frac{1}{4},\frac{3}{4}\right)$.

What are the points of intersection of the parabola and the coordinates axes?

They are $\left(1+\sqrt{2},0\right),\left(1-\sqrt{2},0\right),(0,1),(0,-1)$.

So, we can trace the parabola as in Fig. below.

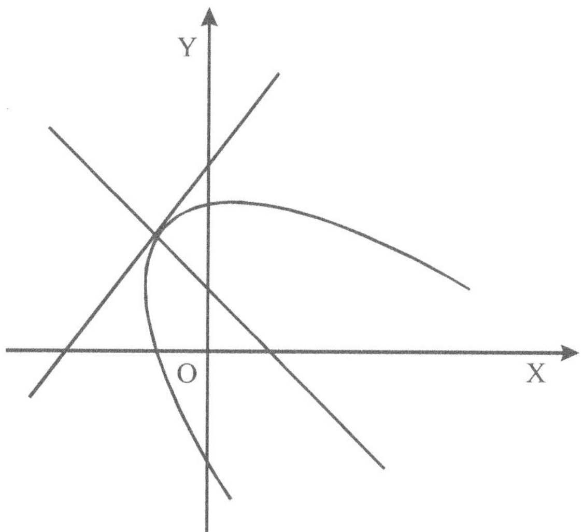

The parabola $x^2+2xy+y^2-2x-1=0$

Q6. Is x + 4y = 0 a tangent to the conic x² + 4xy + 3y² – 5x – 6y + 3 = 0? Find all the tangents to this conic that are parallel to the given line.

Ans. $x+4y=0$ will be a tangent to the given conic if

$$\begin{vmatrix} 1 & 2 & -\frac{5}{2} & 1 \\ 2 & 3 & -3 & 4 \\ -\frac{5}{2} & -3 & 3 & 0 \\ 1 & 4 & 0 & 0 \end{vmatrix} = 0$$

$$\Leftrightarrow -\begin{vmatrix} 2 & 3 & -3 \\ -\frac{5}{2} & -3 & 3 \\ 1 & 4 & 0 \end{vmatrix} + 4\begin{vmatrix} 1 & 2 & -\frac{5}{2} \\ -\frac{5}{2} & -3 & 3 \\ 1 & 4 & 0 \end{vmatrix} = 0$$

$\Leftrightarrow 40 = 0$, which is false.

Thus, the given line is not a tangent to the given conic.

Any line parallel to the given line is of the form $x + 4y + c = 0$. This will be a tangent to the given conic if (15) is satisfied, that is,

$(5c + 28)^2 = 3(3c^2 + 24c + 48)$

$\Leftrightarrow c = -5$ or -8.

Thus, the required tangents are

$x + 4y - 5 = 0$ and $x + 4y - 8 = 0$.

Q7. Find the points of intersection of the parabola $y^2 = 2x$ and the circle $x^2 + y^2 = 1$.

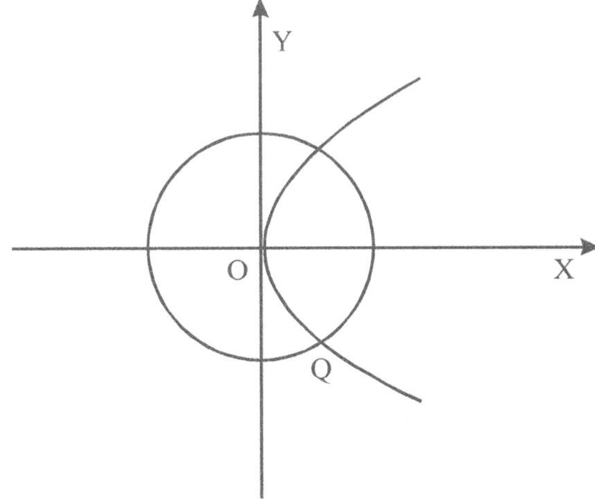

Fig $y^2 = 3x$ and $x^2 + y^2 = 1$ intersect in the points P and Q.

Ans. If (x_1, y_1) is a point of intersection, then $x_1^2 + y_1^2 = 1$ and $y_1^2 = 2x_1$. Eliminating y_1 from these equations, we get

$x_1^2 + 2x_1 = 1$, that is, $(x_1 + 1)^2 = 2$.

So $x_1 = -1 \pm \sqrt{2}$.

Then $y_1^2 = 2x_1$ gives us

$y_1 = \pm\sqrt{2}\left(\sqrt{2}-1\right)^{1/2}$ if $x_1 = -1+\sqrt{2}$, and

$y_1 = \pm\sqrt{2}i\left(\sqrt{2}+1\right)^{1/2}$ if $x_1 = -1-\sqrt{2}$.

Thus, there are only two real points of intersection, namely,

$\left(\sqrt{2}-1, \sqrt{2}\left(\sqrt{2}-1\right)^{1/2}\right)$ and $\left(\sqrt{2}-1, -\sqrt{2}\left(\sqrt{2}-1\right)^{1/2}\right)$.

Q8. If S = 0 and S_1 = 0 are rectangular hyperbolas, then show that S + kS_1 = 0 is a rectangular hyperbola, for all real k.

Ans. Let $S \equiv ax^2 + 2hxy + by^2 + 2gx + 2fy + c = 0$
and $S_1 \equiv a_1x^2 + 2h_1xy + b_1y^2 + 2g_1x + 2f_1y + c_1 = 0$
be rectangular hyperbolas. Then
$a + b = 0$ and $a_1 + b_1 = 0$.

$\therefore (a+b) + k(a_1 + b_1) = 0 \forall k \in \mathbf{R}$

$\Leftrightarrow (a + ka_1) + (b + kb_1) = 0 \forall k \in \mathbf{R}$

$\Leftrightarrow S + kS_1 = 0$ is a rectangular hyperbola $\forall k \in \mathbf{R}$.

Q9. Let $S \equiv \frac{x^2}{9} + \frac{y^2}{4} - 1 = 0$ and $S_1 \equiv xy - 9 = 0$.

Under what conditions on k will S + kS_1 = 0 be

(a) an ellipse?

(b) a parabola?

(c) a hyperbola?

Ans. $S + kS_1 = 0$

$\Leftrightarrow \frac{x^2}{9} - kxy + \frac{y^2}{4} - (1 + 9k) = 0$.

(a) This conic will be an ellipse if

$\left(\frac{1}{9}\right)\left(\frac{1}{4}\right)-\frac{k^2}{4}>0$, that is, $k^2<\frac{1}{9}$.

(b) The conic will be a parabola if

$$k^2=\frac{1}{9} \text{ and } \begin{vmatrix} \frac{1}{9} & -\frac{k}{2} & 0 \\ -\frac{k}{2} & \frac{1}{4} & 0 \\ 0 & 0 & -(1+9k) \end{vmatrix} \neq 0, \text{ that is}$$

if $k= \pm\frac{1}{3}$ and $(1+9k)\left(\frac{1}{36}-\frac{k^2}{4}\right)\neq 0$.

But this can't bve.
So the conic can't be a parabola.

But it will be a pair of lines if $k= \pm\frac{1}{3}$.

(c) The conic will be a hyperbola if $k^2>\frac{1}{9}$.

Q10. Write the equation of a conic through the points of intersection of $4x^2 + 9y^2 = 36$ and $4xy = 9 + 2x$. What is the condition that the conic is a pair of straight lines? [June98, Q2(b)]

Ans. By shifting the origin, the new coordinates x' and y' are related to x and y by

$x = x' - 2$; $y = y' + 1$

Thus the equation becomes,

$(x' - 2)^2 + (y' + 1)^2 + 4(x' - 2) - 2(y' + 1) + 4 = 0$

$x'^2 - 4x' + 4 + y'^2 + 2y' + 1 + 4x' - 8 - 2y' - 2 + 4 = 0$

$\Rightarrow x'^2 + y'^2 - 1 = 0$

$\Rightarrow x'^2 + y'^2 = 1$ ... (i)

Now, rotating the axes through 45°, we get new coordinates x and y given by,

$x'=\frac{x-y}{\sqrt{2}}$ and $y'=\frac{x-y}{\sqrt{2}}$

Thus equation (i), becomes

$\Rightarrow x^2 - 2xy + y^2 + x^2 + 2xy + y^2 = 2$

$\Rightarrow x^2 + y^2 = 1$

Q11. What is the conic represented by [Dec98, Q2] $4x^2 - 4xy + y^2 - 8x + 6y + 5 = 0$? Obtain its centre, if it has one. Also obtain a focus. Hence sketch its curve.

Ans. The given conic is

$4x^2 - 4xy + y^2 - 8x - 6y + 5 = 0$ ... (1)

On compairing this we general equation of second degree

$a = 4, h = -2, b = 1, g = -4\ f = -6, c = 5$

$\Delta = 4\times1\times5 + 2\times-6\times-4\times-2 = 20+96-144-16-20 = -64 \neq 0$

$ab = 4\times1=4,\ h^2 = (-2)^2 = 4$

$\because \Delta \neq 0,\ ab = h^2$

$\therefore$ equation (1) represents parabola

It is non-central. Now rearrange the equation (1)

We add c constant to the equation

$\Rightarrow (2x - y + c)^2 = 8x + 6y - 5 + 4cx - 2cy + c^2$

$\Rightarrow (2x - y + c)^2 = 4(2 + c)x + 2(3 - c)y + c^2 - 5$

$\Rightarrow$ We choose c

$$2\left(\frac{4(2+c)}{2(c-3)}\right) = -1\ \ c = -1$$

$\Rightarrow (2x - y - 1)^2 = 4(x + 2y - 1)$

$$\Rightarrow \left(\frac{2x-y-1}{\sqrt{5}}\right)^2 = \frac{4}{\sqrt{5}}\left(\frac{x+2y-1}{\sqrt{5}}\right)$$

The vertex of this parabola is intersection of

$2x - y - 1 = 0$ and

$x + 2y - 1 = 0$ that is $\left(\frac{3}{5}, \frac{1}{5}\right)$

The focus lies at $\left(\frac{3}{5}, \frac{1}{5}\cos\theta, \frac{1}{5} + \frac{1}{\sqrt{5}}\sin\theta\right)$

Where $\tan\theta = 2$

$\therefore \sin\theta = \frac{2}{\sqrt{5}}, \cos\theta = \frac{1}{\sqrt{5}}$

$\therefore$ The focus lies at $\left(\frac{4}{5}, \frac{3}{5}\right)$

The curve intersect the y-axis in (0, 1) and (0, 5). It does not intersect the x-axis.

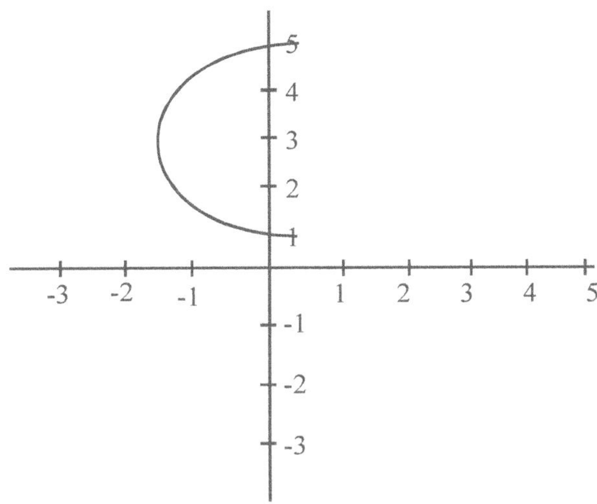

Q12. Is the conic **[June99, Q4]**

$$9x^2 - 24xy + 16y^2 - 18x - 101y + 19 = 0$$

central or not? Find the coordinates of its focus (or foci) and the length of its latus rectum (or its major and minor axes, respectively). Use this information to give a rough sketch of this conic.

Ans. The given conic is

$$9x^2 - 24xy + 16y^2 - 18x - 101y + 19 = 0 \qquad \text{... (1)}$$

$$a = 9,\ b = 16,\ h = -12,\ g = 9,\ f = \frac{-101}{2},\ ab = 9 \times 16 = 144\ h^2 = (-12)^2 = 144$$

$$\Delta = 9 \times 16 \times 0 - 9\left(\frac{-101}{2}\right)^2 - 16 \times 9^2 - 0$$

$\therefore$ (1) is not central because $ab = h^2$

So, it is non-central (discriminant is non-zero)

Thus equation is parabola

$(3x - 4y)^2 = 18x + 101y - 19$

$(3x - 4y + c)^2 = (6c + 18)x + y\,(101 - 8c) + c^2 - 19$

Choose the constant c so that

$3(6c + 18) - 4(101 - 8c) = 0 \qquad c = 7$

Then given equation become

$(3x - 4y + 7)^2 = 15(4x + 3y + 2)$

$$\Rightarrow \left(\frac{3x - 4y + 7}{5}\right)^2 = 3\left(\frac{4x + 3y + 2}{5}\right)$$

Thus, the axis of parabola is

$4x + 3y + 2 = 0$

Vertex is the intersection of

$3x - 4y + 7 = 0$ and $4x + 3y + 2 = 0$

On solving above equation

We get $\left(\frac{-29}{25}, \frac{22}{25}\right)$

The length of lotus rectum is 3 it focus F lies at

$$\left(\frac{-29}{25} + \frac{3}{4}\cos\theta, \frac{22}{25} + \frac{3}{4}\sin\theta\right)$$

Where $\tan\theta = \frac{-4}{3}$

$\therefore$ F is (–0, 71, 0.28)

The curve intersects the y-axis in

$$\frac{101 \pm \sqrt{(101)^2 - 64 \times 19}}{32}$$

That is approximately, $\frac{49}{8}$ and $\frac{3}{16}$ it does not intersect the x-axis

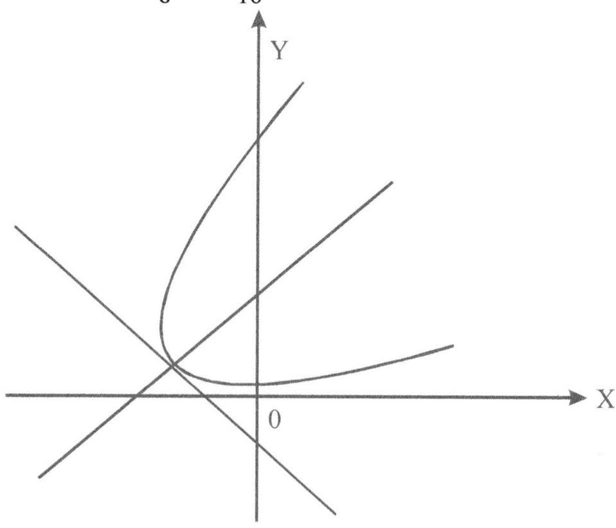

Q13. The equation $9x^2 + 6xy + y^2 + 60x + 20y + 75 = 0$ what shows **[Dec99, Q1(b)]**

Ans. Parabola

Here a = 9, b = 1, h = 3, c = 75, g = 30, f = 10

$\therefore ab - h^2 = 9 \times 1 - 3^2$

$= 0$

The discriminant of conic is

$$\begin{vmatrix} 9 & 3 & 30 \\ 3 & 1 & 10 \\ 30 & 10 & 75 \end{vmatrix} \neq 0$$

Hence given equation is parabola.

Q14. Find the equation of the conic which passes through (1, 1) and the intersection of $x^2 + 2xy + 5y^2 - 7x - 8y + 6 = 0$ with a pair of straight lines $2x - y - 5 = 0$ and $3x + y - 11 = 0$. **[Dec00, Q2(a)]**

Ans. Let $S_1 \equiv x^2 + 2xy + 5y^2 - 7x - 8y + 6 = 0$

$S_2 \equiv (2x - y - 5)(3x + y - 11) = 0$.

Then the required conic is $S_1 + kS_2 = 0$, where we choose k so that (1, 1) lies on the curve. Thus, the curve is

$(1 + 6k)x^2 + (2 - k)xy + (5 - k)y^2 - (7 + 37k)x - (8 - 6k)y + (6 + 55k) = 0$

Since (1, 1) lies on it,

$(1 + 6k) \times 1^2 + (2 - k) \times 1 \times 1 + (5 - k) \times 1^2 - (7 + 37k) \times 1 - (8 - 6k) \times 1 +$

$(6 + 55k) = 0$

$\Rightarrow 1 + 6k + 2 - k + 5 - k - 7 - 37k - 8 + 6k + 6 + 55k = 0$

$\Rightarrow 28k - 1 = 0$

$\Rightarrow k = \frac{1}{28}$

Thus, the conic is

$34x^2 + 55xy + 139y^2 - 233x - 218y + 223 = 0$.

Q15. Identify the curve $x^2 + 4xy + 3y^2 - 5x - 6y + 3 = 0$. If it is central find its centre. Otherwise, find the length of its latus rectum. Further, trace the conic. **[June01, Q5(a)]**

Ans. $x^2 + 4xy + 3y^2 - 5x - 6y + 3 = 0$

Here a = 1, b = 3, h = 2

$\therefore ab - h^2 = 1 \times 3 - 2^2$
$= -1 < 0$
So the given equation is central can be hyperbola or a pair of intersecting lines.

$$\Delta = \begin{vmatrix} 1 & 2 & -5 \\ 2 & 3 & -6 \\ -5 & -6 & 3 \end{vmatrix}$$

$= 1.[9 - 18] - 2[6 - 30] - 5[-12 + 15]$
$= -9 + 48 - 15 = 24 \neq 0$
We can say that equation represents a hyperbola.
It centre is the intersection of $x + hy + g = 0$ and $hx + by + f = 0$
$\Rightarrow x + 2y - 5 = 0$ and $2x\ 3y - 6 = 0$
By solving these two we get
$x = -3, y = 4$
Hence centre is $(-3, 4)$.

Q16. Let $S_1 = 9x^2 + 4y^2 = 1$ and $S_2 \equiv 2xy + 2x + 2y + 1 = 0$. Find K such that $S_1 + KS_2 = 0$ represents a parabola. [Dec02, Q1(a)]

Ans. We have given that,
$S_1 = 9x^2 + 4y^2 = 1$ and
$S_2 = 2xy + 2x + 2y + 1 = 0$
$S_1 + KS_2 = 0$
$9x^2 + 4y^2 - 1 + k(2xy + 2x + 2y + 1) = 0$
$9x^2 + 4y^2 + 2kxy + 2kx + 2ky + k - 1 = 0$
There is a parabola if $ab - h^2 = 0$ and determinant condition is not satisfied.
$a = 9, b = 4, c = 0, g = k, h = k, f = k, h = k,$
$36 - k^2 = 0$ (by $ab - h^2 = 0$)
$k^2 = 36$

$k = \pm 6$

$$\begin{vmatrix} a & h & g \\ h & b & f \\ g & f & c \end{vmatrix} = 0$$

$$\begin{vmatrix} a & k & 1 \\ k & 4 & 1 \\ 1 & 1 & 0 \end{vmatrix} \neq 0$$

$\Rightarrow 9(0 - 1) - k(-1) + 1(k - 4)$

$\Rightarrow -9 + k + k - 4$

$\Rightarrow -9 + 2k - 4$

$\Rightarrow 2k - 13 = 0$

$$k = \frac{13}{2} \neq 0$$

Q17. Reduce the equation

$11x^2 + 2\sqrt{3}\,xy + 9y^2 - 12\sqrt{3}\,x - 12y - 12 = 0$ to the standard form.

Hence identify the curve it represents. **[Dec02, Q4(a)]**

Ans. The given equation is

$$11x^2 + 2\sqrt{3}\,xy + 9y^2 - 12\sqrt{3}\,x - 12y - 12 = 0 \quad \ldots (1)$$

We compare this with general equation and get

Here a = 11

b = 9

$h = \sqrt{3}$

$g = 6\sqrt{3}$

f = -6

c = -12

Now let us rotate the axes through an angle θ, where

$$\tan 2\theta = \frac{2h}{a - b}$$

$$\Rightarrow \frac{2\tan\theta}{1 - \tan^2\theta} = \frac{2\sqrt{3}}{11-9}$$

$$\Rightarrow \frac{2\tan\theta}{1 - \tan^2\theta} = \sqrt{3}$$

$$\Rightarrow 2\tan\theta = \sqrt{3} - \sqrt{3}\tan^2\theta$$

$$\Rightarrow \sqrt{3}\tan^2\theta - 2\tan\theta - \sqrt{3} = 0$$

$$\Rightarrow \sqrt{3}\tan^2\theta - 3\tan\theta + \tan\theta - \sqrt{3} = 0$$

$$\Rightarrow \sqrt{3}\tan\theta\left(\tan\theta - \sqrt{3}\right) + 1\left(\tan\theta - \sqrt{3}\right) = 0$$

$$\Rightarrow \left(\tan\theta - \sqrt{3}\right)\left(\sqrt{3}\tan\theta + 1\right) = 0$$

$\Rightarrow \tan\theta = \sqrt{3}$ or $\tan\theta = -\frac{1}{\sqrt{3}}$

We take $\tan\theta = \sqrt{3}$

$\therefore \sin\theta = \frac{\sqrt{3}}{2}$ and $\cos\theta = \frac{1}{2}$

Equation (1) can transform

$Ax'^2 + By'^2 + 2Gx' + 2Fy' + c = 0$ ... (2)

Where

$A = a\cos^2\theta + 2h\cos\theta\sin\theta + b\sin^2\theta$

$=9.\left(\frac{1}{2}\right)^2 + 2.\sqrt{3}.\frac{1}{2}.\frac{\sqrt{3}}{2} + 11.\left(\frac{\sqrt{3}}{2}\right)^2$

$= \frac{9}{4} + \frac{3}{2} + \frac{33}{4}$

$= \frac{9+6+33}{4}$

$= \frac{48}{4}$

$= 12$

$B = a\sin^2\theta - 2h\sin\theta.\cos\theta + b\cos^2\theta$

$=9.\left(\frac{\sqrt{3}}{2}\right)^2 - 2.\sqrt{3}.\frac{1}{2}.\frac{\sqrt{3}}{2} + 11.\left(\frac{1}{2}\right)^2$

$= \frac{27}{4} - \frac{3}{2} + \frac{11}{4}$

$= \frac{27-6+11}{4}$

$= \frac{32}{4}$

$= 8$

We know that

$ab - h^2 = AB$

$\Rightarrow ab - h^2 = 12 \times 8 \neq 0$

Now both A and B are non-zero

We can write (2) as

$$A\left(X'-\frac{G}{A}\right)^2+B\left(Y'+\frac{F}{B}\right)^2=\frac{G^2}{A}+\frac{F^2}{B}-C$$

Which is a constant K say

Let us shift the origin to $\left(-\frac{G}{A},-\frac{F}{B}\right)$. Then this equation becomes

$AX^2+BY^2=K$ ... (3)

where X and Y are the current co-ordinates if AB = ab – h² > 0 then Equation (3) represents the pair of lines.

$$X=\pm\sqrt{\frac{-B}{A}}Y \text{ if } k=0 \quad \text{... (4)}$$

$$\Rightarrow X=\pm\sqrt{\frac{-8}{12}}Y$$

$$\Rightarrow X^2=\frac{-2}{3}Y^2$$

$$X^2+\frac{2}{3}Y^2=0$$

$$\frac{\frac{X^2}{2}}{3}+\frac{Y^2}{1}=0$$

If k $\neq 0$

$$\frac{\frac{X^2}{k}}{A}+\frac{\frac{Y^2}{k}}{B}=1$$

Since AB = ab – h2

$=11\times 9-\left(\sqrt{3}\right)^2$

= 99 – 3

= 96 > 0

If k > 0 then given equation is ellipse. If k < 0 then it represents empty set.

Q18. Find all the tangents to the conic **[June03, Q5(a)]**

$x^2 + 4xy + 3y^2 - 5x - 6y + 3 = 0$ that are parallel to $y = -\frac{x}{4}$

Ans. General equation

$ax^2 + 2hxy + by^2 + 2gx + 2fy + c = 0$

We know that the condition all tangents

$(prh + pqg - apr - p^2f)^2 = (aq^2 - 2hpq + bp^2)(ar^2 - 2gpr + cp^2)$ ... (1)

In terms of determinants

$$\begin{vmatrix} a & h & g & p \\ h & b & f & q \\ g & f & c & r \\ p & q & r & o \end{vmatrix} = 0 \qquad \text{... (2)}$$

The given equation is

$x^2 + 4xy + 3y^2 - 5x - 6y + 3 = 0$

$y = \frac{-x}{4} \Rightarrow x + 4y = 0$ will be tangent to the given conic if

$$\begin{vmatrix} 1 & 2 & -5/2 & 1 \\ 2 & 3 & -3 & 4 \\ -5/2 & -3 & 3 & 0 \\ 1 & 4 & 0 & 0 \end{vmatrix} = 0$$

$$\Leftrightarrow -\begin{vmatrix} 2 & 3 & -3 \\ -5/2 & -3 & 3 \\ 1 & 4 & 0 \end{vmatrix} + 4\begin{vmatrix} 1 & 2 & -5/2 \\ -5/2 & -3 & 3 \\ 1 & 4 & 0 \end{vmatrix} = 0$$

$\Leftrightarrow$ 40 = 0, which is false.

Thus the given line is not a tangent to the given conic.

Any line parallel to the given line is of the form $x + 4y + c = 0$. This will be a tangent to the given conic if (1) is satisfied, that is,

$(5c + 28)^2 = 3(3c^2 + 24c + 48)$

$\Leftrightarrow c = -5$ or -8

Thus, the required tangents are

$x + 4y - 5 = 0$ and $x + 4y - 8 = 0$

Q19. Trace the conic
$9x^2 - 24xy + 16y^2 - 18x - 101y + 19 = 0$

Ans. We have a = 9, h = -12, b = 16 and $h^2 - ab = 0$

Thus the given conic is a parabola. The given equation can be written as $(3x - 4y)^2 = 18x + 101y - 19$.

We rewrite this equation as

$$(3x - 4y + \lambda)^2 = 18x + 101y - 19 + 6\lambda x - 8\lambda y + \lambda^2$$

$$(3x - 4y + \lambda^2) = 6(\lambda + 3)x + (101 - 8\lambda)y + (\lambda^2 - 19).$$

is a constant to be chosen such that the two lines

Where λ is a constant to be chosen such that the two lines

$3x - 4y + \lambda = 0$,

and $6(\lambda + 3)x + (101 - 8\lambda)y + (\lambda^2 - 19) = 0$ are perpendicular.

Thus $\frac{3}{4}\left[\frac{6\lambda + 18}{8\lambda - 101}\right] = -1$ or $18\lambda + 54 = -32\lambda + 404$ or $\lambda = 7$

Putting $\lambda = 7$ in 1 we get $(3x - 4y + 7)^2 = 60x + 45y + 30 = 15(4x + 3y + 2)$.

The above equation may be written as

$$\left[\frac{3x - 4y + 7}{\sqrt{9 + 16}}\right]^2 = \frac{15}{\sqrt{16 + 9}}\left[\frac{4x + 3y + 2}{\sqrt{16 + 9}}\right]$$

$$\left(\frac{3x - 4y + 7}{5}\right)^2 = 3\left(\frac{4x + 3y + 2}{5}\right)$$

The above equation may be written as

From (2), the following results are obtained :

(i) $3x - 4y + 7 = 0$ is the axis of the parabola.

(ii) $4x + 3y + 2 = 0$ is the tangent at the vertex

(iii) 3 is the latus rectum of the parabola

(iv) Vertex of the parabola is $\left(\frac{-29}{25}, \frac{22}{25}\right)$ given by solving

$3x - 4y + 7 = 0$ and $4x + 3y + 2 = 0$

(v) The slope of the axis $3x - 4y + 7 =$ - is $\tan\theta = \frac{3}{4}$

$\therefore \sin\theta = \frac{3}{5}$ and $\cos\theta = \frac{4}{5}$. We have $a = \frac{1}{4} \to$ (latus rectum) $= \frac{3}{4}$

Focus of the parabola is $S(x_1 + a\cos\theta, y_1 + a\sin\theta)$

$$= S\left[\frac{-29}{25} + \frac{3}{4}\cdot\frac{4}{5}, \frac{22}{25} + \frac{3}{4}\cdot\frac{3}{5}\right] = S\left[\frac{-14}{25}, \frac{133}{100}\right]$$

(vi) Replacing a by – a in the coordinates of S, we get

$$T\left(\frac{-29}{25} - \frac{3}{4}\cdot\frac{4}{5}, \frac{22}{5} - \frac{3}{4}\cdot\frac{3}{5}\right) = T\left(\frac{-44}{25}, \frac{43}{100}\right)$$

The directrix is the line passing through the point T and perpendicular to the axis.

$3x - 4y + 7 = 0$. Its equation is

$$y - \frac{43}{100} = -\frac{4}{3}\left(x + \frac{44}{25}\right) \text{ or } 80x + 60y + 111 = 0.$$

(vii) The parabola meets the y-axis in points given by $16y^2 - 101y + 19 = 0$. Solving, we get y = 6.11, .19 (approx.)

A rough diagram of the curve is shown below

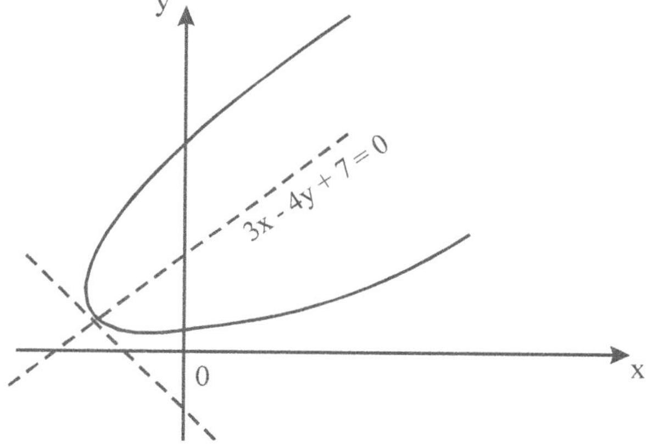

Q20. Trace the conic

$\mathbf{S \equiv x^2 - 24xy - 2y^2 + 10x + 4y = 0}$

Ans. We have a = 1, b = -2, h = -2, g = 5, f = 2 & c = 0

Now $h^2 - ab = 6 > 0 \Rightarrow$ the given conic is a hyperbola.

Step 1. $\partial S/\partial x = 2x - 4y + 10 = 0, \partial S/\partial y = -4x - 4y + 4 = 0$

or $x - 2y + 5 = 0$, $x + y - 1 = 0$

Solving these equation, the centre at the conic is (-1, 2).

Step 2. Shifting the origin to the centre (-1, 2) by means of

$x = X - 1$, $y = Y + 2$ ($x_1 = -1$. $y_1 = 2$).

The given equation of the conic becomes

$X^2 - 2Y^2 - 4XY + c = 0$, $c = gx_1 + fy_1 + c = -1$

$\therefore X^2 - 4XY - 2Y^2 = 1$

$\Rightarrow A = 1,\ B = -2,\ H = -2$.

Step 3. If r be the length of a semi-axis then

$$\frac{1}{r^4} - \frac{1}{r^2}(A+B) + (AB - H^2) = 0$$

or $\frac{1}{r^4} + \frac{1}{r^2} - 6 = 0$ or $6r^4 - r^2 - 1 = 0$

$$\Rightarrow (3r^2+1)(2r^2-1) = 0 \Rightarrow r_1^2 = \frac{1}{2}, r_2^2 = \frac{-1}{3}$$

Length of the transverse axis $= 2r_1 = \sqrt{2}$.

Length of the conjugate axis $= 2\sqrt{-r_2^2} = 2/\sqrt{3}$.

Eccentricity $= \sqrt{\frac{r_1^2 - r_2^2}{r_1^2}} = \sqrt{\frac{5}{3}}$.

Step 4. The equations of the transverse and conjugate axes are

$$\left(A - \frac{1}{r_1^2}\right)X + HY = 0 \text{ and } \left(A - \frac{1}{r_2^2}\right)X + HY = 0$$

$\Rightarrow (1 - 2)\ X - 2Y = 0$ and $(1 + 3)\ X - 2Y = 0$

$\Rightarrow X + 2Y = 0$ and $2X - Y = 0$

$\Rightarrow (x + 1) + 2(y - 2) = 0$ and $2(x + 1) - (y - 2) = 0$

$\Rightarrow X + 2Y = 3$ and $2X - Y + 4 = 0$.

Step 5. The slope of the transverse axis $X + 2Y = 3$ is $\tan\theta = -\frac{1}{2}$

$$\Rightarrow \sin\theta = \frac{-1}{\sqrt{5}}, \cos\theta = \frac{2}{\sqrt{5}}.$$

Also $x_1 = -1, y_1 = 2, e = \sqrt{\frac{5}{3}}, r_1 = \frac{1}{\sqrt{2}}$

The coordinates of the foci are

$$(x_1 \pm r_1 e\cos\theta, y_1 \pm r_1 e\sin\theta)$$

$$=\left(-1\pm\frac{1}{\sqrt{2}}.\sqrt{\frac{5}{3}}.\frac{2}{\sqrt{5}},2\mp\frac{1}{\sqrt{2}}.\sqrt{\frac{5}{3}}.\frac{1}{\sqrt{5}}\right)=\left(-1\pm\sqrt{\frac{2}{3}}.2\mp\frac{1}{\sqrt{6}}\right)$$

Step 6. The given conic meets the x-axis in points (0, 0) and (-10, 0) given by $x^2 - 10x = 0$.

The given conic meets the y-axis in points (0, 0) and (0, 2) given by $-2y^2 + 4y = 0$.

A rough sketch of the hyperbola is shown below:

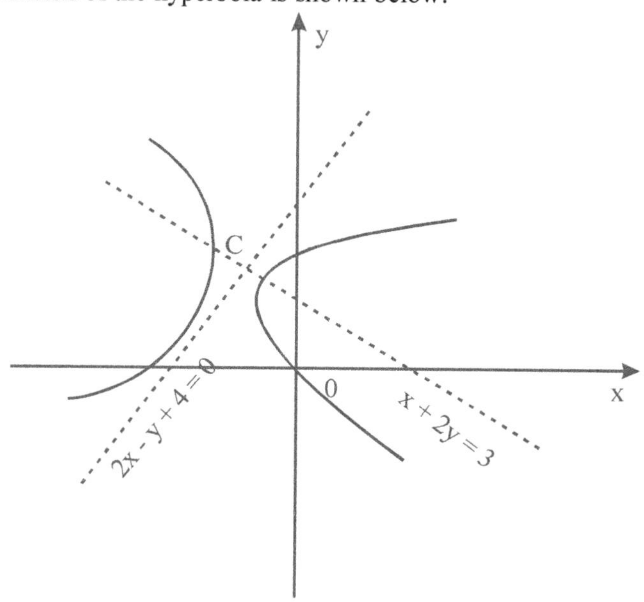

Q21. Trace the curve
$x^2 + xy + y^2 - x + 4y + 3 = 0$

Ans. We have a = b = 1, $h = \frac{1}{2}$, $g = \frac{-1}{2}$, f = 2 and c = 3.

Now $h^2 - ab = -3/4 < 0 \Rightarrow$ the given conic is an ellipse.

Step 1. $\partial S/ax = 2x + y - 1 = 0, \partial S/ax = x + 2y + 4 = 0$

Solving these equations, the centre of the ellipse is (2, -3).

Step 2. Shifting the origin to the centre (2, -3) by means of

$x = X + 2,\ y = Y - 3,\ (x_1 = 2,\ y_1 = -3)$

the given equation of the conic reduces to

$X^2 + XY + Y^2 + C = 0$

Where $c = gx_1 + fy_1 + c = -1 - 6 + 3 = -4$. Thus

$X^2 + XY + Y^2 = 4$ or $\frac{1}{4}x^2 + \frac{1}{4}xy + \frac{1}{4}y^2 = 1$

$A = B = \frac{1}{4}, H = \frac{1}{8}$

Step 3. If r be the length of a semi-axis, then

$$\frac{1}{r^4} - \frac{1}{r^2}(A + B) + (AB - H^2) = 0$$

or $\frac{1}{r^4} - \frac{1}{2r^2} + \frac{3}{64} = 0$ or $3r^4 - 32r^2 + 64 = 0$

$\Rightarrow (3r^2 - 8)(r^2 - 8) = 0 \Rightarrow r_1^2 = 8, r_2^2 = 8/3$

Length of the major axis $= 2r_1 = 4\sqrt{2}$

Length of the minor axis $= 2r_2 = 4\sqrt{\frac{2}{3}}$

Eccetricity $= \frac{\sqrt{r_1^2 - r_2^2}}{r_1^2} = \sqrt{\frac{2}{3}}$

Step 4. The equations of the major and minor axes are

$\left(A - \frac{1}{r_1^2}\right)X + HY = 0$ and $\left(A - \frac{1}{r_2^2}\right)X + HY = 0$

$\Rightarrow \left(\frac{1}{4} - \frac{1}{8}\right)X + \frac{1}{8}Y = 0$ and $\Rightarrow \left(\frac{1}{4} - \frac{3}{8}\right)X + \frac{1}{8}Y = 0$

$\Rightarrow X + Y = 0$ and $(X - Y) = 0$

$X = x - 2, Y = y + 3$

$\Rightarrow (x - 2) + (y + 3) = 0$ and $(x - 2) - (y + 3) = 0$

Thus $x + y + 1 = 0$ and $x - y - 5 = 0$ are the equations of the major axis and minor axis respectively.

Step 5. The slope of the major axis $x + y + 1 = 0$ is $\tan\theta = -1$ i.e. $\theta = -\pi/4$

$\therefore \sin\theta = -1/\sqrt{2}$ and $\cos\theta = 1/\sqrt{2}$

Also $x_1 = 2\ y_1 = -3.\ r_1\ 2\sqrt{2},\ c = \sqrt{\frac{2}{3}}$

The coordinates of the foci are

$\left(x_1 \pm r_1 e \cos\theta, y_1 \pm r_1 e \sin\theta\right)$

$$= \left(2 \pm 2\sqrt{2}.\sqrt{\frac{2}{3}}.\frac{1}{\sqrt{2}}, -3 \mp 2\sqrt{2}.\sqrt{\frac{2}{3}}.\frac{1}{\sqrt{2}}\right)$$

$$= \left(2 \pm 2\sqrt{\frac{2}{3}}, -3 \mp 2\sqrt{\frac{2}{3}}\right)$$

Step 6. The given conic meets the y-axis in points given by
$y^2 + 4y + 3 = 0 \Rightarrow (y + 1)(y + 3) = 0 \Rightarrow y = -1, y = -3$
Thus the ellipse passes through the points (0, -3) and (0, -1).
The given conic does not intersect the x-axis.
Since the discrimination of $x^2 - x + 3 = 0$ is negative.
A rough sketch of the ellipse is shown below

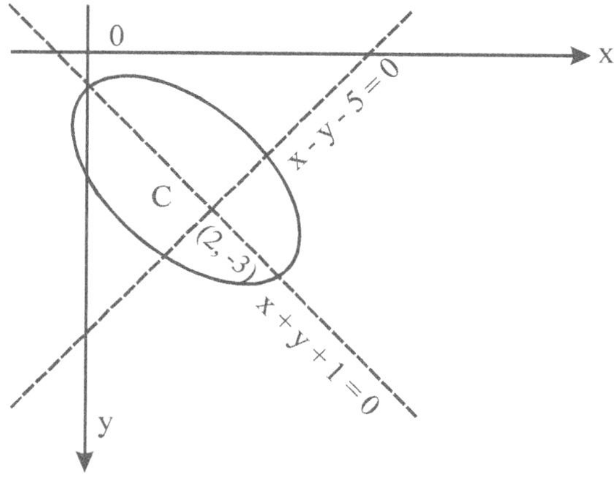

Q22. The centre of the hyperbola $f(x, y) \equiv ax^2 + 2hxy + by^2 + 2gx + 2fy + c = 0$ is (α, β). Show that the equation of the asymptotes is $f(x, y) = f(\alpha, \beta)$

Ans. The equation of the asymptotes is the given conic is
$ax^2 + 2hxy + by^2 + 2gx + 2fy + c + k = 0$
(k being a constant)
Since the asymptotes of a hyperbola pass through the centre.

$\therefore \alpha a^2 + 2h\alpha\beta^2 + 2g\alpha + 2f\beta + c + k = 0$ or $f(\alpha,\beta) + k = 0$ or $k = -f(\alpha,\beta)$

putting this value of k in (1). We obtain

$f(x,y) - f(\alpha,\beta) = 0$ or $f(x,y) = f(\alpha,\beta)$.

Section B

Analytical Geometry (3D)

Chapter-4

Introduction to 3D Co-ordinate Geometry, Straight line, Plane and Sphere

Introduction

If three mutually perpendicular lines meets at a point (o), called three axes i.e. x-axis, y-axis and z-axis and (o) is called origin.

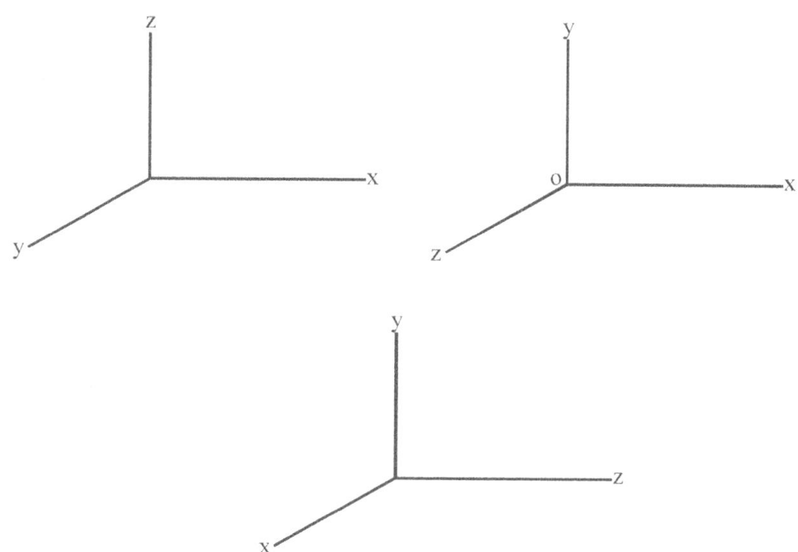

Distance between two points (PQ) when, P $=(x_1,y_1,z_1)$, Q $= (x_2,y_2,z_2)$

$$PQ = \sqrt{(x_1 - x_2)^2 + (y_1 - y_2)^2 + (z_1 - z_2)^2}$$

Division Formula : Let R divides PQ in ratio m:n Internally/Externally

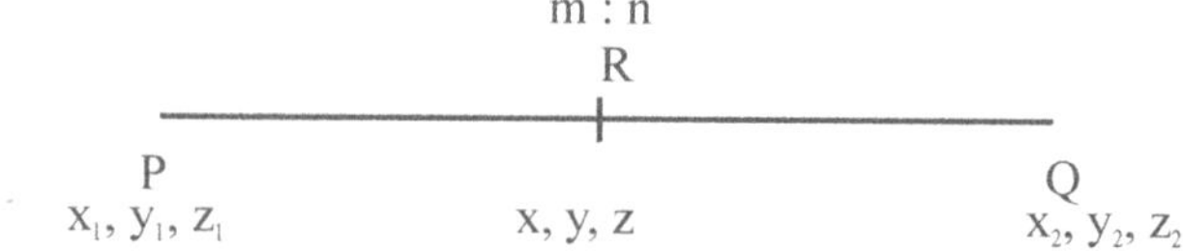

$$R = \frac{mx_2 \pm nx_1}{m \pm n}, \frac{my_2 \pm ny_1}{m \pm n}, \frac{mz_2 \pm nz_1}{m \pm n}$$

Minus sign is used for external division.
If R is mid point then :

$$R = \left(\frac{x_1 + x_2}{2}, \frac{y_1 + y_2}{2}, \frac{z_1 + z_2}{2}\right)$$

Centroid of triangle ABC, when A = (x_1,y_1,z_1), B = (x_2,y_2,z_2), C = (x_3,y_3,z_3) and G be the centroid, G = (x, y, z)

$$G = \left(\frac{x_1 + x_2 + x_3}{3}, \frac{y_1 + y_2 + y_3}{3}, \frac{z_1 + z_2 + z_3}{3}\right)$$

Straight Line :
Direction Cosines (d.c.'s) :

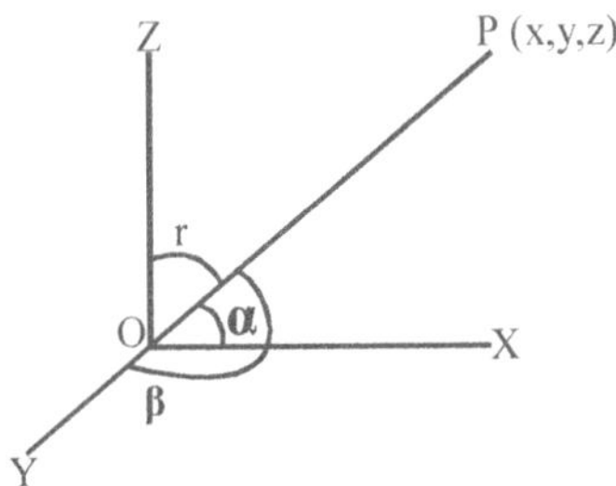

Let OP is a line, makes α, β, γ angle with x,y and z axis respectively.

Then Cosα, Cosβ and Cosγ are the d.c.'s of line OP and also denoted by ℓ, m and n respectively so that ℓ = Cosα, m = Cosβ, n = Cosγ

we have $l^2 + m^2 + n^2 = 1$ i.e. $\text{Cos}^2\alpha + \text{Cos}^2\beta + \text{Cos}^2\gamma = 1$

Direction Ratios (d.r.'s) : Any three numbers (a, b, c) which are proportional to d.c.'s, called d.r.'s i.e.

a α Cosα, b α Cosβ, c α Cosγ or a α l, b α m, c α n then

$$\frac{a}{l} = \frac{b}{m} = \frac{c}{n} = \pm\frac{\sqrt{a^2 + b^2 + c^2}}{\sqrt{l^2 + m^2 + n^2}}$$ and also

$$\therefore l = \frac{a}{\sqrt{a^2 + b^2 + c^2}}, m = \frac{b}{\sqrt{a^2 + b^2 + c^2}}, \frac{c}{\sqrt{a^2 + b^2 + c^2}}$$

$\sum a^2 = a^2 + b^2 + c^2$

$\sum l^2 = l^2 + m^2 + n^2$

d.c.'s and d.r.'s for two points P and Q i.e. for line PQ when P = (x_1, y_1, z_1), Q = (x_2, y_2, z_2)

d.r.'s = $(x_2 - x_1), (y_2 - y_1), (z_2 - z_1)$

$$\text{d.c.'s} = \pm\frac{(x_2 - x_1)}{\sqrt{\sum (x_2 - x_1)^2}}, \pm\frac{(y_2 - y_1)}{\sqrt{\sum (x_2 - x_1)^2}}, \pm\frac{(z_2 - z_1)}{\sqrt{\sum (x_2 - x_1)^2}}$$

where $\sum (x_2 - x_1)^2 = (x_2 - x_1)^2 + (y_2 - y_1)^2 + (z_2 - z_1)^2$

Angle between two lines : Let l_1, m_1, n_1 and l_2, m_2, n_2 are d.c.'s of two lines respectively, and let θ be the angle between them, then :

$\text{Cos}\,\theta = l_1 l_2 + m_1 m_2 + n_1 n_2$

$\text{Sin}\,\theta = \sqrt{(m_1 n_2 - m_2 n_1)^2 + (n_1 l_2 - n_2 l_1)^2 + (l_1 m_2 - l_2 m_1)^2}$

If a_1, b_1, c_1 and a_2, b_2, c_2 are the d.r.'s of two lines then :

$$\text{Cos}\,\theta = \frac{a_1 a_2 + b_1 b_2 + c_1 c_2}{\sqrt{a_1^2 + b_1^2 + c_1^2}\sqrt{a_2^2 + b_2^2 + c_2^2}}$$

$$\text{Sin}\,\theta = \frac{\sqrt{(a_1 b_2 - b_1 a_2)^2 + (b_1 c_2 - b_2 c_1)^2 + (c_1 a_2 - a_2 c_1)^2}}{\sqrt{a_1^2 + b_1^2 + c_1^2}\sqrt{a_2^2 + b_2^2 + c_2^2}}$$

If lines are parallel then,

$\frac{l_1}{l_2} = \frac{m_1}{m_2} = \frac{n_1}{n_2}$ or $\frac{a_1}{a_2} = \frac{b_1}{b_2} = \frac{c_1}{c_2}$, If lines are perpendicular then, $l_1 l_2 + m_1 m_2 + n_1 n_2 = 0$ or

$a_1 a_2 + b_1 b_2 + c_1 c_2 = 0$

Equation of straight line : passing through α, β, γ and having d.c.'s ℓ, m, n is

$$\frac{x - \alpha}{l} = \frac{y - \beta}{m} = \frac{z - \gamma}{n} = r(let)$$

and let a point P lies on this line, then P = $(lr + \alpha, mr + \beta, nr + \gamma)$

Equation of the line passing through point P and Q : P = (x_1, y_1, z_1), Q =

(x_2, y_2, z_2)

$$\frac{x-x_1}{x_2-x_1}=\frac{y-y_1}{y_2-y_1}=\frac{z-z_1}{z_2-z_1}$$

Coplanerity : Three lines with d.c.'s (ℓ_1, m_1, n_1), (ℓ_2, m_2, n_2) and (ℓ_3, m_3, n_3) are coplaner if

$$\begin{vmatrix} l_1 & m_1 & n_1 \\ l_2 & m_2 & n_2 \\ l_3 & m_3 & n_3 \end{vmatrix}=0$$

Plane : A surface, which is, such that the line joining any two points on it lies wholly on it.

General Equation to the plane : Ax + By + cz + D = 0

Equation to the plane when plane passing through point (x_1, y_1, z_1) is : $A(x - x_1) + B(y - y_1) + C(z - z_1) = 0$

Equation of plane in normal form : lx + my + ny = p, where p = length of the normal and l, m, n are d.c.'s.

Equation of plane in intercept form : $\frac{x}{a}+\frac{y}{b}+\frac{z}{c}=1$, where a, b, c are intercepts on x, y, z axis respectively.

Angle between two planes :

Let equation to the planes are :

P $\equiv A_1x+B_1y+C_1z+D_1=0$

Q $\equiv A_2x+B_2y+C_2z+D_2=0$

Let θ be the angle between them,

$$\text{Cos } \theta = \frac{A_1A_2+B_1B_2+C_1C_2}{\sqrt{A_1^2+B_1^2+C_1^2}\,\sqrt{A_2^2+B_2^2+C_2^2}}$$

If planes are perpendicular then $A_1A_2+B_1B_2+C_1C_2 = 0$

If planes are parallel then : $\frac{A_1}{A_2}=\frac{B_1}{B_2}=\frac{C_1}{C_2}$

Equation to the plane through the line of intersection of two given lines : P + λQ = 0, where λ is a constt and will be obtained by passing through given point

Volume of tetrahedron (V), $$V = \frac{1}{6}\begin{vmatrix} x_1 & y_1 & z_1 & 1 \\ x_2 & y_2 & z_2 & 1 \\ x_3 & y_3 & z_3 & 1 \\ x_4 & y_4 & z_4 & 1 \end{vmatrix}$$

Intersection of a straight line and a plane : Let equation to the line is :

$$\frac{x-\alpha}{l}=\frac{y-\beta}{m}=\frac{z-\gamma}{n}=r\,(\text{Let}) \qquad \ldots (1)$$

and equation to the plane is :

$$ax + by + cz + d = 0 \qquad \ldots (2)$$

∴ point have co-ordinate (lr + α , mr + β , nr + γ) and lies on the line. If this point also lies on plane, then

$$(lr+\alpha)\,x + (mr+\beta)y + (nr+\gamma)z + d = 0$$

$$\gamma=\frac{a\alpha+b\beta+c\gamma+d}{al+bm+cn}$$

angle between line and plane is given by :

$$\text{Sin}\,\theta=\frac{la+mb+nc}{\sqrt{a^2+b^2+c^2}}$$

If both are parallel then, $a\ell + bm + nc = 0$.

If both are perpendicular then,

$$\frac{l}{a}=\frac{m}{b}=\frac{n}{c}$$

Sphere : A sphere is a locus of a point, which travels such that the distance from a fixed point along three dimensions remains constant.

Equations of Sphere :

1. General Equation :

$x^2 + y^2 + z^2 + 2ux + 2vy + 2wz + d = 0$

Center C = (–u, –v, –w)

radius r = $\sqrt{u^2+v^2+w^2-d}$

2. Joining the given points as diameter :

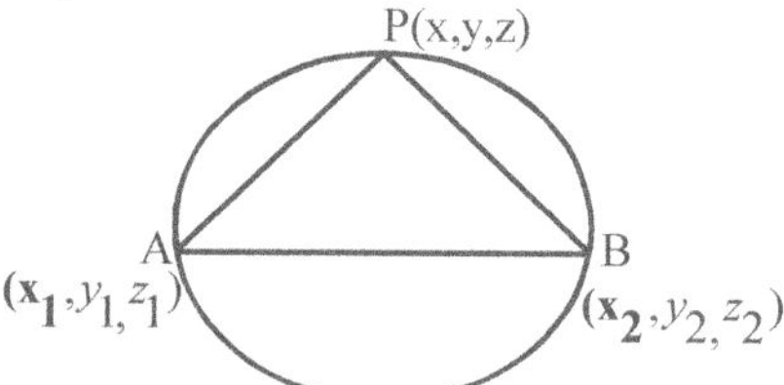

Let A (x_1, y_1, z_1), B (x_2, y_2, z_2) be two given points and Let P(x, y, z) be any point lies on sphere.

d.r.'s of PA = $(x - x_1), (y - y_1), (z - z_1)$

d.r.'s of PB = $(x - x_2), (y - y_2), (z - z_2)$

$\because \angle APB = 90^o$

$\text{Cos } 90 = (x - x_1)(x - x_2) + (y - y_1)(y - y_2) + (z - z_1)(z - z_2)$
(By $\text{Cos}\,\alpha = a_1a_2 + b_1b_2 + c_1c_2$)
$\because$ Cos 90 = 0

$\therefore (x - x_1)(x - x_2) + (y - y_1)(y - y_2) + (z - z_1)(z - z_2) = 0$ which is required equation to the sphere.

3. Where centre (a, b, c) and radius (r) is given : Then Equation to the sphere is :

$$(x - a)^2 + (y - b)^2 + (z - c)^2 = r^2$$

If centre is origin then equation to the sphere is : $x^2 + y^2 + z^2 = r^2$

Plane section of a sphere : Equation to the sphere :

$x^2 + y^2 + z^2 + 2ux + 2vy + 2wz + d = 0$ ... (1)

and equation to the plane is :

$lx + my + nz = p$ ... (2)

Let 0 is the centre of sphere. Let sphere is cut by a plane then there is a

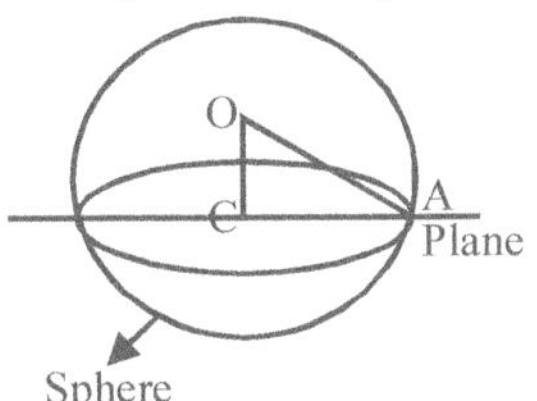

circle with centre C and radius CA. The equation to the circle is given by :

$$(x^2 + y^2 + z^2 + 2ux + 2vy + 2wz + d) + \lambda(lx + my + nz - p) = 0$$

Intersection of two spheres : Let equations of two sphere are :

$$S_1 \equiv x^2 + y^2 + z^2 + 2u_1x + 2v_1y + 2w_1z + d_1 = 0$$

$$S_2 \equiv x^2 + y^2 + z^2 + 2u_2x + 2v_2y + 2w_2z + d_2 = 0$$

then $S_1 + \lambda S_2 = 0$ will represent the equation of intersection of two spheres.

Angle : Let θ be the angle at P then $\text{Cos}\,\theta = \dfrac{r_1^2 + r_2^2 - (c_1c_2)^2}{2r_1r_2}$

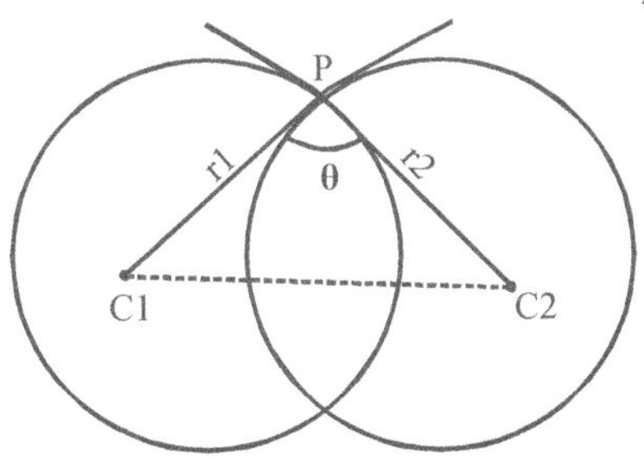

where c_1 and c_2 be their centres, and r_1, r_2 be their radii and c_1c_2 be the distance between both centres and

$$r_1 = \sqrt{u_1^2 + v_1^2 + w_1^2 - d_1}$$

$$r_2 = \sqrt{u_2^2 + v_2^2 + w_2^2 - d_2}$$

$$\therefore Cos\theta = \frac{2u_1u_2 + 2v_1v_2 + 2w_1w_2 - (d_1 + d_2)}{2\sqrt{u_1^2 + v_1^2 + w_1^2 - d_1}\ \sqrt{u_2^2 + v_2^2 + w_2^2 - d_2}}$$

If $\theta = \frac{\pi}{2}$ then, $2u_1u_2 + 2v_1v_2 + 2w_1w_2 = d_1+d_2$

If spherre touches each other then : $c_1c_2 = r_1 + r_2$

Tangent on sphere from a point :

$P = (x_1, y_1, z_1)$

$S = x^2 + y^2 + z^2 + 2ux + 2vy + 2wz + d = 0$

PT be tangent and

$$PT = \sqrt{x_1^2 + y_1^2 + z_1^2 + 2ux_1 + 2vy_1 + 2wz_1 + d}$$

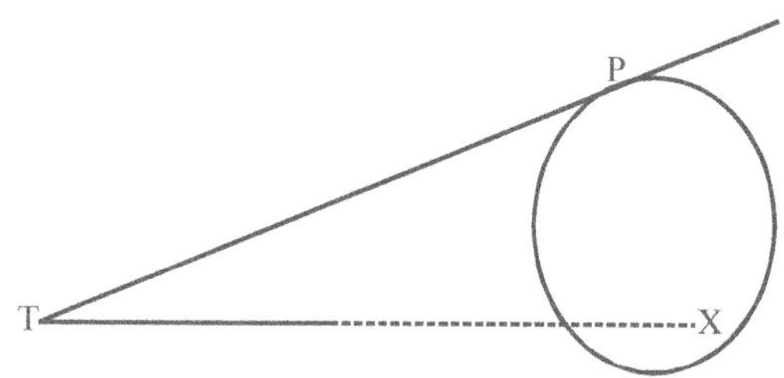

SOLVED EXAMPLES

Q1. If $\cos\alpha$, $\cos\beta$ and $\cos\gamma$ are the direction cosines of a line, show that $\sin^2\alpha + \sin^2\beta + \sin^2\gamma = 2$.

$$\sin^2\alpha + \sin^2\beta + \sin^2\gamma = 1 - \cos^2\alpha + 1 - \cos^2\beta + 1 - \cos^2\gamma$$

Ans. $\sin^2\alpha + \sin^2\beta + \sin^2\gamma = 3 - \left(\cos^2\alpha + \cos^2\beta + \cos^2\gamma\right) = 2$

$(\cos^2\alpha + \cos^2\beta + \cos^2\gamma = 1)$

$\because$ cosα, cosβ, cosγ are d.c's of a line

Q2. Show that the equations of a line through (2, 4, 3) and (–3, 5, 3) are

x + 5y = 22, z = 3.

Ans. The equations are

$$\frac{x+3}{5}=\frac{y-5}{-1}=\frac{z-3}{0}=r\text{, (say,)}$$

– (x + 3) = 5 (y – 5) and z = 3,

x + 5y = 22, z = 3.

Q3. Find the equation of the plane which passes through the points (1, 1, 0), (–2, 2, –1) and (1, 2, 1).

Ans. Equation to the plane is given by

$$\begin{vmatrix} x & y & z & 1 \\ 1 & 1 & 0 & 1 \\ -2 & 2 & -1 & 1 \\ 1 & 2 & 1 & 1 \end{vmatrix}=0$$

Expanding along R_1

$$\Rightarrow x\begin{vmatrix} 1 & 0 & 1 \\ 2 & -1 & 1 \\ 2 & 1 & 1 \end{vmatrix}-y\begin{vmatrix} 1 & 0 & 1 \\ -2 & -1 & 1 \\ 1 & 1 & 1 \end{vmatrix}+z\begin{vmatrix} 1 & 1 & 1 \\ -2 & 2 & 1 \\ 1 & 2 & 1 \end{vmatrix}-\begin{vmatrix} 1 & 1 & 1 \\ -2 & 2 & -1 \\ 1 & 2 & 1 \end{vmatrix}=0$$

$\Rightarrow$ 2x + 3y – 3z = 5.

Q4. Show that the equation of the plane which makes intercepts 2, –1, 5 on the three axes is $\frac{x}{2}+\frac{y}{(-1)}+\frac{z}{5}=1$.

Ans. The points (2, 0, 0), (0, -1, 0), (0, 0, 5) lie on the plane. Thus, its equation is

$$\begin{vmatrix} x & y & z & 1 \\ 2 & 0 & 0 & 1 \\ 0 & -1 & 0 & 1 \\ 0 & 0 & 5 & 1 \end{vmatrix}=0\Rightarrow 5x-10y+2z=10$$

$$\Rightarrow \frac{x}{2}+\frac{y}{(-1)}+\frac{z}{5}=1.$$

Q5. Show that if the sum of the squares of the distances of (a, b, c) from the planes
$x + y + z = 0$, $x = z$ and $x + z = 2y$ is 9, then $a^2 + b^2 + c^2 = 9$.

Ans. We know that

$$\left(\frac{|a+b+c|}{\sqrt{3}}\right)^2 + \left(\frac{|a-c|}{\sqrt{2}}\right)^2 + \left(\frac{|a-2b+c|}{\sqrt{6}}\right)^2 = 9.$$

$\Rightarrow a^2 + b^2 + c^2 = 9.$

Q6. Find the equation of the plane passing through the line $\frac{x+1}{-3} = \frac{y-3}{2} = \frac{z+2}{1}$s and the point (0, 7, –7).

Ans. The line is the intersection of $2(x + 1) = -3(y - 3)$ and $x + 1 = -3(z + 2)$, that is,
$2x + 3y - 7 = 0 = x + 3z + 7.$

Thus, by $(ax + by + cz + d) + k(Ax + By + Cz + D) = 0$, any plane passing through it is of the form
$(2x + 3y - 7) + k(x + 3z + 7) = 0$ for some $k \in \mathbf{R}$.
Since (0, 7, -7) lies on it, we get
$21 - 7 + k(-21 + 7) = 0$, that is, $k = 1$.
Thus, the required plane is
$3x + 3y + 3z = 0$, that is, $x + y + z = 0$.

Q7. Find the equation of the plane passing through (1, 2, 0) and the line $x\cos\alpha + y\cos\beta + z\cos\gamma = 1,\ x + y = z$.

Ans. The equation of the plane passing through the given line is

$$(x\cos\alpha + y\cos\beta + z\cos\gamma - 1) + k(x+y-z) = 0. \quad \text{... (1)}$$

where $k \in \mathbf{R}$ is chosen so that (1, 2, 0) lies on the plane.

$$\therefore (\cos\alpha + 2\cos\beta - 1) + 3k = 0 \Rightarrow k = \frac{1}{3}(1 - \cos\alpha - 2\cos\beta).$$

Thus, the required equation is obtained by putting this value of k in (1) we get

$$(x\cos\alpha + y\cos\beta + z\cos\gamma - 1) + \frac{1}{3}(1 - \cos\alpha - 2\cos\beta)\ (x+y-z) = 0$$

$$3x\cos\alpha + 3y\cos\beta + 3z\cos\gamma - 3 + (1 - \cos\alpha - 2\cos\beta)x$$
$$+(1 - \cos\alpha - 2\cos\beta)y - z(1 - \cos\alpha - 2\cos\beta) = 0$$

$\therefore (3\cos\alpha+1-\cos\alpha-2\cos\beta)x+(3\cos\beta+1-\cos\alpha-2\cos\beta)y+$
$(3\cos\gamma-1+\cos\alpha-2\cos\beta)z-3=0$

$$(2\cos\alpha-2\cos\beta+1)x+(\cos\beta-\cos\alpha+1)y+(3\cos\gamma+\cos\alpha+2\cos\beta)z-3=0$$

Required equation of plane.

Q8. Find the point (or points) of intersection of

$\frac{x+2}{2}=\frac{y+3}{3}=\frac{z+4}{-2}$ and $3x + 2y + 6z = 12$

Ans. Any point on the line is of the form (2k–2, 3k–3, –2k+4), where $k \in \mathbf{R}$. Thus, if there is any point of intersection, it will be given by substituting this triple in $3x + 2y + 6z = 12$.
So, we have
$3(2k - 2) + 2 (3k - 3) + 6 (-2k + 4) = 12$
$\Rightarrow 0 = 0.$
This is true $\forall\, k \in \mathbf{R}$. Thus, for every $k \in \mathbf{R}$, the triple $(2k - 2, 3k - 3, -2k + 4)$ lies in the plane.
This means that the whole line lies in the plane.

Q9. Find the equation of a plane passing through the line of intersection of the planes $7x - 4y + 7z + 16 = 0$ and $4x + 3y - 2z + 13 = 0$, and which is perpendicular to the plane $2x - y - 2z + 5 = 0$.

Ans. The general equation of the plane through the line of intersection is given by
$7x - 4y + 7z + 16 + k (4x + 3y - 2z + 13) = 0.$
$\Rightarrow (7 + 4k)x + (3k - 4)y + (7 - 2k)z + 13k + 16 = 0.$
This will be perpendicular to $2x - y - 2z + 5 = 0$ if
$2(7 + 4k) - (3k - 4) - 2(7 - 2k) = 0$, that is, $k = -\frac{4}{9}$.
Thus, the required equation of the plane is $47x - 48y + 71z + 92 = 0$.

Q10. Show that the angle between the line $\frac{x-a'}{\alpha}=\frac{y-b}{\beta}=\frac{z-c}{\gamma}$ and the plane

$Ax+By+Cz+D=0$ is $\left(\frac{A\alpha+B\beta+C\gamma}{\sqrt{A^2+B^2+C^2}\ \sqrt{\alpha^2+\beta^2+\gamma^2}}\right)$.

Ans. If θ is the angle between the line and the plane, then $\frac{\pi}{2}-\theta$ is the angle between the line and the normal to the plane. Now, A, B, C are the direction ratios of the normal. Thus,

$$\cos\left(\frac{\pi}{2}-\theta\right)=\frac{A\alpha+B\beta+C\gamma}{\sqrt{A^2+B^2+C^2}.\sqrt{\alpha^2+\beta^2+\gamma^2}}.$$

$$\Rightarrow \sin\theta=\frac{A\alpha+B\beta+C\gamma}{\sqrt{A^2+B^2+C^2}.\sqrt{\alpha^2+\beta^2+\gamma^2}}.$$

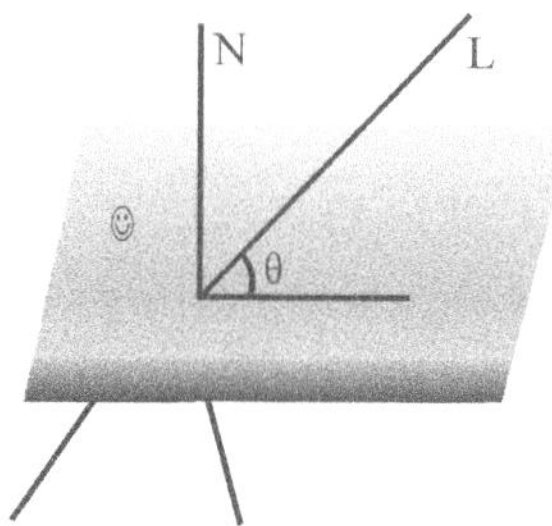

The line L makes an angle θ with plane Π and $(\frac{\Pi}{2}-\theta)$ with normal N to Π

Q11. Find the distance between P (1, 1, –1) and Q (–1, 1, 1). What are the coordinates of the point R that divides PQ in the ratio 3:4?

Ans. PQ = $\sqrt{(1-(-1))^2+(1-1)^2+(-1-1)^2}=\sqrt{8}$

m : n = 3 : 4

The coordinates of R are $=\left(\frac{4\times1+3\times-1}{3+4},\frac{4\times1+3\times1}{3+4},\frac{4\times1+3\times1}{3+4}\right)$

$$=\frac{4-3}{7},\frac{7}{7},\frac{-4+3}{7}$$

$$=\left(\frac{1}{7},1,\frac{-1}{7}\right)$$

Q12. Find the equation of the sphere through the points (0, 0, 0), (0, 1,

–1), (–1, 2, 0) and (1, 2, 3).

Ans. The equation of sphere is :

$x^2 + y^2 + z^2 + 2ux + 2vy + 2wz + d = 0.$

Since the 4 given points lie on it, their coordinates must satisfy this equation. So we get d = 0

$2 + 2v - 2w + d = 0$

$5 - 2u + 4v + d = 0$

$14 + 2u + 4v + 6w + d = 0.$

Solving this system of simultaneous linear equations we get

$$u = -\frac{15}{14},\ v = -\frac{25}{14},\ w = -\frac{11}{14},\ d = 0.$$

Thus, the required sphere is

$7(x^2 + y^2 + z^2) - 15x - 25y - 11z = 0$

Q13. Find the equation of the sphere described on the join of (3, 4, 5) and (1, 2, 3).

Ans. The required equation is

$(x - 3)(x - 1) + (y - 4)(y - 2) + (z - 5)(z - 3) = 0.$

$\Rightarrow x^2 + y^2 + z^2 - 4x - 6y - 8z + 26 = 0.$

Q14. Check if $\frac{x+3}{4} = \frac{y+4}{3} = \frac{z}{5}$ is a tangent to the sphere $x^2 + y^2 + z^2 + 4x + 6y + 10z = 0$.

Ans. $\frac{x+3}{4} = \frac{y+4}{3} = \frac{3}{5} = t$ (let)

$\therefore$ Any point on the line is $(4t - 3, 3t - 4, 5t)$, where $t \in \mathbf{R}$. This will lie on the sphere if

$(4t - 3)^2 + (3t - 4)^2 + 25t^2 + 4(4t - 3) + 6(3t - 4) + 10(5t) = 0.$

$\Leftrightarrow 50t^2 + 36t - 11 = 0$

$$\Leftrightarrow t = \frac{-36 \pm \sqrt{(36)^2 + 2200}}{100}.$$

Since these are real distinct roots, the line will intersect the sphere in two distinct points. Hence, it will not be a tangent to the sphere.

Q15. Find the centre and radius of the circle $x^2 + y^2 + z^2 - 8x + 4y + 8z - 45 = 0,\ x - 2y + 2z = 3$.

Ans. The centre of the sphere is C(4, -2, -4) and its radius is r = $\sqrt{16+4+16+45} = 9$ ·

The distance of the plane from the centre of the sphere is

$$d = \frac{|4+4-8-3|}{\sqrt{1+4+4}} = 1.$$

Thus, the radius of the circle = $\sqrt{r^2 - d^2} = 4\sqrt{5}$ ·

The centre of the circle is the foot of the perpendicular from C onto the plane. To find this, we first need to find the equations of the perpendicular. Its direction ratios are 1, -2, 2. Thus, its equations are

$$\frac{x-4}{1} = \frac{y+2}{-2} = \frac{z+4}{2} .= t \quad \text{(let)}$$

Therefore, any point on the perpendicular is given by (t + 4, -2t – 2, 2t – 4), where $t \in \mathbf{R}$.

This point will be the required centre of the circle if it lies on the plane, that is, if

$$(t + 4) - 2(-2t - 2) + 2(2t - 4) = 3 \Rightarrow t = \frac{1}{3}.$$

Hence, the centre of the circle is $\left(\frac{13}{3}, -\frac{8}{3}, -\frac{10}{3}\right)$.

Q16. Show that 2x – y – 2z = 16 touches the sphere $x^2 + y^2 + z^2 - 4x + 2y + 2z - 3 = 0$, find the point of contact.

Ans. The centre of the sphere is (2, –1, –1) and its radius is

$\sqrt{2^2 + 1^2 + 1^2 + 3} = 3$ ·

The length of the perpendicular from the centre to the plane 2x – y – 2z – 16 = 0 is $\frac{|2.2+1+2-16|}{\sqrt{2^2+1^2+2^2}} = \frac{9}{3} = 3$, which is the same as the radius of the sphere.

So the plane touches the sphere.

Let (x_1, y_1, z_1) be the point of contact. Then the equation of the tangent sphere is

$$xx_1 + yy_1 + zz_1 - 2(x + x_1) + (y + y_1) + (z + z_1) - 3 = 0$$

$$\Rightarrow (x_1 - 2)x + (y_1 + 1)y + (z_1 + 1)z - 2x_1 + y_1 + z_1 - 3 = 0.$$

But this should be the same as the given plane 2x – y – 2z – 16 = 0.

So the coefficients of x, y, z and the constant term in both these equations must be proportional.

$$\therefore \frac{x_1-2}{2}=\frac{y_1+1}{-1}=\frac{z_1+1}{-2}=\frac{2x_1-y_1-z_1+3}{16}$$

$\Rightarrow x_1 = -2y_1$, $z_1 = 1 + 2y_1$, and then

$$\frac{y_1+1}{-1}=\frac{2x_1-y_1-z_1+3}{16}=\frac{-7y_1+2}{16}\Rightarrow 9y_1=-18\Rightarrow y_1=-2.$$

$\therefore x_1 = 4$ and $z_1 = -3$.

Thus, the point of contact is (4, –2, –3).

Q17. Find the angle of intersection of the spheres $x^2 + y^2 + z^2 - 2x + 2y - 4z + 2 = 0$ and $x^2 + y^2 + z^2 = 4$.

Ans. Their centres are C_1 (1, –1, 2) and C_2 (0, 0, 0), respectively.

Both their radii are 2, and $C_1C_2 = \sqrt{(1-0)^2+(1-0)^2+(2-0)^2}$

$$=\sqrt{1+1+4}=\sqrt{6}$$

$$\therefore (C_1C_2)^2=6$$

Thus, the angle of intersection is

$$\cos^{-1}\left(\frac{4+4-6}{2(2)(2)}\right)=\cos^{-1}\left(\frac{1}{4}\right).$$

Q18. Show that the spheres $x^2 + y^2 + z^2 - 2x - 4y - 4z = 0$ and $x^2 + y^2 + z^2 + 10x + 2z + 10 = 0$ touch each other. What is the point of contact?

Ans. Their centres are C_1 (1, 2, 2) and C_2 (-5, 0, -1).

$\therefore C_1C_2 = 7$ = sum of their radii. (C_1C_2, find as Q17, above)

Thus, they touch each other.

The plane $S_1 - S_2 = 0$ is the common tangent plane, where $S_1 = 0$ and $S_2 = 0$ are the two spheres.

This will be $6x + 2y + 3z + 5 = 0$.

The point of contact will be the intersection of the line C_1C_2 with this plane.

Now, C_1C_2 is given by $\frac{x+5}{6}=\frac{y}{2}=\frac{z+1}{3}$. Any point on this is (6t – 5, 2t, 3t – 1). This lies on the tangent plane if $6(6t-5)+2(2t)+3(3t-1)+5=0\Rightarrow$

$$t=\frac{4}{7}.$$

Thus, the point of contact is $\left(\frac{-11}{8},\frac{8}{7},\frac{5}{7}\right)$.

Q19. Find the distance between point P(2, 3, 4) and Q (–1, 2, 3) ?
Ans.

$$PQ=\sqrt{(2-(-1))^2+(3-2)^2+(4-3)^2}$$
$$=\sqrt{9+1+1}\ =\sqrt{11}$$

Q20. Verify that $\frac{\sqrt{l_1+l_2+l_3}}{\sqrt{3}}, \frac{\sqrt{m_1+m_2+m_3}}{\sqrt{3}}, \frac{\sqrt{n_1+n_2+n_3}}{\sqrt{3}}$ can be taken as d.c.'s of a line equally inclinded to three mutually perpendicular lines with d.c.'s $l_1, m_1, n_1; l_2, m_2, n_2; l_3, m_3, n_3$?

Ans. We have

$$l_1^2+m_1^2+n_1^2=1,\ l_2^2+m_2^2+n_2^2=1, l_3^3+m_3^3+n_3^3=1,$$
$$l_1l_2+m_1m_2+n_1n_2=0, l_2l_3+m_2m3+n_2n_3=0,$$
$$l_3l_1+m_3m_1+n_3n_1=0$$

we have given a line L, whose d.c.'s are :

$$\frac{l_1+l_2+l_3}{\sqrt{3}}, \frac{m_1+m_2+m_3}{\sqrt{3}}, \frac{n_1+n_2+n_3}{\sqrt{3}}$$

Let three lines are L_1, L_2, L_3, which makes angles α, β, γ with line L then :

$$\text{Cos}\,\alpha=l_1\left(\frac{l_1+l_2+l_3}{\sqrt{3}}\right)+m_1\left(\frac{m_1+m_2+m_3}{\sqrt{3}}\right)+n_1\left(\frac{n_1+n_2+n_3}{\sqrt{3}}\right)$$

$$=\frac{1}{\sqrt{3}}\left[\left(l_1^2+m_1^2+n_1^2\right)+\left(l_1l_2+m_1m_2+n_1n_2\right)+\left(l_1l_3+m_1m_3+n_1n_3\right)\right]$$

$$=\frac{1}{\sqrt{3}}[1+0+0]\ \text{(from above)}$$

$$=\frac{1}{\sqrt{3}}\quad \therefore \alpha=Cos^{-1}\left(\frac{1}{\sqrt{3}}\right)$$

Similarly we can find, Cos $\beta=\frac{1}{\sqrt{3}}$ = Cos γ

$$\beta=\text{Cos}^{-1}\left(\frac{1}{\sqrt{3}}\right)=\gamma$$

So $\alpha = \beta = \gamma$

Hence L is equally inclinded to the lines L_1, L_2 and L_3.

Q21. If a line makes angles α, β, γ and δ with the four diagonals of a cube, prove that $\cos^2\alpha + \cos^2\beta + \cos^2\gamma + \cos^2\delta = \frac{4}{3}$

Ans. Let 0 be the origin and OA, OB, OC (each = a) be the axes :-
Thus co-ordinate of points are O (0, 0, 0), A (a, 0, 0), B (0, a, 0), C (0, 0, a), D(a, a, a), E (0, a, a), F (a, 0, a), G(a, a,0).

Here OD, AE, FB and CG are four diagonals. Let ℓ, m, n be the d.c.'s of the given line:
Now d.r.'s of OD = a–0, a–0, a–0
= a, a, a

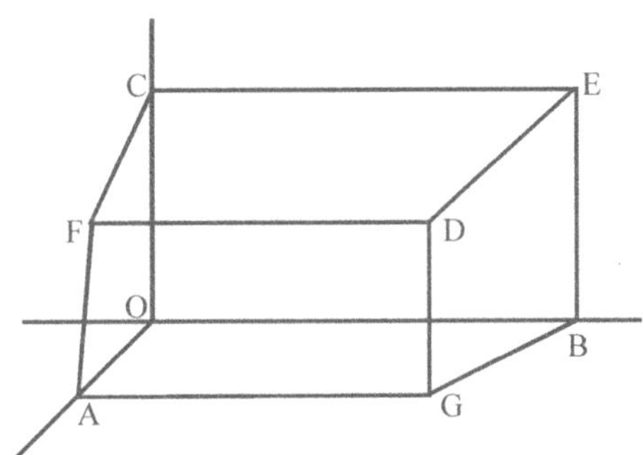

Similarly :
d.r.'s of AE = –a, a, a
d.r.'s of FB = a, –a, a
d.r.'s of CG = a, a, –1

d.c.'s of OD = $\frac{1}{\sqrt{3}}, \frac{1}{\sqrt{3}}, \frac{1}{\sqrt{3}}$

d.c.'s of AE = $-\frac{1}{\sqrt{3}}, \frac{1}{\sqrt{3}}, \frac{1}{\sqrt{3}}$

d.c.'s of FB = $\frac{1}{\sqrt{3}}, -\frac{1}{\sqrt{3}}, \frac{1}{\sqrt{3}}$

d.c.'s of CG = $\frac{1}{\sqrt{3}}, \frac{1}{\sqrt{3}}, -\frac{1}{\sqrt{3}}$

If the given line makes an angle α with OD, β with AE, γ with FB and δ with CG then :

$$\cos\alpha = l\left(\frac{1}{\sqrt{3}}\right) + m\left(\frac{1}{\sqrt{3}}\right) + n\left(\frac{1}{\sqrt{3}}\right)$$

$$\cos\alpha = \frac{1}{\sqrt{3}}(l+m+n) \qquad \text{... (i)}$$

Similarly :

$$\cos\beta = \frac{1}{\sqrt{3}}(-l+m+n) \qquad \text{... (ii)}$$

$$\cos\gamma = \frac{1}{\sqrt{3}}(l-m+n) \qquad \text{... (iii)}$$

$$\cos\delta = \frac{1}{\sqrt{3}}(l+m-n) \qquad \text{... (iv)}$$

Squaring (i), (ii), (iii) and (iv) and adding : $\cos^2\alpha + \cos^2\beta + \cos^2\gamma + \cos^2\delta$

$$= \frac{1}{3}\left[(l+m+n)^2 + (-l+m+n)^2 + (l-m+n)^2 + (l+m-n)^2\right]$$

$$= \frac{1}{3}\left[4(l^2+m^2+n^2)\right] \qquad (\because l^2+m^2+n^2=1)$$

$$= \frac{1}{3}\times[4\times1]$$

$$= \frac{4}{3} \text{ Proved.}$$

Q22. Find the equation to a sphere which has centre (3, 2, -5) and radius 2 units ?

Ans. Equation to the sphere is : $(x-3)^2+(y-2)^2+(z+5)^2=2^2$

$$= x^2+9-6x+y^2+4-4y+z^2+25+10z=4$$

$$= x^2+y^2+z^2-6x-4y+10z+34=0$$

Q23. Find the equation of the sphere whose ends of diameter are (α,β,γ) and (a, b, c) ?

Ans. Equation to the sphere is : $(x-\alpha)(x-a)+(y-\beta)(y-b)+(z-\gamma)(z-c)=0$

$$= x^2 - x(a+\alpha)+\alpha a+y^2-y(b+\beta)+\beta b+z^2-z(c+\gamma)+\gamma c=0$$

$$= x^2+y^2+z^2-(a+\alpha)x-(b+\beta)y-(c+\gamma)z+(\alpha a+\beta b+\gamma c)=0$$

which is required sphere.

Q24. Find the centre and radius of the sphere [June98, Q3(a)]
$x^2 + y^2 + z^2 - 8x + 4y + 8z - 45 = 0$
Hence determine whether the point (1, –2, 0) lies inside or outside the sphere.

Ans. $x^2 + y^2 + z^2 - 8x + 4y + 8z - 45 = 0$

Centre of Sphere

$$\left(\frac{-u}{2}, \frac{-v}{2}, \frac{w}{2}\right)$$

$$= \left(\frac{-(-8)}{2}, \frac{-4}{2}, \frac{-8}{2}\right)$$

= (4, -2, -4)

Radius of sphere

$$\sqrt{u^2 + v^2 + w^2 - d}$$

$$= \sqrt{(4)^2 + (-2)^2 + (-4)^2 + 45}$$

$$= \sqrt{16 + 4 + 16 + 45} = \sqrt{81}$$

= 9

Distance between point to the centre

$$= \sqrt{(1-4)^2 + (-2+2)_2 + (0+4)^2}$$

$$= \sqrt{9+16} = \sqrt{25}$$

$5 < 9$

i.e.(<radius of sphere)

Hence, (4, -2, -4) is lies inside the sphere.

Q25. Find the angle of intersection between the two spheres [June98, Q3(b)]
$x^2 + y^2 + z^2 - 6x - 2y + 2z + 2 = 0$
and $x^2 + y^2 + z^2 - 4x - 8y - 12z + 20 = 0$

Ans. $x^2 + y^2 + z^2 - 6x - 2y + 2z + 2 = 0$ ... (1)

$x^2 + y^2 + z^2 - 4x - 8y - 12z + 20 = 0$ ... (2)

Centres of spheres (1) and (2) are $C_1 \equiv (3, 1, -1)$, $C_2 = (2, 4, 6)$

Then, their radii are

$$r_1 = \sqrt{u_1^2 + v_1^2 + w_1^2 - d_1}$$

$$=\sqrt{(3)^2+(1)^2+(-1)^2-2}$$

$$=\sqrt{9+1+1-2}$$

$$=\sqrt{9}=3$$

and $r_2 == \sqrt{(2)^2+(4)^2+(4)^2-20}$

$$=\sqrt{4+16+36-20}$$

$$=\sqrt{56-20}$$

$$=\sqrt{36}=6$$

Let distance between centres of sphere = d

$$d == \sqrt{(3-2)^2+(1-4)^2+(-1-6)^2}$$

$$d == \sqrt{1+9+49}=\sqrt{59}$$

$d^2 = 59$

Distance between their angle between to the two sphere is

$$\cos\theta=\frac{r_1^2+r_2^2-d^2}{2r_1.r_2}$$

$$\cos\theta=\frac{3^2+6^2-59}{36}$$

$$\cos\theta=\frac{9+36-59}{36}=\frac{45-59}{36}$$

$$\cos\theta=\frac{-14}{36}$$

$$\theta=\cos^{-1}\left(\frac{7}{18}\right)$$

Q26. Find the centre of a sphere through the points of intersection of $x^2 + y^2 + z^2 = 1$ and $2x + y + z = 3$, and which passes through (1, 1, 1).

[Dec98, Q3(a)]

Ans. $x^2 + y^2 + z^2 = 1$ ... (1)

$2x + y + z = 3$ ... (2)

Equation of sphere is given as,

$\Rightarrow x^2 + y^2 + z^2 - 1 + k(2x + y + z - 3) = 0$

it passes through (1, 1, 1) so,

$\Rightarrow 1^2 + 1^2 + 1^2 - 1 + k(2 + 1 + 1 - 3) = 0$

$\Rightarrow 2 + k = 0$

$\Rightarrow k = -2$

$\therefore$ Required equation of sphere is

$x^2 + y^2 + z^2 - 1 - 2(2x + y + z - 3) = 0$

$\Rightarrow x^2 + y^2 + z^2 - 1 - 4x - 2y - 2z + 6 = 0$

$\Rightarrow x^2 + y^2 + z^2 - 4x - 2y - 2z + 5 = 0$

Q27. Find the angle between the lines of intersection of x + y + z = 0 and ayz + bzx + cxy = 0, where a, b, c are real numbers, abc ≠ 0 and a + b + c = 0. [Dec98, Q5(a)]

Ans. The given lines are

$x + y + z = 0$ ... (i)

$ay^2 + bzx + cxy = 0$ ... (ii)

We know that

$$\alpha = \tan^{-1}\left|\frac{2P\sqrt{u^2+v^2+w^2}}{(a+b+c)(u^2+v^2+w^2)-c(u,v,w)}\right|$$

$$\text{where } p^2 = \begin{vmatrix} a & h & g & u \\ h & b & f & v \\ g & f & c & w \\ u & v & w & o \end{vmatrix}$$

Here

u = 1, v = 1, w = 1, a + b + c = 0

$$\alpha = \tan^{-1}\left|\frac{2P\sqrt{1^2+1^2+1^2}}{0(1^2+1^2+1^2)-(a+b+c)}\right|$$

$$\alpha = \tan^{-1}\left|\frac{2P\sqrt{3}}{-a+b+c}\right|$$

$$P^2 = \begin{vmatrix} 0 & a/2 & b/2 & 1 \\ a/2 & 0 & a/2 & 1 \\ b/2 & a/2 & 0 & 1 \\ 1 & 1 & 1 & 0 \end{vmatrix}$$

$$P^2 = 0\begin{vmatrix} 0 & a/2 & 1 \\ a/2 & 0 & 1 \\ 1 & 1 & 0 \end{vmatrix} - a/2\begin{vmatrix} a/2 & b/2 & 1 \\ a/2 & 0 & 1 \\ 1 & 1 & 1 \end{vmatrix}$$

$$+b/2\begin{vmatrix} a/2 & b/2 & 1 \\ 0 & a/2 & 1 \\ 1 & 1 & 0 \end{vmatrix} - 1\begin{vmatrix} a/2 & b/2 & 1 \\ 0 & a/2 & 1 \\ a/2 & 0 & 1 \end{vmatrix}$$

$$= 0 - a/2\left[a/2(0-1) - a/2\left(b/2 - 1\right) + 1\left(b/2 - 0\right)\right]$$

$$+b/2\left[a/2(0-1) - 0(0-1) + 1\left(b/2 - a/2\right)\right]$$

$$-1\left[a/2\left(a/2 - 0\right) - 0\left(b/2 - 0\right) + a/2\left(b/2 - a/2\right)\right]$$

$$= -\frac{a}{2}\left[-\frac{a}{2} - \frac{ab}{4} + \frac{a}{2} + \frac{b}{2}\right] + \frac{b}{2}\left[-\frac{a}{2} + \frac{b}{2} - \frac{a}{2}\right] - \left[\frac{a^2}{4} + \frac{ab}{4} - \frac{a^2}{4}\right]$$

$$-\frac{a^2}{4} + \frac{a^2b}{8} - \frac{a^2}{4} - \frac{ab}{4} - \frac{ab}{4} + \frac{b^2}{4} - \frac{ab}{4} - \frac{a^2}{4} + \frac{ab}{4} - \frac{a^2}{4}$$

$$P^2 = -\frac{4a^2}{4} + \frac{b^2}{4} + \frac{a^2b}{8} - \frac{2ab}{4}$$

$$P^2 = -a^2 + \frac{b^2}{4} + \frac{a^2b}{8} - \frac{ab}{2}$$

$$P^2 = \frac{-8a^2 + 2b^2 + a^2b - 4ab}{8}$$

$$\therefore P^2 = \sqrt{\frac{-8a^2 + 3b^2 + a^2b - 4ab}{2\sqrt{2}}}$$

$$\therefore \alpha = \tan^{-1}\left[\frac{2\sqrt{-8a^2 + 3b^2 + a^2b - 4ab}\left(\sqrt{3}\right)}{2\sqrt{2}(-a + b + c)}\right]$$

Q28. For which values of $\lambda \in R$ does not plane $x + y + z = \lambda$ touch the sphere $x^2 + y^2 + z^2 = 1$? Also find the point of contact for the planes, out of these ones, that touch the sphere. [June99, Q2(a)]

Ans. $x + y + z = \lambda$ touch sphere

$x^2 + y^2 + z^2 = 1$

Distance of plane from centre (0, 0, 0) of sphere = 1

The plane is tangent to the sphere, if the point of contact is (a, b, c) the equation of sphere

$ax + by + cz - 1 = 0$

$x + y + z = \lambda$

$x + y + z - \lambda = 0$

$$\therefore \frac{a}{1} = \frac{b}{1} = \frac{c}{1} = \frac{1}{\lambda}$$

Thus the point of contact is $\left(\frac{1}{\lambda}, \frac{1}{\lambda}, \frac{1}{\lambda}\right)$

Q29. Find the equation of the plane passing through the line of intersection of the planes [June99, Q3(a)]

$7x - 4y + 7z + 16 = 0$ and

$4x + 3y - 2z + 13 = 0$,

and which is perpendicular to the plane

$x - y - 2z + 5 = 0$

Ans. The general equation of the plane through the line of interaction

$(7x + 4y + 7z + 16) + k(4x + 3y - 2z + 13) = 0$

$(7x + 4kx) + (3ky - 4y) + (7z - 2kz) + (13k + 16) = 0$

This will perpendicular to $x - y - 2z + 5 = 0$

$(7 + 4k) - (3k - 4) - 2(7 - 2k) = 0$

$\Rightarrow 7 + 4k - 3k + 4 - 14 + 4k = 0$

$\Rightarrow 7 + k - 10 + 4k = 0$

$\Rightarrow -3 + 5k = 0$

$\Rightarrow 5k = 3$

$k = 3/5$

$\therefore$ The required equation of plane is

$$\Rightarrow (7x - 4y + 7z + 16) + \frac{3}{5}(4x + 3y - 2z + 13) = 0$$

$\Rightarrow 35x - 20y + 35z + 80 + 12x + 9y - 6z + 39 = 0$

$\Rightarrow 23x - 11y + 29z + 119 = 0$

Q30. Find the equation of the sphere passing through the origin and cutting off intercepts a, b and c from the positive directions of the coordinate axes. [Dec99, Q2(b)]

Ans. Let the radius of the given sphere be d and the centre is (α, β, γ).

Since the sphere passes through the origin

The equation of the sphere is

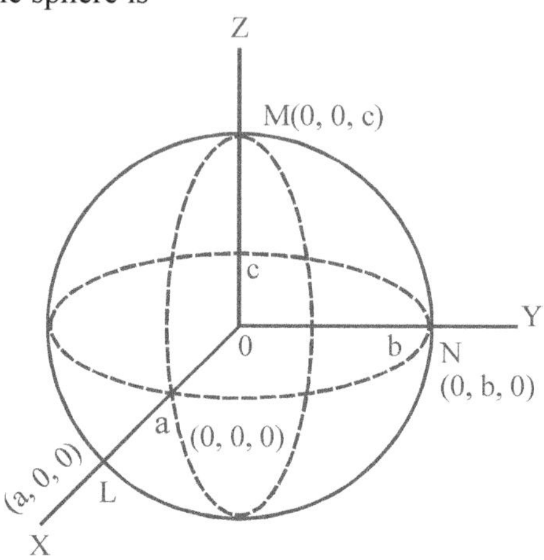

$$(x-\alpha)^2+(y-\beta)^2+(z-\gamma)^2=d^2 \quad \text{... (1)}$$

Since this sphere cuts intercepts a, b, c from axes x, y, z respectively therefore this sphere passes through the points (a, 0, 0), (0, b, 0) & (0, 0, c).

Since sphere passes through (0, 0, 0)

From (1)

$$\alpha^2+\beta^2+\gamma^2=d^2 \quad \text{... (2)}$$

Also since it passes through (a, 0, 0)

$$\therefore (a-\alpha)^2+(0-\beta)^2+(0-\gamma)^2=d^2$$

$$(a-\alpha)^2+\beta^2+\gamma^2=d^2 \quad \text{... (3)}$$

Similarly, it passes through (0, b, 0)

From (1), we have

$$\alpha^2+(b-\beta)^2+\gamma^2=d^2 \quad \text{... (4)}$$

Similarly, for (0, 0, c)

$$\alpha^2+\beta^2+(c-\gamma)^2=d^2 \quad \text{... (5)}$$

(2) – (3), we get

Equation, $\alpha^2-(a-\alpha)^2=0$

or, $\alpha^2 - \left(a^2 + \alpha^2 - 2a\alpha\right) = 0$

or, $\alpha^2 - a^2 - \alpha^2 + 2a\alpha = 0$

or, $2a\alpha - a^2 = 0$

or, $a\left(2\alpha - a\right) = 0$

Since a cannot be zero

$\therefore 2\alpha - a = 0$

or, $\alpha = a/2$

Similarly (2) – (4), we get

$\beta = b/2$

and $\gamma = c/2$

$\therefore$ centre is(a/2, b/2, c/2)

$\therefore$ radius d=$\sqrt{\frac{a^2}{4} + \frac{b^2}{4} + \frac{c^2}{4}}$

$= \sqrt{\frac{a^2 + b^2 + c^2}{4}}$

$= \sqrt{\frac{a^2 + b^2 + c^2}{2}}$

$\therefore$ equation of sphere is

$$\left(x - a/2\right)^2 + \left(y - b/2\right)^2 + \left(2 - c/2\right)^2 = \frac{a^2 + b^2 + c^2}{4}$$

Q31. Find the equation of the sphere having the same centre as $x^2 + y^2 + z^2 - 2x - 4y - 6z - 11 = 0$, but of double the radius.[Dec99, Q3(a)]

Ans. The given sphere is

$x^2 + y^2 + z^2 - 2x - 4y - 6z - 11 = 0$

$\Rightarrow x^2 - 2x + 1 + y^2 - 4y + 4 + z^2 - 6z + 9 - 1 - 4 - 9 - 11 = 0$

$\Rightarrow (x + 1)^2 + (y - 2)^2 + (z - 3)^2 - 25 = 0$

$\Rightarrow (x + 1)^2 + (y - 2)^2 + (z - 3)^2 = 5^2$

Hence centre is (-1, 2, 3) and radius is 5.

Now we have to find out the equation of sphere which centre is same (i) c (-1, 2, 3) and radius is $2 \times 5 = 10$.

Here $x_1 = -1$, $y_1 = 2$, $z_1 = 3$ and r = 10.

Equation of a sphere with centre (x_1, y_1, z_1) and radius r is
$(x - x_1)^2 + (y - y_1)^2 + (z - z_1)^2 = r^2$
$\Rightarrow (x + 1)^2 + (y - 2)^2 + (z - 3)^2 = 10^2$
$\Rightarrow x^2 + 2x + 1 + y^2 - 4y + 4 + z^2 - 6z + 9 - 100 = 0$
$\Rightarrow x^2 + y^2 + z^2 + 2x - 4y - 6z - 86 = 0$
is the required equation of sphere.

Q32. Find the angle between $\frac{x}{1} = 1 - y = \frac{z+1}{2}$ and $y + z = 3$.[June00, Q5(a)]

Ans. $\frac{x}{1} = \frac{1-y}{1} = \frac{z+1}{2}$ and $y + z = 3$

$$\cos\theta = \frac{1\times(0) + 1(1) + 2(1)}{\sqrt{6}\times\sqrt{2}}$$

$$= \frac{0+1+2}{\sqrt{12}} = \frac{3}{\sqrt{12}} = \frac{3}{2\sqrt{3}}$$

$$\frac{3}{2\sqrt{3}} = \frac{3}{2\sqrt{3}} \times \frac{\sqrt{3}}{\sqrt{3}} = \frac{3\sqrt{3}}{6} = \frac{\sqrt{3}}{2}$$

$$\cos\theta = \frac{\sqrt{3}}{2}$$

$$\cos\theta = \cos 30^\circ$$

$$\therefore \theta = 30^\circ$$

Q33. Find the equation of the plane which passes through A(2, 2, 1) and B(3, 4, 2) perpendicular to the plane $2x + 6y + 7z + 5 = 0$. [Dec00, Q2(b)]

Ans. Equation of the plane passing through (2, 2, 1) is given by
$A(x - 2) + B(y - 2) + C(z - 1) = 0$ ... (1)
If it contains (3, 4, 2) then
$A + 2B + C = 0$ ... (2)
Since the plane (1) is perpendicular to the plane
$2x + 6y + 7z + 5 = 0$
We have $2A + 6B + 7C = 0$ ... (3)
Eliminating A, B and C from (1), (2) and (3), we get the equation of the required plane as

$$\begin{vmatrix} x-2 & y-2 & z-1 \\ 1 & 2 & 1 \\ 2 & 6 & 7 \end{vmatrix} = 0$$

$\Rightarrow$ (x – 2) [14 – 6] – 1 × [7y – 14 – 6z + 6] + 2 × [y – 2 – 2z + 2] = 0

$\Rightarrow$ 15x – 16 – 7y + 8 + 6z + 2y – 4z = 0

$\Rightarrow$ 15x – 7y + 2y – 8 = 0

Q34. Find the tangent planer of the sphere **[Dec00, Q3(a)]**
$x^2 + y^2 + z^2 - 4x + 2y - 6z + 5 = 0$
which are parallel to the plane 2x + 2y = z.

Ans. The given sphere is

$x^2 + y^2 + z^2 - 4x + 2y - 6z + 5 = 0$

Here

u = -2, v = 1, w = -3, d = 5

The equation of tangent plane is

xa + yb + zc + u(x + a) + v(y + b) + w(z + c) + d = 0

$\Rightarrow$ xa + yb + zc – 2(x + a) + 1(y + b) – 3(z + c) + 5 = 0

$\Rightarrow$ (a – 2) x + (b + 1) y + (c – 3)z – 2a + b – 3c + 5 = 0 ... (1)

Since equation is parallel to

2x + 2y = z

$\Rightarrow$ 2x + 2y – z = 0

$$\therefore \frac{a-2}{2} = \frac{b+1}{2} = \frac{c-3}{-1} = k \text{ (say)}$$

$\therefore$ a = 2k + 2

b = 2k – 1

c = 3 – k

Put these value in equation (1) we get

(2k + 2 – 2)x + (2k – 1 + 1)y + (3 – k – 3)z – 2(2k + 2) + (2k – 1) – 3(3 + k) + 5 = 0

$\Rightarrow$ 2kx + 2ky – kz – 5k – 9 = 0

This is required plane where $k \in R$.

Q35. Find the projection of AB on CD, where A, B, C, D are points given by (2, 3, 5), (3, 6, 2), (1, –2, 2), (4, 2, 3) respectively. **[Dec00, Q3(b)]**

Ans. The direction ratio of CD are (4 – 1), (2 + 2), (3 – 2)

That is 3, 4, 1

Therefore the direction consine are

$$\frac{3}{\sqrt{3^2+4^2+1^2}}, \frac{4}{\sqrt{3^2+4^2+1^2}}, \frac{1}{\sqrt{3^2+4^2+1^2}},$$

that is $\frac{3}{\sqrt{26}}, \frac{4}{\sqrt{26}}, \frac{1}{\sqrt{26}}$

Hence the projection of AD and CD is

$$(3-2)\times\frac{3}{\sqrt{26}}+(6-3)\times\frac{4}{\sqrt{26}}+(2-5)\times\frac{1}{\sqrt{26}}$$

$$=\frac{3}{\sqrt{26}}+\frac{12}{\sqrt{26}}-\frac{3}{\sqrt{26}}$$

$$=\frac{3+12-3}{\sqrt{26}}$$

$$=\frac{12}{\sqrt{26}}$$

Q36. Find the equation of the sphere through the circle $x^2 + y^2 + z^2 - 2x + 3y + 6 = 0$, $x - 2y + 4z - 9 = 0$ and the centre of the sphere $x^2 + y^2 + z^2 - 2x + 4y - 6z + 5 = 0$ [June01, Q3(a)]

Ans. Let equation of the sphere be

$x^2 + y^2 + z^2 + 2x + 3y + 6 + k(x - 2y + 4z - 9) = 0$ .....(1)

Since it passes through the centre of sphere

$x^2 + y^2 + z^2 - 2x + 4y - 6z + 5 = 0$

Now centre of given sphere is

$C(-u, -v, -w)$

Here $u = -1$, $v = -2$, $w = -3$

Hence, centre is $(1, -2, 3)$

Required sphere is passes through it hence from (1)

$1^2 + (-2)^2 + 3^2 + 2.1 + 3.(-2) + 6 + k[1 - 2.(-2) + 4.3 - 9] = 0$

$\Rightarrow 1 + 4 + 9 + 2 - 6 + 6 + k[1 + 4 + 12 - 9] = 0$

$\Rightarrow 16 + k \times 8 = 0$

$\Rightarrow k = -2$

Hence the equation of sphere is

$x^2 + y^2 + z^2 + 2x + 3y + 6 - 2(x - 2y + 4z - 9) = 0$

$\Rightarrow x^2 + y^2 + z^2 + 2x + 3y + 6 - 2x - 4y + 8z + 18 = 0$

$x^2 + y^2 + z^2 + 7y - 8z + 24 = 0$

Q37. Find the plane passing through the intersection of $6x - 3y - 23 = 0$, $3z + 2 = 0$ and perpendicular to $2x + 3y - 5z + 1 = 0$. **[June01, Q5(b)]**

Ans. The equation of the plane passing through the intersection of two given plane is

$(6x - 3y - 23) + \lambda(3z + 2) = 0$

$6x - 3y + 3\lambda z - 23 + 2\lambda = 0$ ... (1)

Since it is perpendicular

$2x + 3y - 5z + 1 = 0$

$\therefore aa' + bb' + cc' = 0$

$\Rightarrow 6.2 + (-3).3 + 3\lambda.(-5) = 0$

$\Rightarrow 12 - 9 - 15\lambda = 0$

$\Rightarrow \lambda = 3/15 = 1/5$

Putting the value of in λ (1) we get

$$6x - 3y + 3.\frac{1}{5}z - 23 + 2 \times \frac{1}{5} = 0$$

$\Rightarrow 30x - 15y + 3z - 115 + 2 = 0$

$\Rightarrow 30x - 15y + 3z - 113 = 0$

Q38. Check whether the plane $2x + y - 2z - 5 = 0$ is tangent to the sphere $x^2 + y^2 + z^2 - 4y - 6z + 4 = 0$ or not. **[Dec01, Q2(b)]**

Ans. The given sphere is

$x^2 + y^2 + z^2 - 4y - 6z + 4 = 0$

Here u = 0, v = -2, w = -3, d = 4

radius of sphere $= \sqrt{u^2 + v^2 + w^2 - d}$

$= \sqrt{0^2 + (-2)^2 + (-3)^2 - 4}$

$= \sqrt{4 + 9 - 4}$

$= \sqrt{9} = 3$

Centre of sphere is (0, 2, 3)

The length of the perpendicular from centre to the plane

$2x + y - 2z - 5 = 0$ is

$$\frac{|2.0 + 1.(-2) + (-2).(-3) + 4|}{\sqrt{2^2 + 1^2 + (-2)^2}}$$

$$= \frac{|0-2+6+4|}{\sqrt{9}}$$

$$= \frac{8}{3}$$

Which is not same as the radius of sphere. So plane is not touches the sphere. Hence given plane is not tangent to sphere.

Q39. Find the equation of a sphere that passes through (0, 0, 0), (0, 1, –1) and (–1, 2, 0) and whose centre lies on the plane x + y + z = 0.

[June02, Q1(b)]

Ans. Let equation of sphere is

$x^2 + y^2 + z^2 + 2gx + 2fy + 2hz + d = 0$ ... (1)

If it passes through (0, 0, 0).

Then $d = 0$ ... (2)

If it passes through (0, 1, –1)

$0 + 1^2 + (-1)^2 + 2.g.0 + 2.f.1 + 2.h.(-1) + d = 0$

$\Rightarrow 1 + 1 + 2f - 2h + 0 = 0$

$\Rightarrow f - h + 1 = 0$ ... (3)

if it passes through (–1, 2, 0)

$(-1)^2 + 2^2 + 0 + 2.g.(-1) + 2.f.2 + 2.h.0 + 0 = 0$

$\Rightarrow 5 - 2g + 4f = 0$ ... (4)

Again the centre of the sphere is (–g, –f, –h) and this centre lies on the plane $x + y + z = 0$.

We have

$-g - f - h = 0$

$\Rightarrow g + f + h = 0$ ... (5)

$\Rightarrow \frac{5+4f}{2} + f + f + 1 = 0$ [from (3) and (4)]

$\Rightarrow 5 + 4f + 4f + 2 = 0$

$\Rightarrow 8f + 7 = 0$

$\Rightarrow f = \frac{-7}{8}$

$\therefore h = f + 1 = \frac{-7}{8} + 1 = \frac{1}{8}$

$$g = \frac{5+4f}{2} = \frac{5 - \frac{14}{2}}{2}$$

$= \frac{-4}{2} \times \frac{1}{2} = -1$

Putting these value in (1)

$x^2 + y^2 + z^2 - 2x - \frac{-7}{4}y + \frac{1}{4}z = 0$

or $4x^2 + 4y^2 + 4z^2 - 8x - 7y + z = 0$

Q40. Find the angle of intersection between the spheres [Dec02, Q2]
$x^2 + y^2 + z^2 - 2x - 2y - 2z = 1$ and
$x^2 + y^2 + z^2 - 2x - 2y - 1 = 0$

Ans. $x^2 + y^2 + z^2 - 2x - 2y - 2z = 1$

$x^2 + y^2 + z^2 - 2x - 2y - 1 = 0$

Let the sphere $S_1 = x^2 + y^2 + z^2 - 2x - 2y - 2z - 1 = 0$

$u = 1, v = 1, w = 1, d = -1$

c (1, 1, 1) d = –1

$r_1 = \sqrt{u^2 + v^2 + w^2 - d}$

$= \sqrt{1+1+1+1} = \sqrt{4} = 2$

Sphere $S_2 = x^2 + y^2 + z^2 - 2x - 2y - 1 = 0$

$c_2 (1, 1, 0)$ d = –1

$r_2 = \sqrt{1+1+0+1} = \sqrt{3}$

$d = c_1 c_2^2 = 1$

$$\cos\theta = \frac{r_1^2 + r_2^2 - d^2}{2r_1r_2}$$

$$= \frac{4+3-1}{2\times 2\times\sqrt{3}} = \frac{6}{2\times 2\sqrt{3}} = \frac{3}{2\sqrt{3}}$$

$$\cos\theta = \frac{\sqrt{3}}{2}$$

$$\theta = \cos^{-1}\left(\frac{\sqrt{3}}{2}\right)$$

$\theta = 30°$

Q41. Find the equation of the sphere that contains the circle $x^2 + y^2 + z^2$

= 9, x + y – 2z = 4 and passes through the origin. **[June03, Q2(a)]**

Ans. S $x^2 + y^2 + z^2 - 9 = 0$, P $x + y - 2z - 4 = 0$

Let the equation of the sphere be $S + 4\lambda P = 0$

$x^2 + y^2 + z^2 - 9 + \lambda(x + y - 2z - 4) = 0$ where $\lambda \in R$

$x^2 + y^2 + z^2 + \lambda x + \lambda y - 2\lambda z - 4\lambda - 9 = 0$

Since it passes through (0, 0, 0)

$$\lambda = \frac{-9}{4}$$

The required equation is

$$x^2 + y^2 + z^2 + \left(\frac{-9}{4}\right)(x + y - 2z - 4) = 0$$

$4(x^2 + y^2 + z^2) = 9(x + y - 2z)$

$4x^2 + 4y^2 + 4z^2 - 9x + 9y + 18z = 0$

Q42. Find the equation of a plane parallel to the plane 5x – 6y + 7z = 3 and passing through the point (2, 3, 4). **[June03, Q3(a)]**

Ans. $5x - 6y + 7z = 3$

Any plane parallel to $5x - 6y + 7z - 3 = 0$ is if the form

$5x - 6y + 7z - 3 + k = 0$

where $k \in R$.

Since (2, 3, 4) lies on it

$\Rightarrow 5x - 6y + 7z - 3 + k = 0$

$\Rightarrow 5(2) - 6(3) + 7(4) - 3 + k = 0$

$\Rightarrow 10 - 18 + 28 - 3 + k = 0$

$\Rightarrow 10 + 10 - 3 + k = 0$

$\Rightarrow 17 + k = 0$

$k = -17$

Thus, the required plane is

$5x - 6y + 7z - 3 + (-17) = 0$

$5x - 6y + 7z - 3 - 17 = 0$

$5x - 6y + 7z - 20 = 0$

Q43. Obtain the centre and radius of the sphere that contain the circle $x^2 + y^2 + z^2 + 10y - 4z - 8 = 0$, $x + y + z = 3$ as a great circle. **[Dec03, Q1(b)]**

Ans. Given equation of circle

$x^2 + y^2 + z^2 + 10y - 4z - 8 = 0$

$x + y + z = 3$

∴ Then required equation of sphere

$x^2 + y^2 + z^2 + 10y - 4z - 8 + k(x + y + z - 3) = 0$ ... (i)

Since the given circle is a great circle of the sphere, the centre of the sphere must lies on the plan.

$x + y + z - 3 = 0$ ... (ii)

$x^2 + y^2 + z^2 + kx + y(10 + k) + z(-4 + k) - 8 - 3k = 0$ from (i)

$k + (10 + k) + (-4 + k) = 3$ from (ii)

$k + 6 + 2k = 3$

$3k = -3$

$k = -1$

∴ equation of sphere

$x^2 + y^2 + z^2 + 10y - 4z - 8 - (x + y + z - 3) = 0$

$x^2 + y^2 + z^2 + 9y - x - 5z - 5 = 0$

∴ centre of sphere

∴ $2u = -1$

$u = \frac{-1}{2}$

$2v = 9$

$v = \frac{9}{2}$

$2w = -5$

$w = \frac{-5}{2}$

∴ Centre $\left(\frac{1}{2}, -\frac{9}{2}, \frac{5}{2}\right)$

$$\text{Radius} = \sqrt{\frac{1}{4} + \frac{81}{4} + \frac{25}{4} - 5} = \sqrt{\frac{1 + 81 + 25 - 20}{4}} = \frac{\sqrt{86}}{2}$$

Q44. Find the equation of the plane which passes through (1, –1, –3) and its perpendicular to **[Dec03, Q2(c)]**

$$\frac{\mathbf{x - \alpha}}{\mathbf{1}} - \frac{\mathbf{y - \beta}}{\mathbf{3}} = \frac{\mathbf{z - \gamma}}{\mathbf{-2}}$$

Ans. We know that the equation of plane is

$ax + by + cz + d = 0$ ... (i)

∵ plane passes through the point (1, –1, –3)

∴ Direction ratio of line passes through (1, –1, –3) is $(x - 1), (y + 1), (z + 3)$

Also the direction ratio of the normal to the plan is (1, 3, –2)

$\therefore$ direction ratio of (x – 1), (y + 1), (z + 3) and (1, 3, –2) is perpendicular to each other.

$\therefore (x-1)\times 1 + (y+1)\times 3 + (z+3)\times(-2) = 0$

$x - 1 + 3y + 3 - 2z - 6 = 0$

$x + 3y - 2z - 4 = 0$ is required equation of plane.

Q45. The projections of a line segment on the coordinate axes are 2, 1, 5. Find the length of the segment and the direction cosines of the line.

[Dec03, Q3(a)]

Ans. Let CD is a line whose projections on the axis are 2, 1, 5 and whose direction ratio are (l, m, n).

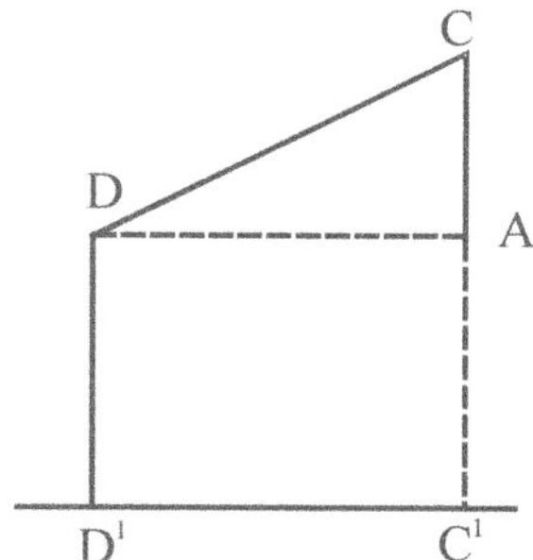

Then

2 = the projection of CD on the x-axis = l.CD

1 = the projection of CD on the y-axis = m.CD

5 = the projection of CD on the z-axis = n.CD

Squaring and adding

$4 + 1 + 25 = (l^2 + m^2 + n^2)\ CD^2$

$30 = CD^2 \qquad [\because l^2 + m^2 + n^2 = 1]$

$CD = \sqrt{30}$

$\therefore l.CD = 2$

$$l = \frac{2}{\sqrt{30}}, m = \frac{1}{\sqrt{30}}, n = \frac{5}{\sqrt{30}}$$

$$\therefore \text{Direction cosine} \left(\frac{2}{\sqrt{30}}, \frac{1}{\sqrt{30}}, \frac{5}{\sqrt{30}}\right).$$

Q46. Check whether the two circles **[June04, Q3(a)]**

$2(z^2 + y^2 + z^2) + 8x - 13y + 17z - 17 = 0,$

$2x + y - 3z + 1 = 0$ and
$x^2 + y^2 + z^2 + 3x - 4y + 3z = 0$, $x - y + 2z = 0$
lie on a sphere. If so, find the equation of the sphere.
Ans. $2(z^2 + y^2 + z^2) + 8x - 13y + 17z - 17 = 0$

$$x^2 + y^2 + z^2 + 4x - \frac{13}{2}y + \frac{17}{2}z - \frac{17}{2} = 0$$

and $2x + y - 3z + 1 = 0$
We get,

$$x^2 + y^2 + z^2 + 4x - \frac{13}{2}y + \frac{17}{2}z - \frac{17}{2} + k(2x + y - 3z + 1) = 0$$

$$x^2 + y^2 + z^2 + x(4 + 2k) - y\left(\frac{13}{2} - k\right) + z\left(\frac{17}{2} - 3k\right)$$

$$-\left(\frac{17}{2} - k\right) = 0 \quad \text{... (i)}$$

$x^2 + y^2 + z^2 + 3x - 4y + 3z + k_1(x - y + 2z) = 0$
$x^2 + y^2 + z^2 + x(3 - k_1) - y[4 + k_1] + z(3 + 2k_1) = 0$ ... (ii)
Comparing equation (i) & (ii) coefficient of x, y and constant
$4 + 2k = 3 + k_1$
$2k - k_1 = -1$ ... (iii)

$$\frac{13}{2} - k = 4 + k_1$$

$$k + k_1 = \frac{13}{2} - 4 = \frac{5}{2}$$

$2k + 2k_1 = 5$ ... (iv)

$$\frac{17}{2} - k = 0$$

$$3k + 2k_1 = \frac{17}{2} - 3 = \frac{11}{2} \quad \text{... (v)}$$

$$k = \frac{17}{2} \quad \text{... (vi)}$$

From equation (iii) and (iv),

$$\begin{aligned} 2k - k_1 &= -1 \\ 2k + 2k_1 &= 5 \\ - \quad - \quad & - \\ \hline -3k_1 &= -6 \end{aligned}$$

$k = \frac{-6}{-3} = 2$

Now putting value of k_1 in equation (iii), we get

$2k - 2 = -1$

$2k = 1$

$k = 1/2$

Therefore sphere passing through both the circles and its equation, we get

$$x^2 + y^2 + z^2 + x\left[4 - 2 \times \frac{1}{2}\right] - y\left[\frac{13}{2} - \frac{1}{2}\right] + 2\left[\frac{17}{2} - \frac{3.1}{2}\right] - \left[\frac{17}{2} - \frac{1}{2}\right] = 0$$

$x^2 + y^2 + z^2 + 5x - 6y + 7z - 8 = 0$ ... (vii)

and $x^2 + y^2 + z^2 + x\,[3 + 2] - y\,[4 + 2] + 2\,[3 + 2.2] = 0$

$x^2 + y^2 + z^2 + 5x - 6y + 7z = 0$ ... (viii)

equation (vii) and (viii) are the required equation.

Q47. Which of the following statements are true:

A. A plane is completely determined if a point on it and the direction ratio of the normal to it are given. [June98, Q1(d)]

Ans. True,

A plane is completely determined if a point o it and direction ratio of the normal to it are given.

B. We can find the equation of a plane if we know even one point that lies on it. [Dec98, Q1(e)]

Ans. False,

Because we can't find the equation of a plane if we know one point that lies on it. We need other containt also only one point is not sufficient to find the equation of a plane.

C. 1/2, 1/4, 1/4 are the direction cosines of a line is 3-dimensional space.

Ans. True,

We know that direction cosine $\cos^2\alpha + \cos^2\beta + \cos^2\gamma = 1$

Given that

$\cos^2\alpha = \frac{1}{2}$

$\cos^2\beta = \frac{1}{4}$

$\cos^2\gamma = \frac{1}{4}$

$\therefore \cos^2\alpha + \cos^2\beta + \cos^2\gamma$

$= \frac{1}{2} + \frac{1}{4} + \frac{1}{4}$

$= \frac{2+1+1}{4} = \frac{4}{4} = 1$

D. The equation of a sphere can be obtained if the end points of any one of its diameters are known. [Dec99, Q1(c)]

Ans. False,

If centre and the diameter is known then equation of sphere is obtained.

E. A plane is completely determined if the direction ratios of the normal to it are given. [June00, Q1(a)]

Ans. False,

Because a plane is completely determined if the direction ratios of the normal to it and angle are given.

F. The lines $\frac{x+1}{2} - \frac{y}{2} = \frac{z-1}{2}$

$\frac{x+3}{5} = \frac{y-5}{-1}$ and z = 3 are perpendicular. [Dec01, Q1(e)]

Ans. False,

$\frac{x+1}{2} - \frac{y}{2} = \frac{z-1}{2}$

$\Rightarrow x + 1 - y = z - 1$

$\Rightarrow x - y - z = 0$ ... (1)

and $\frac{x+3}{2} = \frac{y-5}{-1}$

$\Rightarrow -x - 3 = 5y - 25$

$\Rightarrow -x - 5y + 22 = 0$

$\Rightarrow x + 5y = -22$ ... (2)

and $z = 3$ ... (3)

From (1) and (3)

$x - y = 3$ ... (4)

From (2) and (4)

$a_1 = 1, b_1 = 5, c_1 = 22$

$a_2 = 1, b_2 = -1, c = -3$
Now $a_1a_2 + b_1b_2 + c_1c_2$
$= 1 \times 1 + 5 \times (-1) + 22 \times (-3)$
$= 1 - 5 - 66$
$= -70 \neq 0$
Hence given lines are not perpendicular.

G. Any two planes intersect in a line. **[June02, Q5(i)]**
Ans. False,
Because we know by theorem in general, two conic intersects in four points.

H. $a^2x^2 + by^2 + cz + d = 0$ represents a paraboloid a, b, c, d $\in$ R. **[June02, Q5(v)]**

Ans. False,
We know standard equation of paraboloid is
$ax^2 + by^2 = 2wz$, where $w \neq 0$
The given equation is
$a^2x^2 + by^2 + cz + d = 0$
$\forall$ a, b, c, d $\in$ R
Since $\forall$ c $\in$ R So c = 0 is also. This is not satisfied the condition.

I. If $\cos\alpha$, $\cos\beta$, $\cos\gamma$ are the direction cosines of a line then

$\sin^2\alpha + \sin^2\beta + \sin^2\gamma = 1$ **[June03, Q1(b)]**
Ans. False,
We know that if $\cos\alpha, \cos\beta, \cos\gamma$ are direction cosines of a line then

$\cos^2\alpha + \cos^2\beta + \cos^2\gamma = 1$

J. At any point of a sphere a unique tangent line can be drawn to the sphere **[June03, Q1(c)]**
Ans. False,
If a line intersects a sphere in one point P, it is called a tangent to the sphere at the point P and P is called the point of contact of the tangent. At point P we can draw different tangent line.

K. If the projection of a line segment AB on another line is the line segment CD, then $|AB| = |CD|$ **[June03, Q1(e)]**
Ans. False,
We know that projection of AB,
length $|CD| = |AB| \cos\theta$
where θ is angle between AB and CD.

L. There exists one and only one tangent line to a sphere at any given point of the sphere. [Dec03, Q5(v)]

Ans. Always tangents touches only one point to the any curve.

If it touches more than one point it is interaction of second line which is plane.

M. The direction ratios of $\frac{x-1}{3}=\frac{y}{5}, z=3$ are 3, 5 and 3.[June04, Q5(ii)]

Ans. False,

Because ratio are not satisfy.

$$\frac{x-1}{3}=\frac{y-0}{5}=\frac{z-3}{1}$$

we get

$$\frac{x-x_1}{\alpha}=\frac{y-y_1}{\beta}=\frac{z-z_1}{\gamma}$$

Here $\alpha=3, \beta=5,$ and $\gamma=1$

whose, ration are not satisfy, hence result.

N. The projection of any line segment along the z-axis on the x-axis is 0. [June04, Q5(iii)]

Ans. False,

Because the projection of OP and OX is equal to the sum of the projection of OM, ML and LP on OX, we have

$x = l_1x' + l_2y' + l_3z'$

$y = m_1x' + m_2y' + m_3z'$

$z = n_1x' + n_2y' + n_3z'$

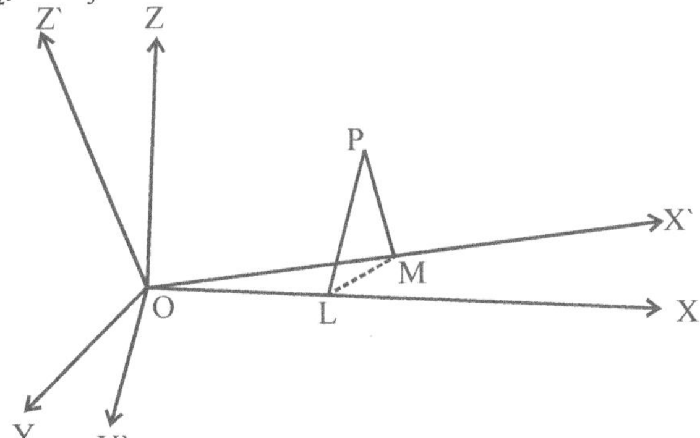

So, we can say that the projection of any line segment along the z-axis on the x-axis is not zero.

Chapter-5

Cone and Cylinder

Cone : A cone is a surface generated by a variable straight line passing through a fixed point and satisfying the condition that intersecting a given curve or touching a given surface. The fixed point is called vertex and the given surface is called guiding curve. The variable line is called the generator of the surface.

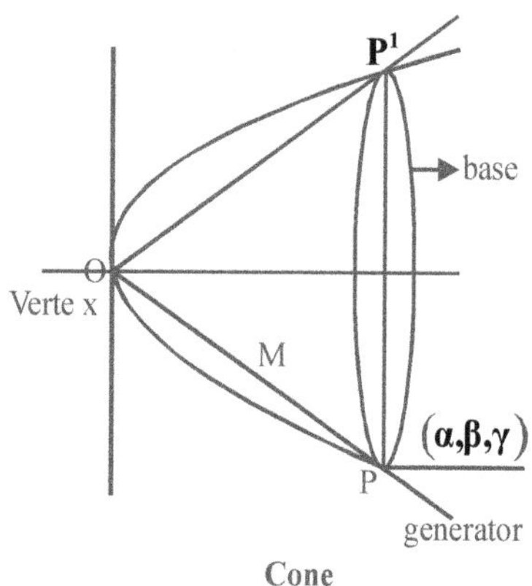

Cone

Equations to the cone:

(i) Cone with vertex at origin :

Let the general equation to the IInd degree in x, y, z be :

$ax^2 + by^2 + cz^2 + 2fyz + 2gzx + 2hxy + 2ux + 2vy + 2wz + d = 0$ ....(1),

represent a cone with vertex at origin O (0, 0, 0).

Let P (α, β, γ) be any point on the cone then equation to the generator is given by :

$$\frac{x-0}{\alpha} = \frac{y-0}{\beta} = \frac{z-0}{\gamma} = r\,(let)$$

Co-ordinate of point M on generator will be, M = $(\alpha r, \beta r, \gamma r)$

Since OP is generator (see figure above) so any point (M) must lie on it so from (1)

$$r^2\left(a\alpha^2+b\beta^2+c\gamma^2+2f\beta\gamma+2g\alpha\gamma+2h\alpha\beta\right)+2r\left(u\alpha+v\beta+c\gamma\right)+d=0$$

Hence, $r\neq 0$

$$a\alpha^2+b\beta^2+c\gamma^2+2f\beta\gamma+2g\alpha\gamma+2h\alpha\beta=0$$
$$u\alpha+v\beta+c\gamma=0,\ d=0$$

We may say that $P(\alpha,\beta,\gamma)$ is a point on plane $u\alpha+v\beta+c\gamma=0$ If u, v, $w\neq 0$. Hence the equation to the cone is :

$$ax^2+by^2+cz^2+2fyz+2gzx+2hxy=0$$

(ii) Equation of cone which passes through co-ordinates axes and vertex is at origin :

We have equation to the cone : $ax^2+by^2+cz^2+2fyz+2gzx+2hxy=0$

d.c.'s of all three co-ordinate axis are 1, 0, 0; 0, 1, 0; 0, 0, 1 using the above equation we get a=0, b=0, c=0, so our required equation of cone is : $fyz+gzx+hxy=0$

(iii) Equation of cone with a given vertex and a given cone for its base :

Let vertex of cone (α,β,γ) and cone is :

$ax^2+by^2+2hxy+2gx+2fy+c=0$.............(1), $z=0$, hence equation to the line through vetex (α,β,γ) is :

$$\frac{x-\alpha}{l}=\frac{y-\beta}{m}=\frac{z-\gamma}{n},$$ where l, m, n are d.c.'s.

This line passes through the plane z = 0 of the point $\left(\alpha-\frac{l\gamma}{n},\beta-\frac{m\gamma}{n},0\right)$ and this point lies on the cone (1) so :

$$a\left(\alpha-\frac{l\gamma}{n}\right)^2+b\left(\beta-\frac{m\gamma}{n}\right)\left(\alpha-\frac{l\gamma}{n}\right)+2g\left(\alpha-\frac{l\gamma}{n}\right)+2f\left(\beta-\frac{m\gamma}{n}\right)+c=0\text{......(2)}$$

where $\frac{l}{n}=\frac{x-\alpha}{z-\gamma}$, $\frac{m}{n}=\frac{y-\beta}{z-\gamma}$ put in (2)

$$a\left[\alpha-\left(\frac{x-a}{z-\gamma}\right)\gamma\right]^2+b\left[\beta-\left(\frac{x-\beta}{z-\gamma}\right)\right]^2+2h\left[\alpha-\left(\frac{x-a}{z-\gamma}\right)\gamma\right]+$$

$$\left[\beta-\left(\frac{x-\beta}{z-\gamma}\right)\gamma\right]+2g\left[a-\left(\frac{y-a}{z-\gamma}\right)\gamma\right]+\left[\beta-\left(\frac{x-\beta}{z-\gamma}\right)\gamma\right]+c=0$$

Hence the required equation of the cone is :

$$a(\alpha z-\gamma x)^2+b(\beta z-\gamma y)^2+2h(\alpha z-\gamma y)+2g(\alpha z-\gamma x)(z-\gamma)+$$
$$2f(\beta z-\gamma y)(z-\gamma)+(z-\gamma)^2=0$$

The angle between the lines in which a plane cuts a cone :

Equation to the plane is

ux+vy+wz = 0 ...(1)

Equation to the cone is :

$ax^2+by^2+cz^2+2fyz+2gzx+2hxy=0$ ...(2)

Let θ be the angle between line and cone. The equation of straight line through O(0, 0, 0) is

$$\frac{x}{l}=\frac{y}{m}=\frac{z}{n}=K\,(let)$$

(x = ℓk, y = mk, z = nk) putting in (2) and (1) :

$$k^2\left(al^2+bm^2+cn^2+2fmn+2z\ln+2hlm\right)=0$$

$k^2\neq 0;\ al^2+bm^2+cn^2+2fmn+2z\ln+2hlm=0$ ...(3)

k(ul+vm+wn) = 0

k$\neq$0, ul + vm + wn = 0 ...(4)

Solving (3) and (4) we get ℓ, m, n, so angle will be found by ℓ, m, n

Tangent to a cone :

Let a straight line is : $\frac{x-\alpha}{l}=\frac{y-\beta}{m}=\frac{z-\gamma}{n}$ ...(1)

Cone is : $ax^2+by^2+cz^2+2fyz+2gzx+2hyx=0$ ...(2)

The line (1) touches cone (2) if

$$l(a\alpha+h\beta+g\gamma)+m(h\alpha+f\gamma+b\beta)+n(g\alpha+f\beta+c\gamma)=0$$

Let equation to a plane : ux + vy + wz = 0 ...(3)

The plane (3) touches cone (2) if :

$$\begin{vmatrix} a & h & g & u \\ h & b & f & v \\ g & f & c & w \\ u & v & w & o \end{vmatrix}=0$$

Right circular cone :

The surface enerated by a line passing through a fixed point (vertex) and makes a constant angle with a fixed line through vertex, called right circular cone. The fixed line is called axis of cone and constant angle is called semi vertical angle (θ)

Let V = (α, β, γ)

P = (x, y, z)

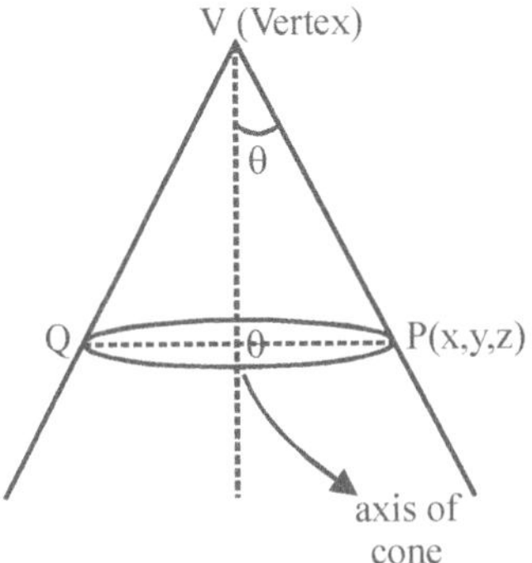

Equation to the axis (vo) :

$$\frac{x-\alpha}{l} = \frac{y-\beta}{m} = \frac{z-\gamma}{n} = k(\text{let})$$

where l, m, n are d.c.'s

d.r.'s of PV = $(x-\alpha),(y-\beta),(z-\gamma)$

$$\therefore \theta = Cos^{-1}\left\{\frac{l(x-\alpha)+m(y-\beta)+n(z-\gamma)}{\sqrt{l^2+m^2+n^2}\ \sqrt{(x-\alpha)^2+(y-\beta)^2+(z-\gamma)^2}}\right\}$$

Standard Equation of cone :

$ax^2 + by^2 + cz^2 = 0 \quad V = (0,0,0)$

Tangent will be

$axx_1 + byy_1 + czz_1 = 0 \qquad P(x_1, y_1, z_1)$

Plane ux + vy + wz = 0, will touch cone if : $bcu^2 + acv^2 + abw^2 = 0$

Equation of pair of tangent from P(x_1, y_1, z_1) is :

$$(ax^2 + by^2 + cz^2)(ax_1^2 + by_1^2 + cz_1^2) = (axx_1 + byy_1 + czz_1)^2$$

Cylinder :

The surface generated by variable straight line moving parallel to a fixed line satisfying the condition of intersecting a given line, curve or touching a given surfaces is called, a cylinder.

Equation to a cylinder through a given conic :

Let the generator of the cylinder is parallel to the line :

$$\frac{x}{l}=\frac{y}{m}=\frac{z}{n} \quad \text{...(1)}$$

Let equation to the conic is :

$$ax^2+2hxy+by^2+2gx+2fy+c=0 \quad \text{...(2)}$$

Let P(α,β,γ) be any point on the cylinder then equation to a generator through P is :

$$\frac{x-\alpha}{l}=\frac{y-\beta}{m}=\frac{z-\gamma}{n} \quad \text{...(3)}$$

Let the generator meets the z = 0, hence co-ordinates of point is $\left(\alpha-\frac{l\gamma}{n},\beta-\frac{m\gamma}{n},0\right)$.

Generator meets the conic if :

$$a\left(\alpha-\frac{l\gamma}{n}\right)^2+2h\left(\alpha-\frac{l\gamma}{n}\right)\left(\beta-\frac{m\gamma}{n}\right)+b\left(\beta-\frac{m\gamma}{n}\right)^2+2g\left(\alpha-\frac{l\gamma}{n}\right)+2f\left(\beta-\frac{m\gamma}{n}\right)$$
$$+c=0$$

The equation of cylinder is obtained by locus of P.

If generator is parallel to z-axis l = 0, m = 0, n = 1

$$ax^2+2hxy+by^2+2gx+2fy+c=0 \quad \text{...(4)}$$

Equation of tangent plane to a cylinder at Point P (α,β,γ) :-

Equation of cylinder is given by (4), then equation to the tangent is :

$$a\alpha x+2h(x\alpha+y\beta)+by\beta+g(x+\alpha)+f(y+\beta)+c=0$$

SOLVED EXAMPLES

Q1. Find equation to the cone on which perpendicular drawn from origin to the tangent plane to the cone $9x^2+11y^2-10zx=0$ lie.

Ans. $9x^2 + 11y^2 - 10zx = 0$ ....(1) compare this (1) with general equation of cone

a = 9, b = 11, c = 0, h = 0, f = 0, g = 5

$A = bc - f^2 = 0$

$B = ac - g^2 = -25$

$C = ab - h^2 = 99$

$F = gh - af = 0$

$G = hf - bg = -55$

$H = fg - ch = 0$

The equation to the required cone is :

$$Ax^2 + By^2 + Cz^2 + 2Fyz + 2Gzx + 2Hxy = 0$$

$$-25y^2 + 99z^2 - 110zx = 0$$

or

$$25y^2 - 99z^2 + 110zx = 0.$$

Q2. Find the equation to the cone with vertex at origin (0, 0, 0) and passes through the points of intersection of curve given by equation; $ax^2+by^2 = 2z$ and $lx + my + nz = p$?

Ans. We have given :

$$ax^2 + by^2 = 2z \qquad ... (1)$$

$$lx + my + nz = p \qquad ... (2)$$

we should make (1) homogenous, so : $ax^2 + by^2 = \frac{2z}{p} \times p$

$$p(ax^2 + by^2) = 2zx(lx + my + nz) \qquad (\text{from}(2))$$

$$p(ax^2 + by^2) = 2(lxz + myz + nz^2)$$

which is required equation to the cone.

Q3. Prove that $a^2x^2 + b^2y^2 + c^2z^2 - 2bcyz - 2cazx - 2abxy = 0$ respect to a cone which touches the co-ordinate planes.

Ans. We have the cone which touches the co-ordinate planes is reciprocal to the cone, which have three axes, normal to the three planes. Now equation to be cone, containing three co-ordinates axes is :

$$f'yz + g'zx + h'xy = 0 \qquad ... (1)$$

Here a = 0, b = 0, c = 0, f = $\frac{f'}{2}$, $h=\frac{h'}{2}$, g = $\frac{g^1}{2}$

A = bc – f² = – $\frac{f^{1^2}}{4}$

B = ac – g = $\frac{g^{1^2}}{4}$

C = ab – h² = $\frac{h^{1^2}}{4}$

F = gh – aF = $\frac{g^1h^1}{4}$

G = hf – bg = $\frac{h^1f^1}{4}$

H = fg – ch = $\frac{f^1g^1}{4}$

the required equation to the cone reciprocal to (1) is :

$Ax^2 + By^2 + Cz^2 + 2Fyz + 2Gzx + 2Hxy = 0$

$$-\frac{f^{1^2}}{4}x^2 - \frac{g^{1^2}}{4}y^2 - \frac{h^{1^2}}{4}z^2 + 2\frac{g^1h^1}{4}yz + 2\frac{h^1f^1}{4}zx + 2\frac{f^1g^1}{4}xy = 0$$

$f^{1^2}x^2 + g^{1^2}y^2 + h^{1^2}z^2 - 2g^1h^1yz - 2h^1f^1zx - 2f^1g^1xy = 0$

which is of the form :

$a^2x^2 + b^2y^2 + c^2z^2 - 2bcyz - 2abxy - 2cazx = 0$

Hence proved.

Q4. Obtain the equation of cylinder if equation of plane and circle is given by :

$$\mathbf{2x - 2y + z = 9}$$
$$\mathbf{x^2 + y^2 + z^2 = 16}$$

Ans. Equation of circle is : $x^2 + y^2 + z^2 = 16$

Equation of plane – 2x – 2y + z = 9

d.r.'s are (2, –2, 1)

the equation of generator of cylinder passing through $P(\alpha, \beta, \gamma)$ be :

$$\frac{x-\alpha}{2}=\frac{y-\beta}{-2}=\frac{z-\gamma}{1}=K(\text{let})$$

Let any point Q lies on cylinder

$Q=(2k+\alpha,-2k+\beta,k+\gamma)$

Q will lies on circle, and also on plane so

$(2k+\alpha)^2+(-2k+\beta)^2+(k+\gamma)^2=16$

$2(2k+\alpha)-2(-2k+\beta)+(k+\gamma)=9$

Eliminating K, we get :

$9\alpha^2+17\beta^2-11\gamma^2-2\beta\gamma-2\alpha\gamma-8\alpha\beta=0$

on generalizing above equation :

$9x^2+17y^2-11z^2-2yz-2zx-8xy=0$

Q5. The axis of a cylinder of radius 3 has equation $\frac{x}{2}=\frac{y+1}{-2}=\frac{z-1}{1}$. find the equation of the cylinder.

Ans. The equation of straight line is :

$\frac{x-0}{2}=\frac{y+1}{-2}=\frac{z-1}{1}$ where

$(\alpha,\beta,\gamma)=(0,-1,+1)\,and$

$(l,m,n)=(2,-2,1)$

Equation to the cylinder is given by :

$[n(y-\beta)-m(z-\gamma)]^2+[l(z-\gamma)-n(x-\alpha)]^2+m[(x-\alpha)-l(y-\beta)]^2$

$=r^2(l^2+m^2+n^2)$

using values of l, m, n, α,β,γ, we have :

$\left[(y+1)-2(z-1)^2\right]+\left[2(z-1)-x\right]^2+\left[2x-2(y+1)\right]^2=81$

$5x^2+5y^2+8z^2-4yz-4zx-8xy-4x-14y-20z-64=0$.

Q6. Find the equation of the cylinder

(a) whose axis is x = 2y = -z and radius is 4.

b) whose axis is $\frac{x-1}{2}=\frac{y}{3}=\frac{z-3}{1}$ and radius is 2.

Ans. a) The equation is $(x^2 + y^2 + z^2 - 16)\left(1+\frac{1}{4}+1\right) = \left(x+\frac{y}{2}-z\right)^2$

$\Leftrightarrow 5x^2 + 8y^2 + 5z^2 - 4xy + 4yz + 8xy - 144 = 0.$

b) The required equation is

$$14\left\{(x-1)^2 + y^2 + (z-3)^2 - 4\right\} = \left\{2(x-1)+3y+(z-3)\right\}^2$$

$\Leftrightarrow 10x^2 + 5y^2 + 13z^2 - 12xy - 6yz - 4xz - 8x + 30y - 74z + 59 = 0.$

Q7. Find the equation of the cylinder having for its base the circle $x^2 + y^2 + z^2 = 9$, $x - y + z = 3$.

Ans. The centre of the sphere is (0, 0, 0), and radius 3. The distance between (0, 0, 0) and the plane $x - y + z = 3$ is $\sqrt{3}$. So the radius of the base circle is $\sqrt{9-3} = \sqrt{6}$

The axis of the cylinder is perpendicular to the plane $x - y + z = 3$ and passes through (0, 0, 0). So its equations are $\frac{x}{1} = \frac{y}{-1} = \frac{z}{1}$.

Then using $\begin{aligned}&\left\{(x-a)^2 + (y-b)^2 + (z-c)^2 - r^2\right\}(\alpha^2+\beta^2+\gamma^2)\\ &= \left\{(x-a)\alpha + (y-b)\beta + (z-c)\gamma\right\}^2\end{aligned}$, we get the required equation as

$3(x^2 + y^2 + z^2 - 6) = (x - y + z)^2$

$\Rightarrow x^2 + y^2 + z^2 + xy + yz - zx - 9 = 0.$

Q8. Find the cone on which the perpendicular drawn from the origin to tangent planes to the cone $19x^2 + 11y^2 + 3z^2 + 6yz - 10zx - 26xy = 0$ lie.

Ans. The required cone is the reciprocal of the given cone. Thus its equation is

$$\begin{vmatrix} 19 & -13 & -5 & x \\ -13 & 11 & 3 & y \\ -5 & 3 & 3 & z \\ x & y & z & 0 \end{vmatrix} = 0$$

$\Leftrightarrow 3x^2 + 4y^2 + 5z^2 + 2yz + 4zx + 6xy = 0.$

Q9. Show that the cones $ax^2 + by^2 + cz^2 = 0$ and $\frac{x^2}{a} + \frac{y^2}{b} + \frac{z^2}{c} = 0$ are

reciprocal.

(Here abc $\neq$ 0.)

Ans. The reciprocal cone of $ax^2 + by^2 + cz^2 = 0$ is given by the determinant equation

$$\begin{vmatrix} a & 0 & 0 & x \\ 0 & b & 0 & y \\ 0 & 0 & c & z \\ x & y & z & 0 \end{vmatrix} = 0$$

$$\Leftrightarrow a\begin{vmatrix} b & 0 & y \\ 0 & c & z \\ y & z & 0 \end{vmatrix} - x\begin{vmatrix} 0 & b & 0 \\ 0 & 0 & c \\ x & y & z \end{vmatrix} = 0$$

$\Leftrightarrow x^2bc + y^2ac + z^2ab = 0$

$\Leftrightarrow \frac{x^2}{a} + \frac{y^2}{b} + \frac{z^2}{c} = 0$, dividing throughout by abc.

This is the required equation.

Q10. Find the equation of the tangent plane at the point $\left(\frac{1}{7}, \frac{1}{4}, 1\right)$ to the cone 5yz – 8zx – 3xy = 0.

Ans. The required equation is

$$x\left\{-\frac{3}{2}\left(\frac{1}{4}\right) - 4(1)\right\} + y\left\{-\frac{3}{2}\left(\frac{1}{7}\right) + \frac{5}{2}(1)\right\} + z\left\{(-4)\left(\frac{1}{7}\right) + \frac{5}{2}\left(\frac{1}{4}\right)\right\} = 0.$$

$\Leftrightarrow -245x + 128y + 3z = 0.$

Q11. Show that if a + b + c = 0, then the cone

$$\mathbf{C(x,y,z) \int ax^2 + by^2 + cz^2 + 2fyz + 2gzx + 2hxy = 0}$$

has infinitely many sets of three mutually perpendicular generators.

Ans. Let $\frac{x}{\alpha} = \frac{y}{\beta} = \frac{z}{\gamma}$ be any generator of the cone. Then, by equation of cone is $ax^2 + by^2 + cz^2 + 2fyz + 2gzx + 2hxy = 0$ and we know that $C(\alpha, \beta, \gamma) = 0$. Therefore, using the fact that a + b + c = 0 and

$c(u,v,w)=(a+b+c)(u^2+v^2+w^2)$,

we see that the plane $\alpha x+\beta y+\gamma z=0$ intersects the cone in two mutually perpendicular generators, say L and L'.

Now $\frac{x}{\alpha}=\frac{y}{\beta}=\frac{z}{\gamma}$ is normal to the plane $\alpha x+\beta y+\gamma z=0$. Thus, it is perpendicular to both L and L'. Thus, these three lines form a set of three mutually perpendicular generators of the cone.

Note that we chose $\frac{x}{\alpha}=\frac{y}{\beta}=\frac{z}{\gamma}$ arbitrarily. Thus, for each generator chosen we get a set of three mutually perpendicular generators. Hence, the cone has infinitely many such sets of generators.

Q12. Find the angle between the lines of intersection of $3x + y + 5z = 0$ and $6yz - 2zx + 5xy = 0$.

Ans. The required angle is

$$\alpha=\tan^{-1}\left|\frac{2P\sqrt{3^2+1^2+5^2}}{0-6(1)(5)+2(5)(3)-5(3)(1)}\right|.$$

where $$P^2=\begin{vmatrix} 0 & \frac{5}{2} & -1 & 3 \\ \frac{5}{2} & 0 & 3 & 1 \\ -1 & 3 & 0 & 5 \\ 3 & 1 & 5 & 0 \end{vmatrix}=\frac{225}{4}$$

$$\therefore P=\frac{15}{2}.$$

$$\therefore \alpha=\tan^{-1}\sqrt{35}.$$

Q13. If $\frac{u^2}{a}+\frac{v^2}{b}+\frac{w^2}{c}=d$, show that $ax^2 + by^2 + cz^2 + 2ux + 2vy + 2wz + d = 0$ represents a cone.

Ans. Substituting the value of d in the equation, we can write it as

$$a\left(x+\frac{u}{a}\right)^2+b\left(y+\frac{\text{v}}{\text{b}}\right)^2+c\left(z+\frac{w}{c}\right)^2=0.$$

which is a homogeneous equation of degree 2 in $x+\frac{u}{a}, y+\frac{\text{v}}{\text{b}}, z+\frac{w}{c}$.

Thus, it is a cone with vertex at $\left(-\frac{u}{a},-\frac{\text{v}}{\text{b}},-\frac{w}{c}\right)$.

Q14. Which of the following equations represents a cone?
3x + 4y + 5z = 0; $x^2 + y^2 + z^2 = 9$; $3(x^2 + y^2 + z^2) = xy$; xyz = yz + zx + xy.
Ans. Only $3(x^2 + y^2 + z^2) = xy$.

Q15. A homogeneous equation of the second degree in 3 variables represents a cone whose vertex is at the origin. Prove it.
Ans. Let the given equation be
$ax^2 + by^2 + cz^2 + 2fyz + 2gzx + 2hxy = 0$. ...(1)
Let P(α,β,γ) be a point on this surface and O the origin. Then OP is given by the equations $\frac{x}{\alpha}=\frac{y}{\beta}=\frac{z}{\gamma}=r$ (say).

So any point on OP is $(r\alpha, r\beta, r\gamma)$. Since P lies on (1),

$a\alpha^2+b\beta^2+c\gamma^2+2f\beta\gamma+2g\gamma\alpha+2h\alpha\beta=0$. ...(2)
Multiplying (2) throughout by r^2, we get

$$a(r\alpha)^2+b(r\beta)^2+c(r\gamma)^2+2f(r\beta)(r\gamma)+2g(r\gamma)(r\alpha)+2h(r\alpha)(r\beta)=0.$$

Thus, $(r\alpha, r\beta, r\gamma)$ also lies on (1), for any $r \in \mathbf{R}$. In particular, O lies on (1). So, the line OP lies on the surface given by (1). In other words, OP is a generator of (1). Thus, the surface (1) is generated by lines through the origin. Each of these lines will also pass through any curve obtained by intersecting (1) by a plane, and any of these curves can be treated as a base curve. Thus, (1) represents a cone with the origin as vertex.

Q16. Find the equation of the cone passing through $2x^2 + 3y^2 + 4z^2 = 1$ and x + y + z = 1.
Ans. $2x^2 + 3y^2 + 4z^2 = (x + y + z)^2$
$\Leftrightarrow x^2 + 2y^2 + 3z^2 - 2xy - 2yz - 2zx = 0$.

Q17. Find the equation of the cone with vertex at the origin and base curve

(a) the parabola $y^2 = 4ax$, $z = 3$,

(b) the ellipse $\frac{y^2}{3}+\frac{z^2}{5}=1$, $x=-2$.

Ans. (a) $y^2 = 4ax\left(\frac{z}{3}\right) \Leftrightarrow 3y^2 - 4azx = 0$.

(b) $\frac{x^2}{4}-\frac{y^2}{3}-\frac{z^2}{5}=0$.

Q18. Show that the equation of the right circular cone with vertex at (a, b, c), axis $\frac{x-a}{\alpha}=\frac{y-b}{\beta}=\frac{z-c}{\gamma}$ and semi-vertical angle θ is

$$\left[\alpha(x-a)+\beta(y-b)+\gamma(z-c)\right]^2 \left(\alpha^2+\beta^2+\gamma^2\right)\left\{(x-a)^2+(y-b)^2+(z-c)^2\right\}\cos^2\theta$$

Ans. Let P (x, y, z) be any point on the cone. Since V (a, b, c) is its vertex, the direction ratios of PV are x – a, y – b, z – c. Also, the direction ratios of the axis of the cone are α, β, γ.

$$\therefore \cos\theta = \frac{\alpha(x-a)+\beta(y-b)+\gamma(z-c)}{\sqrt{\alpha^2+\beta^2+\gamma^2}\sqrt{(x-a)^2+(y-b)^2+(z-c)^2}}.$$

On squaring and cross multiplying we get

$$\left[\alpha(x-a)+\beta(y-b)+\gamma(z-c)\right]^2$$

$$\left(\alpha^2+\beta^2+\gamma^2\right)\left\{(x-a)^2+(y-b)^2+(z-c)^2\right\}\cos^2\theta$$

Q19. Obtain the equation of a cylinder having for its base the circle $x^2 + y^2 - z^2 = 16$. $2x - 2y + z = 9$ [June98, Q5(a)]

Ans. The centre of the sphere is (0, 0, 0) and radius 4. The distance between (0, 0, 0) and the plane 2x – 2y + 2 = 9 is 3.

So, the radius of the base circle is $=\sqrt{16-9}=\sqrt{7}$.

The axis of the cylinder is perpendicular to the plane 2x – 2y + 2 = 9 and passes through (0, 0, 0). So its equations are $\frac{x}{2}=\frac{4}{-2}=\frac{z}{1}$.

The using equation

$$\{(x-a)^2+(y-b)^2+(z-c)^2\}(\alpha^2+\beta^2+\gamma^2)$$

$$=\{(x-a)\alpha+(y-b)\beta+(z-c)\gamma\}^2$$

We get the required equation

$$\{(x-0)^2+(y-0)^2+(z-0)^2-(\sqrt{7})^2\}((2)^2+(-2)^2+(1)^2)$$

$$=\{(x-0)2+(y-0)\times(-2)+(z-0)1\}^2$$

$(x^2 + y^2 + z^2 - 7)(4 + 4 + 1) = (2x - 2y + z)^2$
$9(x^2 + y^2 + z^2 - 7) = (2x)^2 + (2y)^2 + (z)^2 + 2.2x(-2y) + 2.-2y.z + 2.2x.2$
$9x^2 + 9y^2 + 9z^2 - 49 = 4x^2 + 4y^2 + z^2 - 8xy - 4yz + 4xz$
$5x^2 + 5y^2 + 5z^2 + 8xy + 4yz - 4xz - 49 = 0$

Q20. Define a cylinder. Find the equation of a right circular cylinder whose axis is x = 2y = -z and radius is 2. [Dec98, Q4(a)]

Ans. See definition in chapter

The equation of axis x = 2y = – z
r = 2

$$\frac{x}{1}=\frac{y}{1/2}=\frac{z}{-1}$$

The equation of right circular cylinder with radius r

$$\Rightarrow\{(x-a)^2+(y-b)^2+(z-c)^2-r^2\}(\alpha^2+\beta^2+\gamma^2)=0$$

$$\Rightarrow\{(x-a)\alpha+(y-b)\beta+(z-c)\gamma\}^2=0$$

$$\{(x-0)^2+(y-0)^2+(z-0)^2-2^2\}\left(1+\frac{1}{4}+1\right)=0$$

$$\Rightarrow\left\{(x-0).1+(y-0).\frac{1}{2}+(z-0).\frac{1}{2}+(z-0).(-1)\right\}^2=0$$

$$\Rightarrow(x^2+y^2)+z^2-4).\frac{9}{4}=(x+y/2-z)^2$$

$\Rightarrow 5x^2 + 8y^2 + 5z^2 - 4xy + 4yz + 4yz + 8xy - 36 = 0$

Q21. Find the equation of the right circular cone whose vertex (–1, 1, 0)

axis is $\frac{x+1}{3} = y-1 = -z$ and semi-vertical angle is 60°. Further, find the conic obtained by intersecting the cone by a plane parallel to the yz-plane. **[June99, Q5(b)]**

Ans. Let the P(x', y', z') be any point in the cone

Equation of axis is :

$$\frac{x+1}{3} = \frac{y-1}{1} = \frac{-z}{1}$$

d.e.'s are

$$\frac{3}{\sqrt{3^2+1^2+1^2}}, \frac{1}{\sqrt{3^2+1^2+1^2}}, \frac{-1}{\sqrt{3^2+1^2+1^2}}$$

$$\frac{3}{\sqrt{11}}, \frac{1}{\sqrt{11}}, \frac{-1}{\sqrt{11}}$$

Supposed Direction ratios are

x' – 1, y' + 1, z' – 0

∴ Direction cosine are

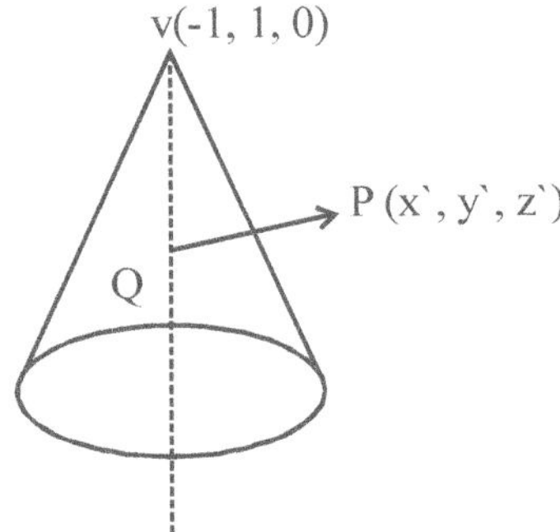

$$\frac{x'-1}{\sqrt{(x-1)^2+(y-1)^2+(z'-0)^2}}$$

$$\frac{y'+1}{\sqrt{(x'+1)^2+(y+1)^2+z'^2}}, \frac{z'-0}{\sqrt{(x'-1)^2+(y'+1)^2+z'^2}}$$

Now

$$\cos 60^\circ = \frac{3(x'-1)+1(y'+1)-1(z'-0)}{\sqrt{11}\sqrt{(x'-1)^2+(y'+1)^2+(z'-0)^2}}$$

$$\Rightarrow \frac{1}{2} = \frac{3x'+y'-z'-2}{\sqrt{11}\sqrt{(x'-1)^2+(y'+1)^2+(z'-0)^2}}$$

$$\Rightarrow (x'-1)^2+(y'-1)^2+(z'-0)^2 = \frac{2}{\sqrt{11}}(3x'+y'-z'-2)^2$$

$\therefore$ The required of cone is

$$(x-1)^2+(y+1)^2+(z-0)^2 = \frac{2}{\sqrt{11}}(3x+y-z-2)^2$$

Q22. Find the equation of a right circular cylinder of radius 2, whose axis is the line $\frac{x-1}{2}=\frac{y-2}{1}=\frac{z-3}{2}$. **[Dec99, Q5(a)]**

Ans. $\frac{x-1}{2}=\frac{y-2}{1}=\frac{z-3}{2}$ radius = 2

Let P(x, y, z) be any point as the cylinder A point on the axis of the cylinder A(1, 2, 3) and direction ratio (2, 1, 2).
The equation of a right circular cylinder is

$$\left\{(x-a)^2+(y-b)^2+(z-c)^2-r^2\right\}\left(\alpha^2+\beta^2+\gamma^2\right)=\left[(x-a).\alpha+(y-b).\beta+(z-c)\gamma\right\}^2$$

$$\Rightarrow\left\{(x-1)^2+(y-2)^2+(z-3)^2-(2)^2\right\}\left(2^2+1^2+2^2\right)=\left[(x-1).2+(y-2).1+(z-3).2\right]^2$$

$$\Rightarrow\left\{\left(x^2-2x+1\right)+\left(y^2-4y+4\right)+\left(z^2-6z+9\right)-4\right\}9=\left[2x-2+y-2+2z-6\right]^2$$

$$\Rightarrow\left\{\left(x^2+y^2+z^2-2x-4y-6z+1+4+9\right)-4\right\}9=\left[2x+y+2z-2-2-6\right]^2$$

$$\Rightarrow\left\{x^2+y^2+z^2-2x-4y-6z+10\right\}9=\left(2x+y+2z-10\right)^2$$

Q23. Find the equation of the cone whose vertex is at the origin and which passes through the curve given by the equations
$y^2 + z^2 = b^2$, $x = a$
Also identify the sections of the cone by the planes parallel to the xy-plane. **[Dec99, Q4(a)]**

Ans. The given curve is

$y^2 + z^2 = b^2$

$$\Rightarrow \frac{y^2}{b^2} + \frac{z^2}{b^2} = 1 \qquad ...(1)$$

$x = a$

$$\Rightarrow \frac{x}{a} = 1$$

$$\Rightarrow \frac{x^2}{a^2} = 1 \qquad ...(2)$$

Subtract (1) from (2)

$$\frac{x^2}{a^2} - \frac{y^2}{b^2} - \frac{z^2}{b^2} = 0$$

This is required equation of cone.

Q24. Find the cone on which the perpendiculars drawn from the origin to the tangent planes to the cone $9x^2 + 11y^2 - 10zx = 0$ lie.

[June01, Q2(b)]

Ans. The given equation is

$9x^2 + 11y^2 - 10zx = 0$

$a = 9,\ b = 11,\ c = 0$

$$\therefore h = 0,\ f = 0,\ g = \frac{-10}{2} = -5$$

The required cone is the reciprocal of the given cone. Thus it equation is

$$\begin{vmatrix} a & h & g & x \\ h & b & f & y \\ g & f & c & z \\ x & y & z & 0 \end{vmatrix} = 0$$

$$\Rightarrow \begin{vmatrix} 9 & 0 & -5 & x \\ 0 & 11 & 0 & y \\ -5 & 0 & 0 & z \\ x & y & z & 0 \end{vmatrix} = 0$$

$$\Rightarrow 9\begin{vmatrix} 11 & 0 & y \\ 0 & 0 & z \\ y & z & 0 \end{vmatrix} - 0\begin{vmatrix} 0 & -5 & x \\ 0 & 0 & z \\ y & z & 0 \end{vmatrix} + (-5)\begin{vmatrix} 0 & -5 & x \\ 11 & 0 & y \\ y & z & 0 \end{vmatrix}$$

$$-x\begin{vmatrix} 0 & -5 & x \\ 11 & 0 & y \\ 0 & 0 & z \end{vmatrix} = 0$$

$$\Rightarrow 9\left[11\times(-z)^2 + y.0\right] - 0 - 5\left[-11.(-xz) + y(-5y)\right] - x\left[-11\times(-5y)\right] = 0$$

$\Rightarrow$ -99z – 55xz + 25y^2 – 25xy = 0

$\Rightarrow$ 25y^2 – 55xz – 55xy – 99z = 0

This is required equation.

Q25. Find the equation of right circular cone whose vertex is (1, – 1, 0), axis is $\frac{x-1}{2} = \frac{y+1}{2} = z - 3$ and semi-vertical angle is $\frac{\pi}{4}$. [Dec01, Q3(a)]

Ans.

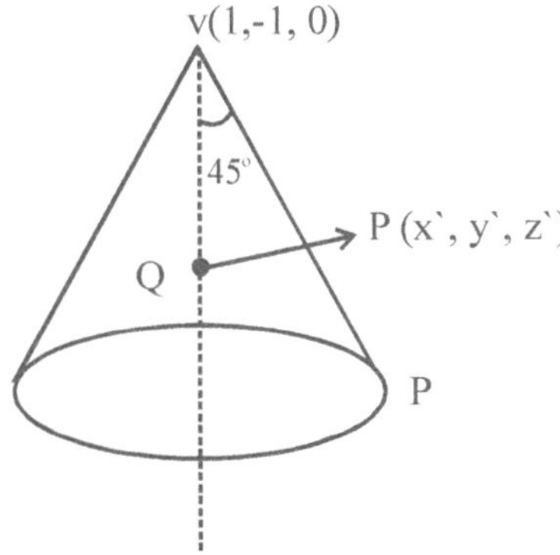

Given vertex point is (1, -1, 0) and axis is $\frac{x-1}{2} = \frac{y+1}{2} = z - 3$ and angle is $\frac{\pi}{4}$ = 45°.

Let P(x', y', z') be any point on the cone.

Hence direction cosine of the axis VQ, are

$$\frac{2}{\sqrt{2^2+2^2+1^2}}, \frac{2}{\sqrt{2^2+2^2+1^2}}, \frac{1}{\sqrt{2^2+2^2+1^2}},$$

i.e. $\frac{2}{3}, \frac{2}{3}, \frac{1}{3}$

Direction ratio's of VP are

x' – 1, y' + 1, z' – 0

$\therefore$ d.e.'s are

$$\frac{x'-1}{\sqrt{(x'-1)^2+(y'+1)^2+z'^2}}, \frac{y'-1}{\sqrt{(x'-1)^2+(y'+1)^2+z'^2}},$$

$$\frac{z}{\sqrt{(x'-1)^2+(y'+1)^2, z'^2}}$$

Now

$$\cos 45° = \frac{2.(x'-1)+2.(y'+1)+1.z'}{3.\sqrt{(x'-1)^2+(y'+1)^2+z'^2}}$$

$$\Rightarrow \frac{1}{\sqrt{2}} = \frac{2x'-2+2y'+2+z'}{3\sqrt{(x'-1)^2+(y'+1)^2+z'^2}}$$

$$\Rightarrow (x'-1)^2 + (y'+1)^2 + z'^2 = \frac{2}{9}(2x' + 2y' + z')^2$$

$\therefore$ The equation of cone is

$$(x-1)^2 + (y+1)^2 + z^2 = \frac{2}{9}(2x + 2y + z)^2$$

Where we have generalized the equation changing (x', y', z') by (x, y, z).

Q26. Consider the cone C $\equiv$ 3xy + z (8x – 5y) = 0 One of a set of 3 mutually perpendicular generators of C is x = y, y + z = 0. Find the equations of the other two generators. [June03, Q4(a)]

Ans. x – y + k(y + z) = 0, k $\in$ R gives any plane through the given line. This will cut the given cone in perpendicular lines if

$$3\times1\times(k-1)+k\times[8\times1-5.(k-1)]=0$$

$$\Rightarrow 3k-3+k\times(8-5k+5)=0$$

$\Rightarrow 3k - 3 + 13k - 5k^2 = 0$

$\Rightarrow 16k - 3 - 5k^2 = 0$

$\Rightarrow 5k^2 - 16k + 3 = 0$

$\Rightarrow (5k - 1)(k - 3) = 0$

$\Rightarrow k = \frac{1}{5}, 3$

Thus the planes are

$x - y + 3(y + z) = 0$

$\Rightarrow x + 2y + 3z = 0$

and $x - y + \frac{1}{5}(y + z) = 0$

$\Rightarrow 5x - 4y + z = 0$

Now $x + 2y + 3z = 0$ intersects the cone in two perpendicular lines of which one is given one which lies on the plane. Therefore, the other one has to be the normal to plane at (0, 0, 0). This is $\frac{x}{1} = \frac{y}{2} = \frac{z}{3}$ so this will be another of the required set of mutually perpendicular generators. Similarly, the third generated will be the normal to $5x - 4y + z = 0$ at (0, 0, 0) that is $\frac{x}{5} = \frac{y}{-4} = \frac{z}{1}$.

Q27. Find the equation of a cylinder whose generators have directional ratios 1, –2, 3 and whose base curve is the ellipse $x^2 + 2y^2 + 1$, $z = 3$.

[Dec03, Q3(b)]

Ans. The equation of the curve are

$x^2 + 2y^2 + 1, z = 3$ ... (1)

give cosine is 1, -2, 3

Let a point $P(x_1, y_1, z_1)$ on the cylinder. The equation of the cylinder. Thus equation of the generator through the point $P(x_1, y_1, z_1)$ which is a line parallel to the given line (2) are

$$\frac{x - x_1}{1} = \frac{y - y_1}{2} = \frac{z - z_1}{3} \quad \text{... (2)}$$

The generator (2) meets the plane

x = 3 is the point given by

$$\frac{x - x_1}{1} = \frac{y - y_1}{2} = \frac{3 - z_1}{3} \quad \text{... (3)}$$

i.e. $\left(x_1 - \frac{1}{3}z_1 + 1, y_1 + \frac{2}{3}, z_1 - 2, 3\right)$

Since the generator (3) mets the conic (1) hence the point

$$\left(x_1 - \frac{1}{3}z_1 + 1, y_1 + \frac{2}{3}, z_1 - 2, 3\right)$$

will satisfy the equation of the given by (1) and so we have

$$\left(x_1 - \frac{1}{3}z_1 + 1\right)^2 + \left(y_1 + \frac{2}{3}, z_1 - 2\right)^2 = 1$$

$(3x_1 - z_1 + 3)^2 + 2\ (3y_1 + 2z_1 - 6)^2 = 9$

$9x^2 + z^2 + 9 - 6zx + 18x - 6z + 2(9y^2 + 4z^2 + 36 + 12yz - 36y - 24z) = 9$

or $9x^2 + 18y^2 + 9z^2 + 2yz - 6zx + 18x - 7zy - 48z + 72 = 0$

or $3x^2 + 6y^2 + 3z^2 + 8yz + 2zx + 6x - 24y - 16z + 24 = 0$

It is required equation of cylinder.

Q28. Find the cone on which the perpendiculars drawn from the origin to the tangent planes to the cone $19x^2 + 11y^2 + 6yz = 0$ lie.

[June04, Q2(a)]

Ans. Given the equations

$19x^2 + 11y^2 + 6yz = 0$

Here

$ax^2 + by^2 + cz^2 + 2hxy + 2fyz + 2gzx + 2gzx + d = 0$

Comparing

Here

$a = 19, b = 11, c = 0$

$h = 0, f = 3, g = 0$

The required cone is reciprocal of the given cone. Thus it is equation

$$\begin{vmatrix} a & h & g & x \\ h & b & f & y \\ g & f & c & z \\ x & y & z & 0 \end{vmatrix} = \begin{vmatrix} 19 & 0 & 0 & x \\ 0 & 11 & 3 & y \\ 0 & 3 & 0 & z \\ x & y & z & 0 \end{vmatrix}$$

$$\Rightarrow 19\begin{vmatrix} 11 & 3 & y \\ 3 & 0 & z \\ y & z & 0 \end{vmatrix} - 0\begin{vmatrix} 0 & 3 & y \\ 0 & 0 & z \\ x & z & 0 \end{vmatrix} + 0\begin{vmatrix} 0 & 11 & y \\ 0 & 3 & z \\ x & y & 0 \end{vmatrix} - x\begin{vmatrix} 0 & 11 & 3 \\ 0 & 3 & 0 \\ x & y & z \end{vmatrix}$$

$19[11(0 - z^2) - 3(0 - yz) + y(3z - 0)] - x[0(3z - 0) - 0(112 - 3y) + x(0 - 9)]$

$= 0$

$19[-11z^2 + 3yz + 3yz] - x[-9x] = 0$

$19[-11z^2 + 6yz] + 9x^2 = 0$

$9x^2 - 209z^2 + 114yz = 0$

Q29. Prove that any tangent plane to a right circular cylinder is parallel to the axis of the cylinder. [June04, Q4(b)]

Ans. If equation of cylinder $ax^2 + 2hxy + by^2 + 2gx + 2fy + c = 0$

$\therefore$ The equation of tangent at the point (x_1, y_1, z_1) is

$axx_1 + h(xy_1 + x_1y) + byy_1 + y(x + x_1) + f(y + y_1) + c = 0$

$\therefore$ the line through the point $p(x_1, y_1, z_1)$

$$\frac{x - x_1}{l} = \frac{y - y_1}{m} = \frac{z - z_1}{n} = r$$

This equation is a tangent line to the cylinder

$\therefore$ r must be zero

$\therefore$ forf(x, y) = 0 cylinder is parallel to z-axis

f(y, z) = 0 cylinder is parallel to x-axis.

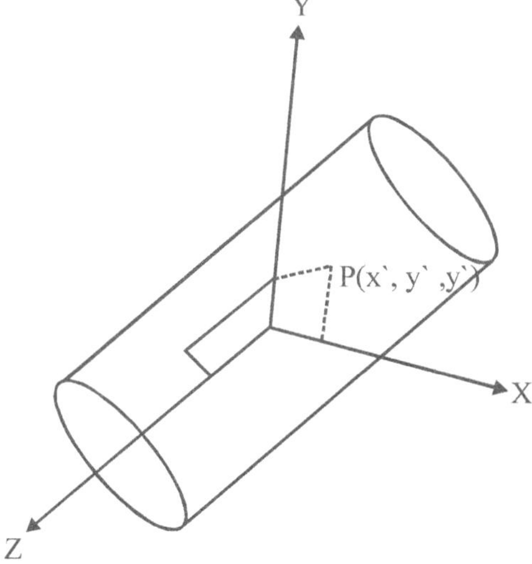

Chapter-6

General Theory of Conicoid and Central Conicoid

Conicoid : These are the surfaces in three dimensional space similar to conic section in two dimensional space. General equation (given below) of second degree represents equation of the conicoid :

$$ax^2 + by^2 + cz^2 + 2fyz + 2hxy + 2gzx + 2ux + 2vy + 2wz + d = 0 \qquad ...(1)$$

In case : If a = b = c = 1, f = g = h = 0 then (1) given equation of sphere :

$$x^2 + y^2 + z^2 + 2ux + 2vy + 2wz + d = 0$$

In case : If u = v = w = d = 0, then (1) gives the equation to the cone :

$$ax^2 + by^2 + cz^2 + 2fyz + 2gzx + 2hxy = 0$$

III case : If a = b = 1, h = 0, z = k, then (1) gives equation to the right circular cylinder

$$x^2 + y^2 + 2ux + 2vy + d = 0,\ z = k$$

Note : Conicoids are of two types :

(i) Central conicoids : The conicoide which have centre called central conicoids as ellipsoid, cone etc..

(ii) Noncentral conicoids : Having no centre. These are cylinder, paraboloid (also are of two types elloptic paraboloid & hyperbolic paraboloid e.g. dish antenas).

Transformation of axes This is done by two ways :

I. By change of origin.

II. By rotation of axes.

I. By change of origin : In this transformation is done through shifting of origin to another point without changing the direction of the axes. The equation of transformations are given by :

$x = x^1+a$, $y = y^1+b$, $z = z^1+c$

II. By rotating of axes : The transformation of a co-ordinate system in which the direction of axes is changed without shifting the origin. The equation of transformation are given by the following table :

	x	y	z
x'	l_1	m_1	n_1
y'	l_2	m_2	n_2
z'	l_3	m_3	n_3

where l_i, m_i, n_i, i = 1, 2, 3 are the direction consines of the axes.

- A conicoid remains a conicoid under a translation or rotation of axes.
- There is a Cartesian coordinate system in which the equation of a conicoid with a centre takes the standard form : $ax^2+by^2+cz^2+d = 0$

Definition of a central conicoid : The necessary any sufficient condition for the conicoid to $ax^2+by^2+cz^2+2fyz+2gzx+2hxy+2ux+2vy+2wz+d = 0$ to have a centre

$$\text{is} \begin{vmatrix} a & h & b \\ h & b & f \\ g & f & c \end{vmatrix} \neq 0$$

The standard form of a central conicoid is :

$ax^2+by^2+cz^2+d = 0$, $abc \neq 0$

If $d \neq 0$, then there are four categories, as given in the table below :

Table : Standard Form of central conicoids

Type	Standard form
Cone	$ax^2 + by^2 + cz^2 = 0$
Imaginary ellipsoid	$\frac{x^2}{a^2}+\frac{y^2}{b^2}+\frac{z^2}{c^2}=-1$
Hyperboloid of one sheet	$\frac{x^2}{a^2}+\frac{y^2}{b^2}-\frac{z^2}{c^2}=1$ $\frac{x^2}{a^2}-\frac{y^2}{b^2}+\frac{z^2}{c^2}=1$ $-\frac{x^2}{a^2}+\frac{y^2}{b^2}+\frac{z^2}{c^2}=1$
Hyperboloid of two sheet	$\frac{x^2}{a^2}-\frac{y^2}{b^2}-\frac{z^2}{c^2}=1$ $-\frac{x^2}{a^2}+\frac{y^2}{b^2}-\frac{z^2}{c^2}=1$ $-\frac{x^2}{a^2}-\frac{y^2}{b^2}+\frac{z^2}{c^2}=1$

The condition for a line to a tangent to the central conicoid $ax^2+by^2+cz^2+d = 0$ at (x_0, y_0, z_0) is $ax_0\alpha+by_0\beta+cz_0\gamma=0$, where α,β,γ are the equation ratios of the line.

The equation of the tangent plane to a central conicoid $ax^2+by^2+cz^2 = 1$ at a point (x_0, y_0, z_0) is $axx_0 + byy_0 + czz_0 = 1$.

The condition that the plane $ux+vy+wz=p$ is a tangent to the central conicoid $ax^2+by^2+cz^2=1$ is

$$\frac{u^2}{a}+\frac{v^2}{b}+\frac{w^2}{c}=p^2$$

A planar section of a central conicoid is a conic section.

Paraboloid : The standard form of a non central conicoid is $ax^2+by^2+2wz+d = 0$, if $w = 0$, the equation represents a cylinder and pair of straight lines. If $w \neq 0$ the surfaces represented by the equation called a paraboloid. The standard equation of a paraboloid is : $ax^2+by^2 = 2wz$, $w \neq 0$. There are two types of paraboloids

When a and b are of the same signs, we get an elliptic paraboloid.

When a and b are of opposite signs, we get a hyperbolic paraboloid.

The condition for a line with direction ratios a, b, g to be a tangent to the central conicoid $ax^2+by^2 = 2z$ at (x_0, y_0, z_0) is $ax_0\alpha + by_0\beta = \gamma$

The equation of the tangent plane to the paraboloid $ax^2+by^2 = 2z$ at a point (x_0, y_0, z_0) is $axx_0+byy_0 = (z+z_0)$.

The condition that the plane ux + vy + wz = 0 is a tangent plane to the paraboloid $ax^2+by^2 = 2z$ is :

$$\frac{u^2}{a}+\frac{v^2}{b}+2wp=0$$

Note : The plannar section of a paraboloid is a conic section.

SOLVED EXAMPLES

Q1. Find the centre of the conicoid [June98, Q4(b)]
$x^2 + 2y^2 - 7z^2 + 2x + 8y - 14z + 1 = 0$
Reduce the conicoid to its standard form and then given a rough sketch of it.

Ans. The given equation is

$x^2 + 2y^2 - 7z^2 + 2x + 8y - 14z + 1 = 0$

Here a = 1, b = 2, c = -7, u = 2, v = 8, and w = -14, h = g = f = 0

We know (x, y, z) is centre if

$ax + hy + gz + 4 = 0$

$hx + by + fz + v = 0$

$gx + fy + cz + w = 0$ have solution.

We put the value we get

$x + 2 = 0$

$2y + 8 = 0$

$-7z - 14 = 0$

$\Rightarrow x = -2, y = -4, z = 2$

Hence centre is (-2, -4, 2).

Now we shift the origin from (0, 0, 0) to (-2, -4, 2). The equation of transformation are

$x = x' - 2, y = y' - 4, z' + 2$

Substitute x, y, z in given equation.

$(x' - 2)^2 + 2(y' - 4)^2 - 7(z' + 2)^2 + 2(z' - 2) + 8(y' - 4) - 14(z' + 2) + 1 = 0$

$\Rightarrow x'^2 - 4x' + 4 + 2y'^2 - 16y' + 16 - 7z'^2 - 28z' - 28 + 2x' - 4 + 8y' - 32 - 14z' - 28 + 1 = 0$

$\Rightarrow x'^2 + 2y'^2 - 7z'^2 - 2x' - 8y' - 42z' - 71 = 0$
Hence reduced equation is
$x^2 + 2y^2 - 7z^2 - 2x - 8y - 42z - 71 = 0$

Q2. Find the equation of the sections of the conicoid $2x^2 + y^2 - z^2 = 1$ by the plane $3x + 4y + 5z = 0$. **[Dec99, Q3(b)]**

Ans. We have to find the section of conicoid
$2x^2 + y^2 - z^2 = 1$ by the plane $3x + 4y + 5z = 0$
We know that now, if the conicoid is given by
$ax^2 + by^2 + cz^2 = 1$ and plane is given by $ux + vy + wz = p$ then the section will be a hyperbola, parabola or an ellipse
$\Rightarrow bcu^2 + cav^2 + abw^2 < 0$
$\Rightarrow bcu^2 + cav^2 + abw^2 = 0$
$\Rightarrow bcu^2 + cav^2 + abw^2 > 0$
Since $2x^2 + y^2 - z^2 = 1$; and $3x + 4y + 5z = 0$
$a = 2, b = 1, c = -1,$
$u = 3, v = 4, w = 5$
Then $bcu^2 + cav^2 + abw^2$
$\Rightarrow -9 - 32 + 50 > 0$
Therefore the section is an ellipse
This equation is not we can obtain the condition by eliminating either x, y or z from the equation
$2x^2 + y^2 - z^2 = 1$ and $3x + 4y + 5z = 0$
Since it is lengthy, we have not include it here.

Q3. Identify the conic obtained by intersecting the hyperboloid $9x^2 + 6y^2 - 14z^2 = 3$ and $x + y + z = 1$. **[June99, Q2(b)]**

Ans. The given hyperboloid is
$9x^2 + 6y^2 - 14z^2 = 3$

$$\therefore a = 3, b = 2, c = \frac{-14}{3}$$

$u = v = w = 1$
Thus, $bcu^2 + cav^2 + abw^2$

$$= 2 \times \frac{-14}{3} - 14 + 6 < 0$$

$$= \frac{-28}{3} - 8 < 0$$

A planner section of a central conical need not be a central conic the section is a hyperbola.

Q4. Reduce the equation
$5x^2 + 3y^2 + 3z^2 - 2xy + 2yz - 2zx + 12x + 10y + 2z + 20 = 0$
to standard form. To do so, after applying a suitable translation, you should rotate the system so that the direction ratios of the new axes are 0, 1, –1; 1, 1, 1; – 2, 1, 1. [June99, Q3(b)]

Ans. $5x^2 + 3y^2 + 3z^2 - 2xy + 2yz - 2zx + 12x + 10y + 2z + 20 = 0$
We first check whether the conicoid represented by this equation has centre
$a = 5, b = 3, c = 3, h = -1, g = -1, f = 1, u = 6, v = 5, w = 1, d = 20$
The system of equation for transformation are given by
$ax + hy + gz + u = 0$
$hx + by + fz + v = 0$
$gx + fy + cz + w = 0$
Therefore
$5x - y - z + 6 = 0$ ...(i)
$-x + 3y + z + 5 = 0$ ...(ii)
$-x + y + 3z + 1 = 0$ ...(iii)
From equation (ii) and (iii)
$5x - y - z = -6$
$\underline{-x + y + 3z = -1}$
$4x \quad -2z = -7$ ...(iv)
Again we take equation (i)3 and add equation (iii)
$15x - 3y - 3z = -18$
$\underline{-x + 3y + z = -5}$
$14x \quad -2z = -23$ ...(v)

Now, again we taken
$14x - 2z = -23$
$\underline{4x + 2z = -7}$
$18x \quad = -30$

$$x = \frac{-30}{18} = \frac{-5}{3}$$

$$x = \frac{-5}{3}$$

We put $x = \frac{-5}{3}$ in equation

$14x - 2z = -23$

$$14\times\frac{-5}{3}-2z=-23$$

$$\frac{70}{3}-2z=-23$$

$$\frac{-70-6z}{3}=\frac{-23}{1}$$

$\Rightarrow -70-6z=-69 \qquad \Rightarrow -6z=-69+70$

$\Rightarrow -6z=1, \qquad z=\frac{1}{6}$

Now, we put all value in equation

$5x-y-z=-6$

$$\Rightarrow 5\times\left(\frac{-5}{3}\right)-y+\frac{1}{6}=-6$$

$$\Rightarrow \frac{-25}{3}-y+\frac{1}{6}=-6$$

$$-y=-6-\frac{1}{6}+\frac{25}{3} \quad \Rightarrow \quad -y=\frac{-37+50}{6}\Rightarrow y=\frac{-13}{6}$$

$\left(x=\frac{-5}{3},\ y=\frac{-13}{6},\ z=\frac{-1}{6}\right)$ is centre

Now shifting the origin to the centre. Then we get the new equation

$5x^2+3y^2+3z^2-2xy+2yz-2zx+d'=0$

where

$$d`=5\left(\frac{-5}{3}\right)^2+3\left(\frac{-13}{6}\right)+3\left(\frac{-1}{6}\right)^2-2\left(\frac{-5}{3}\right)\left(\frac{-13}{6}\right)+2\left(\frac{-13}{6}\right).$$

$$\left(\frac{-1}{6}\right)-2\left(\frac{-1}{6}\right)\left(\frac{-5}{3}\right)+12\left(\frac{-5}{3}\right)+10\left(\frac{-13}{6}\right)+2\left(\frac{-1}{6}\right)+20$$

We apply the rotation of axes. The equation of transformation are direction cosine the new axes are (0, 1, -1)(1, 1, 1)(-2, 1, 1)

$x=y'-2z'$

$y=x'+y'-2z'$

$z=-x'+y'+z'$

Substituting for (x, y, z) equation is conicoid, we get

$5x^2 + 3y^2 + 3z^2 - 2xy + 2yz - 2zx + d' = 0$

$5(y' - 2z')^2 + 3(x' + y' - 2z')^2 + 3(-x' + y' + z')^2 - 2(y' - 2z')$

$(x' + y' - 2z') + 2(x' + y' - 2z')(-x' + y' + z') - 2(-x' + y' + z')$

$(y' - 2z') + d' = 0$

Q5. Sketch the surface defined by

$$\frac{-x^2}{16} + \frac{y^2}{9} + \frac{z^2}{9} = 1$$ **[June99, Q5(a)]**

Ans. The surface is

$$\frac{-x^2}{16} + \frac{y^2}{9} + \frac{z^2}{9} = 1$$

$\Rightarrow ax^2 + by^2 + cz^2 = -d$

$$\Rightarrow \frac{-x^2}{-\frac{d}{a}} + \frac{-y^2}{-\frac{d}{a}} + \frac{-z^2}{-\frac{d}{c}} = 1$$

$$\Rightarrow \frac{-x^2}{\frac{1}{16}} + \frac{y^2}{-\frac{1}{9}} + \frac{z^2}{-\frac{1}{9}} = 1$$

$$\therefore a = \sqrt{\frac{1}{-16}} = \frac{1}{4}$$

$$b = \sqrt{\frac{1}{-9}} = \frac{1}{3}$$

$$c = \sqrt{\frac{1}{-9}} = \frac{1}{3}$$

$a > 0, b > 0, c < 0, d < 0$

$$\frac{-x^2}{16} + \frac{y^2}{16} + \frac{z^2}{9} = 1$$

It is one sheet hyperboloid

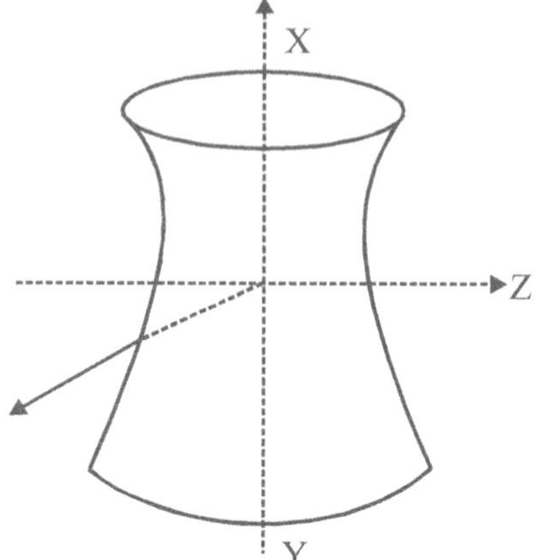

The hyperboloid of one sheet $\frac{-x^2}{16}+\frac{y^2}{9}+\frac{z^2}{9}=1$

Q6. Find the equation of the tangent planes to the conicoid x² + 3y² – 3z² = 1 which pass through the lines 7x + 10y + 3z = 0 and x + y – 5z + 5 = 0. **[Dec99, Q3(b)]**

Ans. $x^2 + 3y^2 - 3z^2 = 1$

Equation of a plane passing through the given line

$7x + 10y + 3z + \lambda (x + y - 5z + 5) = 0$

λ is a real number plane is tangent plane to the coincoid equation of plane

$$\Rightarrow \frac{xx_0}{1}+\frac{3yy_0}{1}-\frac{3zz_0}{1}=1$$

Comparing the coefficient we get

$$\Rightarrow \frac{x_0}{7+\lambda}+\frac{3y_0}{10+\lambda}-\frac{3z_0}{3-5\lambda}=\frac{1}{5\lambda}$$

$$\Rightarrow x_0=\frac{7+\lambda}{5\lambda}, y_0=\frac{10+\lambda}{15\lambda}, z_0=\frac{3-5\lambda}{15\lambda}$$

where λ is real

$\Rightarrow$ since (α,β,γ) lies on the coincoid

$\Rightarrow x^2 + 3y^2 - 3z^2 = 1$

$$\Rightarrow \left(\frac{7+\lambda}{5\lambda}\right)^2+3\left(\frac{10+\lambda}{15\lambda}\right)^2-3\left(\frac{3-5\lambda}{15\lambda}\right)=1$$

$$\Rightarrow \frac{49+14\lambda+\lambda^2}{25\lambda^2}+\frac{3\left(100+20\lambda+\lambda^2\right)}{225\lambda^2}-\frac{3\left(9-30\lambda+25\lambda^2\right)}{225\lambda^2}=1$$

$$\Rightarrow \frac{441+126\lambda+9\lambda^2+300+60\lambda+3\lambda^2-27+90\lambda-75\lambda^2}{225\lambda^2}=1$$

$$-288\lambda^2+276\lambda+714=0$$

Q7. Reduce the equation **[Dec99, Q2(b)]**
$4x^2 + y^2 - z^2 + 4x + 4y + 6z - 8 = 0$
to standard form. Hence identify the surface represented by it.
Ans. The given equation is
$4x^2 + y^2 - z^2 + 4x + 4y + 6z - 8 = 0$
$\Rightarrow 4x^2 + 4x + 1 + y^2 + 4y + 4 - z^2 + 6z - 9 - 1 - 4 + 9 - 8 = 0$
$\Rightarrow (2x + 1)^2 + (y + 2)^2 - (z - 3)^2 - 4 = 0$
$\Rightarrow (2x + 1)^2 + (y + 2)^2 - (z - 3)^2 = 4$

$$\Rightarrow \frac{4\left(x+\frac{1}{2}\right)^2}{4}+\frac{(y+2)^2}{4}-\frac{(z-3)^2}{4}=1$$

$$\Rightarrow \frac{\left(x+\frac{1}{2}\right)^2}{1}+\frac{(y+2)^2}{4}-\frac{(z-3)^2}{4}=1$$

Shifting the origin to $\left(-\frac{1}{2},-2,3\right)$ the equation reduced to

$$\frac{x^2}{1}+\frac{y^2}{4}-\frac{z^2}{4}=1$$

This is hyperboloid.

Q8. Consider the hyperbolic paraboloid given by
$y^2 - 2z^2 = x$
(i) What are its sections by the planes y = 0 and x = 1/
(ii) Sketch the surface described by the given equation. [Dec99, Q4(b)]
Ans. (i)

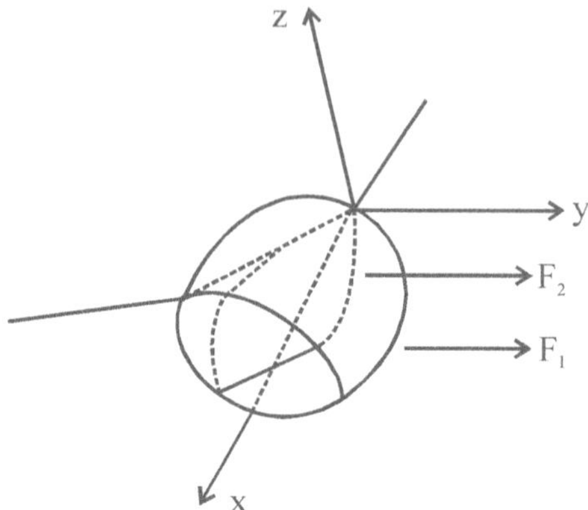

F_1 and F_2 are sections obtained by intersecting the elliptic paraboloid with the planes y = 0 and x = 1.

(ii)

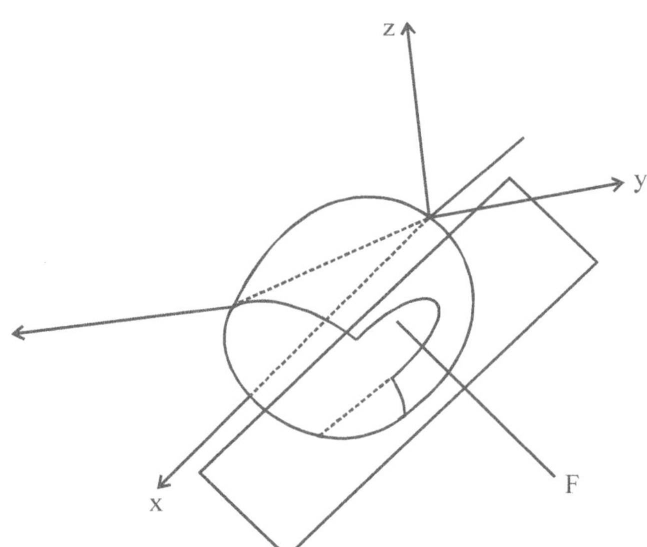

F is the section of the hyperbolic paraboloid $y^2 - 2z^2 = x$.

Q9. Obtain the equation of the right-circular cone with vertex at (1, 0, 1) and passing through the point (1, 1, 1). The axis of the cone is equally inclined to the coordinated axes. [June00, Q2(a)]

Ans. Since axis of the cone is esqually inclined i.e. $\theta = 45°$

direction ratio $\alpha = \beta = \gamma = \cos 45° \times \sqrt{2} = 1$

(Let k= $\sqrt{2} \in R$)

v(1, 0, 1) and p(1, 1, 1)

a = 1, b = 0, c = 1

$$\therefore \cos\theta = \frac{\alpha(x-a)+\beta(y-b)+\gamma(z-c)}{\sqrt{\alpha^2+\beta^2+\gamma^2}\sqrt{(x-a)^2+(y-b)^2+(z-c)^2}}$$

$$\Rightarrow \cos 45° = \frac{1.(x-1)+1.(y-0)+1.(z-1)}{\sqrt{1+1+1}\times\sqrt{(x-1)^2+(y-0)^2+(z-1)^2}}$$

$$\Rightarrow \frac{1}{\sqrt{2}} = \frac{x-1+y+z-1}{\sqrt{3}\times\sqrt{(x-1)^2+y^2+(z-1)^2}}$$

$$\Rightarrow \frac{\sqrt{3}}{\sqrt{2}}\times\sqrt{(x-1)^2+y^2+(z-1)^2} = (z+y+z-2)$$

$$\Rightarrow \frac{3}{2}\left[(x-1)^2+y^2+(z-1)^2\right] = (z+y+z-2)^2$$

This is required equation.

Q10. Find the centre of the conicoid
$4x^2 - y^2 + 2z^2 + 12x - 11y + 6z + 4 = 0$
Also reduce the equation to standard form. **[Dec00, Q4(a)]**

Ans. The given conicoid is

$4x^2 - y^2 + 2z^2 + 12x - 11y + 6z + 4 = 0$

Here a = 4, b = –1, c = 2, f = 0, g = 0,

h = 0, u = 6, $v = -\frac{11}{2}$, w = 3, d = 0

We have to see whether the following system of linear equation is consistent or not

ax + hy + gz + u = 0

hx + by + fz + v = 0

gx + fy + cz + w = 0

4x + 0 + 0 + 6 = 0

$$x = \frac{-6}{4} = \frac{-3}{2}$$

and $0 + (-1).y + 0 - \frac{11}{2} = 0$

$$\Rightarrow -y - \frac{11}{2} = 0$$

$$\Rightarrow y = \frac{-11}{2}$$

and 0 + 0 + 2z + 3 = 0

$$\Rightarrow z = \frac{-3}{2}$$

Hence centre is $\left(\frac{-3}{2}, \frac{-11}{2}, \frac{-3}{2}\right)$ or (p, q, r) let

Now we shift the origin to the centre we know

$ax'^2 + by'^2 + cz'^2 + 2fz' + 2gz'x' + 2hx'y' + 2u'x' + 2v'y' + 2w'z' + d' = 0$

Put the value a, b, c, f, g, h we get

$4x'^2 - y'^2 + 2z'^2 + 2u'x' + 2v'y' + 2w'z' + d' = 0$ .....(A)

We know

$u' = (ap + hq + gr) + u$

$$= \left(4 \times \left(\frac{-3}{2}\right) + 0 + 0\right) + 6$$

$= -6 + 6 = 0$

$v' = (hp + bp + fr) + v$

$$= \left[0 + (-1) \times \left(\frac{-11}{2}\right) + 0\right] + \frac{-11}{2}$$

$$= \frac{11}{2} - \frac{11}{2} = 0$$

$w' = (gp + fq + cr) + w$

$$= \left(0 + 0 + 2 \times \left(\frac{-3}{2}\right)\right) + 3$$

$= -3 + 3 = 0$

$d' = ap^2 + bq^2 + cr^2 + 2fqr + 2grp + 2hpq + 2up + 2vq + 2wr + d$

$$= 4\left(\frac{-3}{2}\right)^2 (-1)^2 \left(\frac{-11}{2}\right)^2 + 2 \times \left(\frac{-3}{2}\right)^2 + 0 + 0 + 0 + 2.6\left(\frac{-3}{2}\right)$$

$$+2.\left(\frac{-11}{2}\right)\left(\frac{-11}{2}\right) + 2.3\left(\frac{-3}{2}\right)$$

$$= 9 - \frac{121}{4} + \frac{9}{2} - 18 + \frac{121}{2} - 9$$

$$= \frac{121}{2} + \frac{9}{2} - 18$$

$$= \frac{121 + 9 - 36}{2}$$

$$= \frac{94}{2} = 47$$

Put these value in (A)

$4x'^2 - y'^2 + 2z'^2 + 47 = 0$

This is required equation.

Q11. Find the conic obtained by intersecting the conicoid

$$\frac{x^2}{3} + \frac{y^2}{7} = 4z$$

with the plane x = y? If it is central, find its foci and directions, if it is not central, find its vertex, focus and the length of the latus rectum. Roughly sketch the curve also. **[Dec00, Q5(a)]**

Ans. The conicoid is

$$\frac{x^2}{3} + \frac{y^2}{7} = 4z$$

$\Rightarrow 7x^2 + 3xy - 84z = 0$

$x_0 = 0,\ y_0 = 0,\ z_0 = 0$

$a = 1,\ b = 1,\ c = 0,\ w = -84$

So we get the system has unique solution. The conicoid has a unique centre. As we know A conicoid is called a central conicoid if it has a unique centre. Hence given conicoid is central.

The given conicoid

$$\frac{x^2}{3} + \frac{y^2}{7} = 4z$$

is hyperbolic paraboloid with the principal planes x = 0, y = 0.

Q12. Find the cone on which the perpendiculars drawn from the origin to the tangent planes to the cone $9x^2 + 11y^2 - 10zx = 0$ lie. **[June01, Q2(b)]**

Ans. The given equation is

$9x^2 + 11y^2 - 10zx = 0$

$a = 9.\ b = 11,\ c = 0$

$\therefore h = 0,\ f = 0,\ g = \dfrac{-10}{2} = -5$

The required cone is the reciprocal of the given cone. Thus it equation is

$$\begin{vmatrix} a & h & g & x \\ h & b & f & y \\ g & f & c & z \\ x & y & z & 0 \end{vmatrix} = 0$$

$$\Rightarrow \begin{vmatrix} 9 & 0 & -5 & x \\ 0 & 11 & 0 & y \\ -5 & 0 & 0 & z \\ x & y & z & 0 \end{vmatrix} = 0$$

$$\Rightarrow 9\begin{vmatrix} 11 & 0 & y \\ 0 & 0 & z \\ y & z & 0 \end{vmatrix} - 0\begin{vmatrix} 0 & -5 & x \\ 0 & 0 & z \\ y & z & 0 \end{vmatrix} + (-5)\begin{vmatrix} 0 & -5 & x \\ 11 & 0 & y \\ y & z & 0 \end{vmatrix} - x\begin{vmatrix} 0 & -5 & x \\ 11 & 0 & y \\ 0 & 0 & z \end{vmatrix} = 0$$

$$\Rightarrow 9\left[11\times(-z) + y.0\right] - 0 - 5\left[-11.(-xz) + y(-5y)\right] - x\left[-11\times(-5y)\right] = 0$$

$$\Rightarrow -99z - 55xz + 25y^2 - 25xy = 0$$

$$\Rightarrow 25y^2 - 55xz - 55xy - 99z = 0$$

This is required equation.

Q13. Find the centre of the conicoid
$3x^2 + 5y^2 + 3z^2 + 2x + 12y + 10z + 20 = 0$
Reduce it to standard form. **[June01, Q3(b)]**

Ans. $3x^2 + 5y^2 + 3z^2 - 2yz + 2zx - 2xy + 2x + 12y + 10z + 20 = 0$

First we check the conicoid represented by this equation has centre.

$a = 3,\ b = 5,\ c = 3,\ h = -1,\ g = 1,\ f = -1,\ u = 1,\ v = 6,\ w = 5$ and $d = 20$.

The system of equation for transformation are given by

$3x - y + z + 1 = 0$

$-x + 5y - z + 6 = 0$

$x - y + 3z + 5 = 0$

Solving these equation we get

$x=-\frac{1}{6}, y=-\frac{5}{3}$ and $z=-\frac{13}{6}$

Hence centre is $\left(-\frac{1}{6},-\frac{5}{3},-\frac{13}{6}\right)$

Now we shift be origin to the centre. Then we get the new equation as
$\Rightarrow 3x^2 + 5y^2 + 3z^2 - 2yz + 2zx - 2xy + d' = 0$
This is the standard form of the given conicoid

Q14. Identify the conic obtained by intersecting the ellipsoid $x^2 + 4y^2 + z^2 = 4$ and the plane $y + z + 1 = 0$. Also give the rough sketch of the conic obtained. **[Dec01, Q2(a)]**

Ans. The given ellipsoid is
$x^2 + 4y^2 + z^2 = 4$

$$\Rightarrow \frac{x^2}{4}+\frac{y^2}{1}+\frac{z^2}{4}=1$$

Here a = 4, b = 1, c = 4
The given plane is
$y + z + 1 = 0$
Here u = 0, v = 1, w = 1
Now

$$\frac{u^2}{a}+\frac{v^2}{b}+\frac{w^2}{c}$$

$$=\frac{0}{4}+\frac{1^2}{1}+\frac{1^2}{4}$$

$$=0+1+\frac{1}{4}$$

$$=\frac{5}{4}>0 \qquad (>1)$$

Hence conic is ellipse.

Q15. Is the conicoid
$C \equiv x^2 + 2y^2 - 7z^2 + 2x + 8y - 14z + 1 = 0$
central? Given reasons for your answer. If C is central, reduce it to its standard form and identify the conicoid it represents. Otherwise, alter the coefficient of x^2 inn the equation of C to get a central conicoid, and

then identify the new conicoid you get. **[June02, Q2(b)]**

Ans. The given conicoid is

$x^2 + 2y^2 - 7z^2 + 2x + 8y - 14z + 1 = 0$

Here

a = 1, b = 2, c = 7

f = 0, g = 0, h = 0

u = 1, v = 4, w = –7, d = 1

The given conicoid is central

$$\text{if} \begin{vmatrix} a & h & g \\ h & b & f \\ g & f & c \end{vmatrix} \neq 0$$

$$\begin{vmatrix} a & h & g \\ h & b & f \\ g & f & c \end{vmatrix} = \begin{vmatrix} 1 & 0 & 0 \\ 0 & 2 & 0 \\ 0 & 0 & -7 \end{vmatrix}$$

$$= 1.[-14 - 0]$$

$$= -14 \neq 0$$

Hence given conicoid is central.

According to theorem we reduced to conicoid to its standard form

$ax^2 + by^2 + cz^2 + d = 0$

$\Rightarrow x^2 + 2y^2 - 7z^2 + 1 = 0$

$$\Rightarrow \frac{-x^2}{14} - \frac{y^2}{7} + \frac{z^2}{2} = \frac{1}{14}$$

$$\Rightarrow \frac{-x^2}{196} - \frac{y^2}{98} + \frac{z^2}{28} = 1$$

This represent hyperboloid.

Q16. Reduce the section of the conicoid

$xy - z^2 - 10z = 21$

by the plane x = y + z to standard form. Hence identify the conic you get. Also find the eccentricity of the conic. **[June02, Q3]**

Ans. The given section of conicoid is

$xy - z^2 - 10z = 21$

and plane x = y + z

$\therefore$ a = 0, b = 0, c = –1

u = 1, v = -1, w = –1

Then $bcu^2 + cav^2 + abw^2$

= 0 + 0 + 0

= 0

Therefore section is parabola.

Since, it is parabola therefore eccentricity

e = 1.

Q17. Check whether the plane 2x – y + z = 0 is a tangent plane to the cone generated by the normals to the tangent planes at (0, 0, 0) to the cone $5yz + x^2 - 3y^2 = 0$. [June02, Q4(b)]

Ans. The given cone is

$5yz + x^2 - 3y^2 = 0$

$\therefore$ a = 1, b = –3, c = 0

f = 5/2, g = 0, h = 0

The given tangent plane is

2x – y + z = 0

u = 2, v = –1, w = 1

Now we have to check whether it is normal tangent plane to given cone at (0, 0, 0) or not.

$\therefore$ We have to show

$$\begin{vmatrix} a & h & g & u \\ h & b & f & v \\ g & f & c & w \\ u & v & w & 0 \end{vmatrix} = 0$$

$$\therefore \begin{vmatrix} a & h & g & u \\ h & b & f & v \\ g & f & c & w \\ u & v & w & 0 \end{vmatrix} = \begin{vmatrix} 1 & 0 & 0 & 2 \\ 0 & -3 & 5/2 & -1 \\ 0 & 5/2 & 0 & 1 \\ 2 & -1 & 1 & 0 \end{vmatrix}$$

$$= 1.\begin{vmatrix} -3 & 5/2 & -1 \\ 5/2 & 0 & 1 \\ -1 & 1 & 0 \end{vmatrix} - 2.\begin{vmatrix} 0 & 0 & 2 \\ -3 & 5/2 & 1 \\ 5/2 & 0 & 1 \end{vmatrix}$$

$$= -3[0-1] - 5/2[0+1] - 1.[5/2-0] - 2.2[0-25/4]$$

$$= 3 - \frac{5}{2} - \frac{5}{2} + 25$$
$= 3 - 5 + 25$
$= 23 \neq 0$
Hence given tangent plane is not a tangent plane to given cone.

Q18. Find the equation of a cylinder whose generators have directional ratios 1, –2, 3 and base curve is the ellipse $x^2 + 2y^2 = 1$, z = 3.
[Dec02, Q2(a)]

Ans. Direction ratios are 1, –2, 3

Let (α, β, γ) be any point in the cylinder.

So, the equation of the generator through (α, β, γ) is

$$\frac{x-\alpha}{1}, \frac{y-\beta}{-2}, \frac{z-\gamma}{3} = r \text{ (say)}$$

For it is parallel to given line any point $(\alpha + r, \beta - 2r, \gamma + 3r)$
For some value of r this point must lie on the guiding curve.

$\therefore (\alpha + r)^2 + 2(\beta + 2r)^2 = 1, \gamma + 3r = 3$
Eliminating r and we get

$$\left(\frac{3-\gamma}{3} + \alpha\right)^2 + 2\left(\beta + 2\frac{3-\gamma}{3}\right)^2 = 1$$

$$(3 - \gamma + 3\alpha)^2 + 2(3\beta + 6 - 2\gamma)^2$$

Replacing (α, β, γ) by (x, y, z) for generalizing and we get
$(3 - z + 3x^2) + 2(3y + 6 - 2z)^2 = 9$
$\Rightarrow 9 + z^2 + 9x^2 - 6z - 6zx + 18x + 18y^2 + 72 + 8z^2 + 72y - 48z + 24yz = 9$
$\Rightarrow 9x^2 + 18y^2 + 9z^2 + 24yz - 6zx + 18x + 72y - 54z + 72 = 0$
$\Rightarrow 3(x^2 + 2y^2 + z^2) - 18yz - 2zx + 6x + 24y - 18z + 24 = 0$
$3x^2 + 6y^2 + 3z^2 - 8yz - 2zx + 6x + 24y - 18z + 24 = 0$
which is required equation of cylinder.

Q19. Show that the plane x + y – 2z = 1 touches the paraboloid $ax^2 + by^2 = 2z$ if $\frac{1}{a} + \frac{1}{b} = 4$. Under what conditions on a and b will the paraboloid be an elliptic paraboloid? **[Dec02, Q2(b)]**

Ans. The plane x + y – 2z = 1

The plane ux + vy + wz = 9 will be tangent plane to the paraboloid

$ax^2 + by^2 = 2z$

$$\text{if}\frac{u^2}{a}+\frac{v^2}{b}+2pw=0$$

a = 1, b = 2, u = 1, v = 1, w = –2, p = 1

$$\Rightarrow\frac{1}{1}+\frac{1}{2}+2.1(-2)$$

$$\Rightarrow 1+\frac{1}{2}+(-4)\quad\Rightarrow 1+\frac{1-8}{2}$$

$$\Rightarrow 1+\frac{(-7)}{2}=1-\frac{7}{2}\qquad\Rightarrow\frac{2-7}{2}=\frac{-5}{2}$$

Q20. Reduce the equation

$11x^2+2\sqrt{3}xy+9y^2-12\sqrt{3}x-12y-12=0$ to the standard form. Hence identify the curve it represents.

Ans. The given equation is

$$11x^2+2\sqrt{3}xy+9y^2-12\sqrt{3}x-12y-12=0$$

In the form

$ax^2 + 2hxy + by^2 + 2gx + 2fy + c = 0$ ...(1)

Here a = 11

b = 9

h = $\sqrt{3}$

g = $6\sqrt{3}$

f = –6

c = –12

Now let us rotate the axes through an angle, where

$$\tan 2\theta=\frac{2h}{a-b}$$

$$\Rightarrow\frac{2\tan\theta}{1-\tan^2\theta}=\frac{2\sqrt{3}}{11-9}$$

$$\Rightarrow\frac{2\tan\theta}{1-\tan^2\theta}=\sqrt{3}$$

$\Rightarrow 2\tan\theta = \sqrt{3} - \sqrt{3}\tan^2\theta$

$\Rightarrow \sqrt{3}\tan^2\theta - 2\tan\theta - \sqrt{3} = 0$

$\Rightarrow \sqrt{3}\tan^2\theta - 3\tan\theta + \tan\theta - \sqrt{3} = 0$

$\Rightarrow \sqrt{3}\tan\theta\left(\tan\theta - \sqrt{3}\right) + 1\left(\tan\theta - \sqrt{3}\right) = 0$

$\Rightarrow \left(\tan\theta - \sqrt{3}\right)\left(\sqrt{3}\tan\theta + 1\right) = 0$

$\Rightarrow \tan\theta = \sqrt{3}$ or $\tan\theta = -\frac{1}{\sqrt{3}}$

We take $\tan\theta = \sqrt{3}$

$\therefore \sin\theta = \frac{\sqrt{3}}{2}$ and $\cos\theta = \frac{1}{2}$

Equation (1) can transform

$Ax'^2 + By'^2 + 2Gx' + 2Fy' + c = 0$ ...(2)

Where

$A = a\cos^2\theta + 2h\cos\theta\sin\theta + b\sin^2\theta$

$= 9.\left(\frac{1}{2}\right)^2 + 2.\sqrt{3}.\frac{1}{2}.\frac{\sqrt{3}}{2} + 11.\left(\frac{\sqrt{3}}{2}\right)^2$

$= \frac{9}{4} + \frac{3}{2} + \frac{33}{4}$

$= \frac{9+6+33}{4}$

$= \frac{48}{4}$

$= 12$

$B = a\sin^2\theta - 2h\sin\theta.\cos\theta + b\cos^2\theta$

$= 9.\left(\frac{\sqrt{3}}{2}\right)^2 - 2.\sqrt{3}.\frac{1}{2}.\frac{\sqrt{3}}{2} + 11.\left(\frac{1}{2}\right)^2$

$= \frac{27}{4} - \frac{3}{2} + \frac{11}{4}$

$$= \frac{27 - 6 + 11}{4}$$

$$= \frac{32}{4}$$

$= 8$

We know that

$ab - h^2 = AB$

$\Rightarrow ab - h^2 = 12 \times 8 \neq 0$

Now both A and B are non-zero

We can write (2) as

$$A\left(X' - \frac{G}{A}\right)^2 + B\left(Y' + \frac{F}{B}\right)^2 = \frac{G^2}{A} + \frac{F^2}{B} - C$$

Which is a constant K say

Let us shift the origin to $\left(-\frac{G}{A}, \frac{F}{B}\right)$. Then this equation becomes

$AX^2 + BY^2 = K$ ...(3)

where X and Y are the current co-ordinates if $AB = ab - h^2 > 0$ then Equation (3) represents the pair of lines.

$$X = \pm\sqrt{\frac{-B}{A}Y} \text{ if } k = 0 \quad \text{... (4)}$$

$$\Rightarrow X = \pm\sqrt{\frac{-8}{12}Y}$$

$$\Rightarrow X^2 = \frac{-2}{3}Y^2$$

$$X^2 + \frac{2}{3}Y^2 = 0$$

$$\frac{X^2}{\frac{2}{3}} + \frac{Y^2}{1} = 0$$

If $k \neq 0$

$$\frac{\frac{X^2}{k}}{A} + \frac{\frac{Y^2}{k}}{B} = 1$$

Since AB = ab – h^2

$$= 11 \times 9 - \left(\sqrt{3}\right)^2$$

= 99 – 3

= 96 > 0

If k > 0 then given equation is ellipse. If k < 0 then it represents empty set.

Q21. Give a rough sketch of the conicoid represented by $3x^2 - 5y^2 + 7z^2 = 1$. Also list 2 properties that you used for sketching it.[Dec02, Q4(b)]

Ans. $3x^2 - 5y^2 + 7z^2 = 1$

Case 1:- (d = 0) in this case the equation reduce to $ax^2 + by^2 + cz^2 = 0$.

$3x^2 - 5y^2 + 7z^2 = 1$

Case 2:- ($d \neq 0$) and a, b, c are the same sign) in this case there are no real value of (x, y, z) which satisfy $3x^2 - 5y^2 + 7z^2 = 1$

Because for any $(x, y, z) \in R^3$, the left hand side is either positive or negative never zero. An Imaginary conicoid an imaginary conicoid, in fact it represent on imaginary conicoid ellipsoid.

Case 3:- ($d \neq 0$ and two of the four coefficient a, b, c and d are same sign)

$3x^2 - 5y^2 + 7z^2 = 1$

$$\frac{\frac{x^2}{1}}{3} - \frac{\frac{y^2}{1}}{5} + \frac{\frac{z^2}{1}}{7} = 1$$

The number $\frac{1}{3}, \frac{1}{5}, \frac{1}{7}$ are positive

$x = \sqrt{3}, y = \sqrt{5}, z = \sqrt{7}$

The conicoid generate by this equation is called a hyperboloid of one sheet because a > 0, b < 0, c > 0, d > 0.

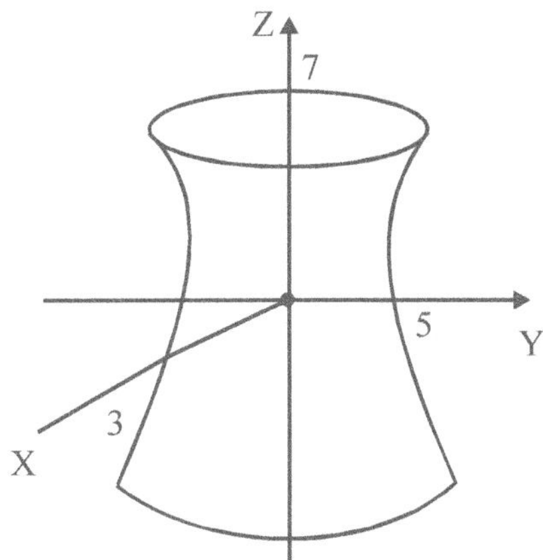

Q22. Give a rough sketch of the conicoid represented by $4y^2 - 9x^2 - 4z^2 = 1$. Also list two properties that you used for sketching it. [June03, Q2(c)]

Ans. $4y^2 - 9x^2 - 4z^2 = 1$

$-9x^2 + 4y - 4z^2 = 1$

Case 1:- (d = 0): In this case the equation reduce to $ay^2 + bx^2 + c = 0$

Case 2:- ($d \neq 0$ and a, b, c, d are of same sign)

In this case there are no real value of (x, y, z) which satisfy

$-9x^2 + 4y - 4z^2 = 1$

This is because for any $(x, y, z) \in R^3$, the left hand side is either positive or negative never zero. On imaginary conicoid an imaginary conicoid infact, it represent on imaginary ellipsoid.

Case 3:- ($d \neq 0$ and two of the four coefficient a, b, c and d are same sign)

Let assume that a < 0, b > 0 and c < 0

$-9x^2 + 4y^2 - 4z^2 = 1$

$$\frac{x^2}{-\frac{1}{9}} + \frac{y^2}{-\frac{1}{4}} - \frac{z^2}{-\frac{1}{4}} = 1$$

the number $-\frac{1}{9}, \frac{1}{4}$ and $-\frac{1}{4}$ are positive a = -3, 2, -2

The conicoid generated by this equation, is called a hyperboloid of one sheet because –a < 0, b > 0, c > 0, d > 0.

Q23. Reduce the equation

$3x^2 + 5y^2 + 3z^2 - 2yz + 2zx - 2xy + 2x + 12y + 10z + 20 = 0$

to standard form by shifting the origin to the centre and then rotating

the system so that the direction ratios to the new axes are –1, 0, 1; 1, 1, 1; 1, –2, 1. **[June03, Q3(b)]**

Ans. $3x^2 + 5y^2 + 3z^2 - 2yz + 2zx - 2xy + 2x + 12y + 10z + 20 = 0$

First we check the conicoid represented by this equation has centre.

$a = 3, b = 5, c = 3, h = -1, g = 1, f = -1, u = 1, v = 6, w = 5$ and $d = 20$.

The system of equation for transformation are given by

$3x - y + z + 1 = 0$

$-x + 5y - z + 6 = 0$

$x - y + 3z + 5 = 0$

Solving these equation we get

$$x = -\frac{1}{6}, y = -\frac{5}{3} \text{ and } z = -\frac{13}{6}$$

Hence centre is $\left(-\frac{1}{6}, -\frac{5}{3}, -\frac{13}{6}\right)$

Now we shift be origin to the centre. Then we get the new equation as

$\Rightarrow 3x^2 + 5y^2 + 3z^2 - 2yz + 2zx - 2xy + d' = 0$

$3x^2 + 5y^2 + 3z^2 - 2yz + 2zx - 2xy + d' = 0$

where

$$d' = 3\left(-\frac{1}{6}\right)^2 + 5\left(\frac{-5}{3}\right)^2 + 3\left(\frac{-13}{6}\right)^2 - 2\left(\frac{-5}{3}\right)\left(\frac{-13}{6}\right)$$

$$+2\left(\frac{-13}{6}\right)\left(\frac{-1}{6}\right) - 2\left(\frac{-1}{6}\right)\left(\frac{-5}{3}\right) + 2\left(\frac{-1}{6}\right)$$

$$+12\left(\frac{-5}{3}\right) + 10\left(\frac{-13}{6}\right) + 20$$

Now we apply the rotation of axes. The equation of transformation are

$x = -x' + y' + z'$

$y = y' - 2z'$

$z = x' + y' + z'$

Substituting for x, y, z in the given equation of the conicoid

$3(x' + y' + z')^2 + 5(y' - 2z')^2 + 3(x' + y' + z')^2$

$-2(y' - 2z')(x' + y' + z') + 2(x' + y' + z')(-x' + y' + z')$

$-2(-x' + y' + z')(y' - 2z') + d = 0$

$\Rightarrow 4x'^2 + 9y'^2 + 36z'^2 + d' = 0$

This is the standard form of the given coincoid.

Q24. Consider the cone $C \equiv 3xy + z(8x - 5y) = 0$ One of a set of 3

mutually perpendicular generators of C is x = y, y + z = 0. Find the equations of the other two generators. [June03, Q4(a)]

Ans. $x - y + k(y + z) = 0$, $k \in R$ gives any plane through the given line. This will cut the given cone in perpendicular lines if

$$3 \times 1 \times (k-1) + k \times [8 \times 1 - 5.(k-1)] = 0$$

$$\Rightarrow 3k - 3 + k \times (8 - 5k + 5) = 0$$

$\Rightarrow 3k - 3 + 13k - 5k^2 = 0$

$\Rightarrow 16k - 3 - 5k^2 = 0$

$\Rightarrow 5k^2 - 16k + 3 = 0$

$\Rightarrow (5k - 1)(k - 3) = 0$

$$\Rightarrow k = \frac{1}{5}, 3$$

Thus the planes are

$x - y + 3(y + z) = 0$

$\Rightarrow x + 2y + 3z = 0$

and $x - y + \frac{1}{5}(y + z) = 0$

$\Rightarrow 5x - 4y + z = 0$

Now $x + 2y + 3z = 0$ intersects the cone in two perpendicular lines of which one is given one which lies on the plane. Therefore, the other one has to be the normal to plane at (0, 0, 0). This is $\frac{x}{1} = \frac{y}{2} = \frac{z}{3}$ so this will be another of the required set of mutually perpendicular generators. Similarly, the third generated will be the normal to $5x - 4y + z = 0$ at (0, 0, 0) that is $\frac{x}{5} = \frac{y}{-4} = \frac{z}{1}$

Q25. Find all the tangents of the conic $x^2 + 4xy + 3y^2 - 5x - 6y + 3 = 0$ that are parallel to $y = -\frac{x}{4}$ [June03, Q5(a)]

Ans. General equation

$ax^2 + 2hxy + by^2 + 2gx + 2fy + c = 0$

We know that the condition all tangents

$(prh + pqg - aqr - p^2f)^2 = (aq^2 - 2hpq + bp^2)(ar^2 - 2gpr + cp^2)$ ...(1)

In terms of determinants

$$\begin{vmatrix} a & h & g & p \\ h & b & f & q \\ g & f & c & r \\ p & q & r & o \end{vmatrix} = 0 \qquad ....(2)$$

The given equation is

$x^2 + 4xy + 3y^2 - 5x - 6y + 3 = 0$

$y = \frac{-x}{4} \Rightarrow x + 4y = 0$ will be tangent to the given conic if

$$\begin{vmatrix} 1 & 2 & -5/2 & 1 \\ 2 & 3 & -3 & 4 \\ -5/2 & -3 & 3 & 0 \\ 1 & 4 & 0 & 0 \end{vmatrix} = 0$$

$$\Leftrightarrow -\begin{vmatrix} 2 & 3 & -3 \\ -5/2 & -3 & 3 \\ 1 & 4 & 0 \end{vmatrix} + 4\begin{vmatrix} 1 & 2 & -5/2 \\ -5/2 & -3 & 3 \\ 1 & 4 & 0 \end{vmatrix} = 0$$

$\Leftrightarrow 40 = 0$, which is false.

Thus the given line is not a tangent to the given conic.

Any lines parallel to the given line is of the form $x + 4y + c = 0$. This will be a tangent to the given conic if (1) is satisfied, that is,

$(5c + 28)^2 = 3(3c^2 + 24c + 48)$

$\Leftrightarrow c = -5$ or -8

Thus, the required tangents are

$x + 4y - 5 = 0$ and $x + 4y - 8 = 0$

Q26. Identify the conic section formed by taking the planar section of the paraboloid $\frac{x^2}{2} - \frac{y^2}{3} = z$ by the plane $3(x - y) + 4z + 2 = 0$.

[Dec03, Q4(a)]

Ans. Equation of paraboloid $\frac{x^2}{2} - \frac{y^2}{3} = z$

$\therefore 3x^2 - 2y^2 = 6z$

equation of plane

$3(x - y) + 4z + 2 = 0$

$3x - 3y + 4z + 2 = 0$

$\therefore x = 3$

$v = 3$

$w = 4$

$\therefore w \neq 0$

But a = 3, b = –2

which is opposite sign

$\therefore$ Given section of paraboloid is hyperbola.

Q27. Reduce $x^2 + 2yz - 4x + 6y + 2z = 0$ to standard form by shifting the origin to (2, –1, 3), and then rotating the axes to get a new system in which the direction ratios of the new axes are 0, –1, 1; $\sqrt{2}$, 1, 1; $\sqrt{2}$, –1, –1 with respect to the original coordinate system. [Dec03, Q4(b)]

Ans. Given equation

$x^2 + 2yz - 4x + 6y + 2z = 0$ ...(i)

$\therefore a = 1, b = 0, c = 0, f = 1, g = 0, h = 0, x = -2, v = 3, w = 2$

Shifting the origin from (0, 0, 0) to (2, -1, -3).

We get new equation

$x^2 + 2yz + d' = 0$

where

$d' = 3(2)^2 + 2(-1)(-3) - 4(2) + 6(-1) + 2(-3)$

$= 12 + 6 - 8 - 6 - 6 = 18 - 20 = -2$

$\therefore x^2 + 2yz - z = 0$ ...(ii)

Now we apply a rotation of axes to the new equation, we note that the direction cosines of the new axes are 0, –1, 1; $\sqrt{2}$, 1, 1; $\sqrt{2}$, –1, –1.

$\therefore x = -y' + z'$

$y = \sqrt{2}x + y' + z'$

$z = x\sqrt{2} - y' - z'$

Substituting these equation in the given equation of the conicoid from (ii)

$$\left(-y' - z'\right)^2 + 2\left(\sqrt{2}x + y' + z'\right)\left(x\sqrt{2} - y' - z'\right) - 2 = 0$$

$$y'^2 + z'^2 - 2y'z' + 2\left(2\sqrt{2}x' + 2y' + 2z'\right)\left(x'\sqrt{2} - y' - z'\right) - 2 = 0$$

$$y'^2 + z'^2 - 2y'z' + 4x'^2 - 2\sqrt{2}x'y' - 2\sqrt{2}x'z' + 2\sqrt{2}x'y'$$

$-2y'^2 - 2y'z' + 2\sqrt{2}x'z' - 2z'y' - 2z'^2 = 0$

$4x'^2 - y'^2 - 2z'^2 - 6y'z' = 0$

So the original equation of conicoid

$4x^2 - y^2 - 2z^2 - 6yz = 0$

Q28. Find the equations of the tangent planes to the conicoid $x^2 + 5y^2 + 3z^2 = 6$, which pass through the line $x + 2y - 3 = 0$, $5y - 3z = 0$.

[June04, Q2(b)]

Ans. The plane through the given line

$x + 2y - 3 + k(5y - 3z) = 0$

$\Rightarrow x + y(2 + 5k) - 3kz - 3 = 0$ ...(i)

Where K is the real number since this plane is a tangent plane to the given conicoid

$\therefore$ The plane must be of the form

$$\frac{xx'}{6} + \frac{5yy'}{6} + \frac{3zz'}{6} = 1$$

Comparing the coefficient of x, y, z with equation (i)

$$\frac{x'}{1} = \frac{5y'}{2+5k} = \frac{3z'}{-3k} = \frac{6}{3}$$

$\therefore$ (x', y', z') lies on the given conicoid

$\Rightarrow 4 + 5(4 + 10k)^2 + 3(-2k)^2 = 6$

$\Rightarrow 4 + 5(16 + 100k^2 + 80k) + 12k^2 = 6$

$\Rightarrow 4 + 80 + 512k^2 + 400k + 12k^2 = 6$

$512k^2 + 400k + 72 = 0$

$64k^2 + 50k + 9 = 0$

$\Rightarrow 64k^2 + 18k + 32k + 9 = 0$

$2k(32k + 9) + (32k + 9) = 0$

$(2k + 1)(32k + 9) = 0$

$$k = \frac{-1}{2}$$

$$k = \frac{-9}{32}$$

$\therefore$ The required equation is of tangent put value of k in equation (i)

$$x + 2y - 3 - \frac{1}{2}(5y - 3z) = 0$$

$2x - 4y - 6 - 5y + 3z = 0$

2x – 4y + 32 – 6 = 0

and $x+2y-3-\frac{9}{32}(5y-3z)=0$

32x + 64y – 96 – 45y + 272 = 0

$\therefore$ 32x + 19y + 176 = 0

QUESTION PAPERS
MTE-05

MTE-5 : ANALYTICAL GEOMETRY
December, 2001

Note : Question no. 5 is **compulsory.** Do any **three** questions out of questions no. 1 to 4. No calculators are allowed.

Q1. Which of the following statements are true? Justify your answer. **10**

(a) A paraboloid is a conicoid for which all the planar sections are parabolas.
(b) The equation $x^2 + 3xy + y^2 = 0$ represents a pair of real straight lines.
Refer to Chapter-1, Q.No.-14(f)

(c) The cone
$$19x^2 + 11y^2 + 3x^2 + 6yz - 10zx - 26xy = 0$$
has three mutually perpendicular generators.

(d) The point $\left(-\frac{1}{\sqrt{2}}, \frac{1}{\sqrt{3}}\right)$ **lies outside the ellipse** $2x^2 + 3y^2 = 1$.

(e) The lines $\frac{x+1}{2} = \frac{y}{2} = \frac{z-1}{2}$

$\frac{x+3}{5} = \frac{y-5}{-1}$ **and** $z = 3$ **are perpendicular.**
Refer to Chapter-4, Q.No.-47

Q2. (a) Identify the conic obtained by intersecting the ellipsoid $x^2 + 4y^2 + z^2 = 4$ and the plane $y + z + 1 = 0$. Also give the rough sketch of the conic obtained. **3**
Refer to Chapter-6, Q.No.-14

(b) Check whether the plane $2x + y - 2z - 5 = 0$ is tangent to the sphere $x^2 + y^2 + z^2 - 4y - 6z + 4 = 0$ or not. **2**
Refer to Chapter-4, Q.No.-38

Q3. (a) Find the equation of right circular cone whose vertex is (1, -1, 0), axis is $\frac{x-1}{2} = \frac{y+1}{2} = z - 3$ and semi-vertical angle is $\frac{\pi}{4}$. **2**
Refer to Chapter-5, Q.No.-25

(b) For the hyperbola $16x^2 - 25y^2 = 9$ find the vertices, eccentricity, foci, length of axes and the asymptotes. **3**

Refer to Chapter-2, Q.No.-24

Q4. (a) Is the conicoid $C \equiv 3x^2 - y^2 - z^2 + 6yz - 6x + 6y - 2z - 2 = 0$ central? If so, find its centre. If not, alter one coefficient in the equation for C to get a central conicoid and find the centre of the new conicoid. Also find the transformed equation of the conicoid C when the origin is shifted to the centre. **3**

(b) Find the equation of a right circular cylinder of radius 2 and whose axis passes through the point (1, 2, 3) and has direction ratios 2, –3, 6. **2**

Q5. (a) Find the foot of the perpendicular from the point (2, 3, –5) to the plane $x + y + z = 1$. **2**

(b) Reduce the following equations to the Cartesian form and hence identify the curves they represent: **3**

(i) $r \cos\left(\theta - \frac{\pi}{4}\right) = \sqrt{2}$

(ii) $r^2 = 3r \sin\theta$

Refer to Chapter-2, Q.No.-25

MTE-5 : ANALYTICAL GEOMETRY
June, 2002

Note : Question no. 5 is **compulsory.** Do any **three** questions out of questions no. 1 to 4. No calculators are allowed.

Q1. (a) Let ABCD be a square the length of whose sides is b. Take AB and AD as coordinate axes. Find the equation of the circle that passes through the vertices of the square. 2

(b) Find the equation of a sphere that passes through (0, 0, 0), (0, 1, –1) and (-1, 2, 0) and whose centre lies on the plane $x + y + z = 0$. 3

Q2. (a) Obtain the equation of an ellipse whose eccentricity is 1/2, one focus is (–1, 1) and the corresponding directrix is $x - y + 3 = 0$. 2

Refer to Chapter-2, Q.No.-26

(b) Is the conicoid

$C \equiv x^2 + 2y^2 - 7z^2 + 2x + 8y - 14z + 1 = 0$

central? Given reasons for your answer. If C is central, reduce it to its standard form and identify the conicoid it represents. Otherwise, alter the coefficient of x^2 in the equation of C to get a central conicoid, and then identify the new conicoid you get. 3

Refer to Chapter-6, Q.No.-15

Q3. Reduce the section of the conicoid

$xy - z^2 - 10z = 21$

by the plane $x = y + z$ to standard form. Hence identify the conic you get. Also find the eccentricity of the conic. 5

Refer to Chapter-6, Q.No.-16

Q4. (a) Find the equations of the tangents to the ellipse $4x^2 + 3y^2 = 24$ drawn parallel to $y = 2x$. 2

Refer to Chapter-2, Q.No.-27

(b) Check whether the plane $2x - y + z = 0$ is a tangent plane to the cone generated by the normals to the tangent planes at (0, 0, 0) to the cone $5y^2 + x^2 - 3y^2 = 0$. 3

Refer to Chapter-6, Q.No.-17

Q5. Which of the following statements are true? Give reasons for your answers, either by a short proof or a counter example. **10**

(i) Any two planes intersect in a line.

Refer to Chapter-4, Q.No.-47(g)

(ii) Given a right circular cylinder, there is only one plane that intersects it in a circle.

(iii) The projection of the line segment joining (2, 0, 0) and (0, 1, 0) on the z-axis is 0.

(iv) The equation $y^2 + z^2 + 2ux + 2vy + d = 0$ represents a surface that is symmetric about the origin.

(v) $a^2x^2 + by^2 + cz + d = 0$ represents a paraboloid a, b, c, d $\in$ R.

Refer to Chapter-4, Q.No.-47(h)

Whatever you do, do with determination. You have one life to live; do your work with passion and give your best. Whether you want to be a chef, doctor, actor, or a mother, be passionate to get the best result.

MTE-5 : ANALYTICAL GEOMETRY
December, 2002

Note : Question no. 5 is **compulsory.** Do any **three** questions out of questions no. 1 to 4. No calculators are allowed.

Q1. (a) Let $S_1 = 9x^2 + 4y^2 = 1$ and
$S_2 \equiv 2xy + 2x + 2y + 1 = 0$. Find K such that
$S_1 + KS_2 = 0$ represents a parabola. 3

Refer to Chapter-3, Q.No.-16

(b) Find the angle of intersection between the spheres
$x^2 + y^2 + z^2 - 2x - 2y - 2z = 1$ and
$x^2 + y^2 + z^2 - 2x - 2y - 1 = 0$ 2

Refer to Chapter-4, Q.No.-40

Q2. (a) Find the equation of a cylinder whose generators have direction ratios 1, -2, 3 and base curve is the ellipse $x^2 + 2y^2 = 1, z = 3$ 2½

Refer to Chapter-6, Q.No.-18

(b) Show that the plane $x + y - 2z = 1$ touches the paraboloid $ax^2 + by^2 = 2z$ if $\frac{1}{a} + \frac{1}{b} = 4$. Under what conditions on a and b will the paraboloid be an elliptic paraboloid? 2½

Refer to Chapter-6, Q.No.-19

Q3. (a) Find the equation of the normal to $y^2 = 4ax$ at the point of contact of the tangent $y = mx + \frac{a}{m}$. 2

(b) Find the equations of the planes which contain the line $7x + 10y - 30 = 0, 5y - 3z = 0$ and touch the conicoid $7x^2 + 5y^2 + 3z^2 = 60$. 3

Q4. (a) Reduce the equation
$11x^2 + 2\sqrt{3}xy + 9y^2 - 12\sqrt{3}x - 12y - 12 = 0$ to the standard form.
Hence identify the curve it represents. 3

Refer to Chapter-3, Q.No.-17

(b) Give a rough sketch of the conicoid represented by $3x^2 - 5y^2 + 7z^2 = 1$. Also list 2 properties that you used for sketching it.

Refer to Chapter-6, Q.No.-21

Q5. Which of the following statements are true? Give reasons for your answer. **10**

(i) Under a rotation of axes, a non-degenerate conic can become a degenerate conic.

(ii) $2x + 3y = 9z - 5$ represents a line.

(iii) Any plane intersects a given ellipsoid in a real ellipse.

(iv) Any tangent plane to a cone intersects the cone in only one point.

(v) The direction ratios of the line $\frac{x-2}{1} = \frac{y+1}{3}$, $z = 2$ are 1, 3, 1.

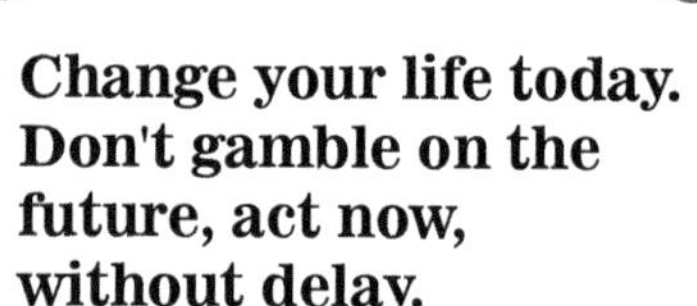

Change your life today. Don't gamble on the future, act now, without delay.

Lighten up, just enjoy life, smile more, laugh more, and don't get so worked up about things.

MTE-5 : ANALYTICAL GEOMETRY

June, 2003

Note : Question no. 5 is **compulsory.** Do any **three** questions out of questions no. 1 to 4. No calculators are allowed.

Q1. Which of the following statements are true? Justify your answer. **10**

(a) Under a rotation of the coordinate axes through 30°, the slope of the line y = x – 1 does not change.
Refer to Chapter-1, Q.No.-14(g)

(b) If cos α, cos β, cos γ are direction cosines of a line then $\sin^2\alpha + \sin^2\beta + \sin^2\gamma = 1$
Refer to Chapter-4, Q.No.-47(i)

(c) At any point of a sphere a unique tangent line can be drawn to the sphere
Refer to Chapter-4, Q.No.-47(j)

(d) Any line the intersects a conic in only one point is a tangent to that conic.

(d) If the projection of a line segment AB on another line is the line segment CD, then |AB| = |CD|.
Refer to Chapter-4, Q.No.-47(k)

Q2. (a) Find the equation of the sphere that contains the circle $x^2 + y^2 + z^2 = 9$, $x + y - 2z = 4$ and passes through the origin. **1½**
Refer to Chapter-4, Q.No.-41

(b) The difference between the focal distances of a hyperbola is 2 and its eccentricity is $\sqrt{2}$ Find its equation. **1½**
Refer to Chapter-2, Q.No.-28

(c) Give a rough sketch of the conicoid represented by $4y^2 - 9x^2 - 4z^2 = 1$. Also list two properties that you used for sketching it. **2**
Refer to Chapter-4, Q.No.-47(h)

Q3. (a) Find the equation of a plane parallel to the plane $5x - 6y + 7z = 3$ and passing through the point (2, 3, 4). **1**
Refer to Chapter-4, Q.No.-42

(b) Reduce the following
$3x^2 + 5y^2 + 3z^2 - 2yz + 2zx - 2xy + 2x + 12y + 10z + 20 = 0$
to standard form by shifting the origin to the centre and then rotating the system so that the direction ratios to the new axes are
$-1, 0, 1; 1, 1, 1; 1, -2, 1.$ 4

Refer to Chapter-6, Q.No.-23

Q4. (a) Consider the cone $C \equiv 3xy + z(8x - 5y) = 0$ One of a set of 3 mutually perpendicular generators of C is $x = y, y + z = 0$. Find the equations of the other two generators. 3½

Refer to Chapter-6, Q.No.-24

(b) Give an example, with justification, of a curve which is symmetric with respect to the line $y = x$ but not symmetric with respect to either of the coordinate axes. 1½

Refer to Chapter-1, Q.No.-16

Q5. (a) Find all the tangents to the conic 2½

$x^2 + 4xy + 3y^2 - 5x - 6y + 3 = 0$ that are parallel to $y = -\frac{x}{4}$

Refer to Chapter-3, Q.No.-18

(b) Find the equation of the right circular cylinder whose base curve is the section of $x^2 + y^2 + z^2 = 16$ by the plane $2x - y + z = 0$ 2½

MTE-5 : ANALYTICAL GEOMETRY
December, 2003

Note : Question no. 5 is **compulsory.** Do any **three** questions out of questions no. 1 to 4. No calculators are allowed.

Q1. (a) The angle between the lines joining the foci of an ellipse to an extremely of the minor axis is 90°. If the major axis of the ellipse has length $2\sqrt{2}$, find the equation of the ellipse. **2½**

Refer to Chapter-2, Q.No.-29

(b) Obtain the centre and radius of the sphere that contains the circle $x^2 + y^2 + z^2 + 10y - 4z - 8 = 0, x + y + z = 3$ as a great circle. **2½**

Refer to Chapter-4, Q.No.-43

Q2. (a) Show that the line y = x + 2 is a tangent to $y^2 = 8x$. Also find the point of contact and the equation of the normal at this point. **1½**

Refer to Chapter-2, Q.No.-30

(b) Find the equation of a cone with vertex (1, 1, 1) and whose generates touch the sphere
$x^2 + y^2 + z^2 = 1$ **2½**

(c) Find the equation of the plane which passes through (1, -1, -3) and its perpendicular to

$$\frac{x-\alpha}{1}-\frac{y-\beta}{3}=\frac{z-\gamma}{-2}.$$ **1**

Refer to Chapter-4, Q.No.-44

Q3. (a) The projections of a line segment on the coordinate axes are 2, 1, 5. Find the length of the segment and the direction cosines of the line. **2**

Refer to Chapter-4, Q.No.-45

(b) Find the equation of a cylinder whose generators have direction ratios 1, -2, 3 and whose base curve is the ellipse $x^2 + 2y^2 + 1, z = 3$. **3**

Refer to Chapter-5, Q.No.-27

Q4. (a) Identify the conic section formed by taking the planar section of the paraboloid $\frac{x^2}{2}-\frac{y^2}{3}=z$ by the plane $3(x-y)+4z+2=0$. 1½

Refer to Chapter-6, Q.No.-26

(b) Reduce $x^2+2yz-4x+6y+2z=0$ to standard form by shifting the origin to (2, -1, -3), and then rotating the axes to get a new system in which the direction ratios of the new axes are 0, -1, 1; $\sqrt{2}$, 1, 1; $\sqrt{2}$, −1, -1 with respect to the original coordinate system. 3½

Refer to Chapter-6, Q.No.-27

Q5. Which of the following statements are true? Give reasons for your answers. 10

(i) Every planar section of a hyperboloid is a hyperbola.

(ii) The direction ratios of $x+2=\frac{y-5}{2}$, $z=5$ are (1, 2, 1).

(iii) The curve $(x-1)^2=y+1$ is symmetric about the line $x=1$.

(iv) Under a rotation or a translation of the axes, the equation of a conicoid remains unchanged.

(v) There exists one and only one tangent line to a sphere at any given point of the sphere.

Refer to Chapter-4, Q.No.-47(L)

MTE-5 : ANALYTICAL GEOMETRY
June, 2004

Note : Question no. 5 is **compulsory.** Do any **three** questions out of questions no. 1 to 4. No calculators are allowed.

Q1. (a) Find the equation of a line perpendicular to the line $2y + x + 1 = 0$ and passing through $(2, -1)$. **2**

Refer to Chapter-1, Q.No.-15

(b) Reduce the following equation to standard form, and hence identify the object it represents.

$25x^2 + 4y^2 - z^2 = 50x + 2z + 12 - 16y$. **3**

Q2. (a) Find the cone on which the perpendicular drawn from the origin to the tangent planes to the cone $19x^2 + 11y^2 + 6yz = 0$ lie. **2**

Refer to Chapter-5, Q.No.-28

(b) Find the equations of the tangent planes to the conicoid $x^2 + 5y^2 + 3z^2 = 6$, which pass through the line $x + 2y - 3 = 0$, $5y - 3z = 0$. **3**

Refer to Chapter-6, Q.No.-28

Q3. (a) Check whether the two circles

$2(z^2 + y^2 + z^2) + 8x - 13y + 17z - 17 = 0$,

$2x + y - 3z + 1 = 0$

and

$x^2 + y^2 + z^2 + 3x - 4y + 3z = 0$, $x - y + 2z = 0$

lie on a sphere. If so, find the equation of the sphere. **3**

Refer to Chapter-4, Q.No.-46

(b) Show that the product of the distances from any point on a hyperbola to the asymptotes of the hyperbola is a constant. **2**

Refer to Chapter-2, Q.No.-31

Q4. (a) Reduce $r = (4 + \cot\theta)\,\text{cosec}\,\theta$ to Cartesian form. Identify the conic it represents *after reducing* it to standard form. **2**

Refer to Chapter-2, Q.No.-32

(b) Prove that any tangent plane to a right circular cylinder is parallel to the axis of the cylinder. **3**

Refer to Chapter-5, Q.No.-29

Q5. Which of the following statements are true? Give reasons for your answers. **10**

(i) The eccentricity of the conic $2x^2 + 3y^2 = 1$ is greater than 1.

(ii) The direction ratios of $\frac{x-1}{3} = \frac{y}{5}$, $z = 3$ are 3, 5 and 3.

(iii) The projection of any line segment along the z-axis on the x-axis is 0.

(iv) If a curve is symmetric with respect to the z-axis, it remains so even after applying a rotation to the axes.

(v) All the planar sections of a hyperboloid are hyperbolas.

MTE-5 : ANALYTICAL GEOMETRY
December, 2005

Note : Question no. 5 is **compulsory.** Do any **three** questions out of questions no. 1 to 4. No calculators are allowed.

Q1. (a) Reduce the equation
$5x^2 - 2xy + 5y^2 + 2x - 10y - 7 = 0$
to standard form. Hence identify the object it represents. **3**

(b) Find the cone on which the perpendiculars drawn from the origin to the tangent planes to the cone
$3x^2 + 4y^2 + 5z^2 + 2yz + 4zx + 6xy = 0$ lie. **2**

Q2. (a) Find the eccentricity, the foci and the length of the latus rectum of $5x^2 + 4y^2 = 2$. **3**

(b) What is the surface represented by
$12x^2 - 17y^2 + 7z^2 = 7$?
Determine the points of intersection of the line

$$\frac{-(x+5)}{3} = y - 4 = \frac{1}{7}(z-11)$$

with this surface. **2**

Q3. (a) Find the equation, centre and radius of the sphere having the circle
$x^2 + y^2 + z^2 = 16,\ 2x - 3y + 6z = 7$

as a great circle. **$2\frac{1}{2}$**

(b) Prove that the section of
$ax^2 + by^2 = 2z$ by $ux + vy + wz = p$
is a conic section. Further, under what conditions on w, a and b is the conic section a parabola? **$2\frac{1}{2}$**

Q4. (a) Show that the conic
$(a^2 + b^2)(x^2 + y^2) = (bx + ay - ab)^2$

is a parabola of latus rectum $\frac{2ab}{\sqrt{a^2+b^2}}$ **$2\frac{1}{2}$**

(b) Obtain the equation of the plane which is perpendicular to 4x + 5y – 3z = 8 and contains the line

x + y + z = 6, 2x + 3y + 4z + 5 = 0 $2\frac{1}{2}$

Q5. Are the following statements *true* of *false*? Give reasons for your answer. **10**

(i) The line $y = x\tan\theta + a\cot\theta$ is a tangent to the parabola $y^2 = 4ax$.

(ii) The direct cosines of

$$\frac{2x-1}{5} = \frac{y+3}{-2}, 2z = 1$$

are proportional to $5_1 - 2, \frac{1}{2}$.

(iii) A hyperbola consists of two parabolas.

(iv) For any line segment AB, the projection of AB on the x-axis is the same as its projection on the y and z axes.

(v) If three generators of a cone are mutually perpendicular, then the vertex of the cone is the origin.

MTE-5 : ANALYTICAL GEOMETRY
June, 2006

Note : Question no. 5 is **compulsory.** Do any **three** questions out of questions no. 1 to 4. No calculators are allowed.

1. (a) Find the equation of the parabola with focus $(1, -1)$ and directrix $x + y - 3 = 0$. **2**

(b) Obtain the equations of the spheres which pass through the circle
$x^2 + y^2 + z^2 = 5$, $x + 2y + 3z = 3$
and touch the plane $4x + 3y = 15$. **3**

2. (a) Find the equation of the right circular cylinder whose axis is

$\frac{x-1}{2} = y - 2 = \frac{z-3}{2}$ and radius is 2. **2**

(b) Reduce $x^2 + y^2 - 4z^2 + 4x - 6y - 8z = 13$ to standard form. Hence identify the object is represents. Also draw a rough sketch of the surface in standard form. **3**

3. (a) Check whether the conicoid
$3x^2 - 5y^2 + 3z^2 - 2yz + 2zx - 2xy + 2x + 12y + 10z + 20 = 0$ is cemral. **3**

(b) The tangents to an ellipse at two distinct point E and F meet at a point A. Show that the line joining A to the centre of the ellipse bisects the chord EF. **3**

4. (a) Reduce $25x^2 + 4y^2 - z^2 = 50x + 2z + 12 - 16y$ to standard form. Hence identify the object it represents. **3**

(b) Find the equation of the right circular cone with vertex $(1, 1, 3)$ axis parallel to $x = \frac{y}{2} = \frac{z}{2}$ and with one of its generators having direction ratios $2, 1, -1$. **2**

5. Are the following statements are true or false? Give reasons for your answers. **10**

(i) The lines with direction cosines proportional to 2, 3, 4; 1, –2, 1 are perpendicular to each other.

(ii) The intersection with any plane parallel to the xy plane of the paraboloid $3x^2 - y^2 = 4z$ is a hypenola.

(iii) A curve is symmetric about the x-axis if it is symmetric with respect to the origin.

(iv) y = x + 5 represents a line in three-dimensional space.

(v) A cylinder retrains a cylinder under rotation of axes.

MTE-5 : ANALYTICAL GEOMETRY
December, 2006

Note : Question no. 5 is **compulsory.** Do any **three** questions out of questions no. 1 to 4. No calculators are allowed.

1. (a) Find the eccentricity of the ellipse with its foci on the y-axis, and whose minor axis is equal to one half of its major axis. **2**

Ans. e = ?

Major axis =2a

Minor axis =2b

Given that minor axis $= \frac{\text{major axis}}{2}$

$$2b = \frac{2a}{2}$$

a=2b

we know that $b^2 = a^2 (1 - e^2)$

$b^2 = (2b)^2 (1 - e^2)$

$b^2 = 4b^2 (1 - e^2)$

$$\frac{1}{4} = 1 - e^2$$

$$e^2 = 1 - \frac{1}{4}$$

$$e^2 = \frac{3}{4}$$

$$e = \frac{\sqrt{3}}{2} (\angle 1)$$

(b) Check whether the spheres

$$\mathbf{x^2 + y^2 + z^2 - 2x + 2y - 4z + 5 = 0}$$

and $x^2 + y^2 + z^2 - 4x + 6y + 9 = 0$

touch each other. If they do, find their point of contact. If they don't touch each other, find the equation of their circle of intersection. **3**

Ans. $S \equiv x^2 + y^2 + z^2 - 2x + 2y - 4z + 5 = 0$ ... (1)

a=1, b=1, c=1, u=–1, v=1, w=–2, d=5

$r_1 = \sqrt{u^2 + v^2 + w^2 - d} = \sqrt{(-1)^2 + (1)^2 + (-2)^2 - 5}$

$= \sqrt{1+1+4-5}$

$r_1 = 1$

Centre $C_1 = (1, -1, 2)$

$S^1 \equiv x^2 + y^2 + z^2 - 4x + 6y + 9 = 0$ ...(2)

$a = 1,\ b = 1,\ c = 1,\ u = -2,\ v = 3,\ w = 0,\ d = 9$

$C_2 = (2, -3, 0)$

$r_2 = \sqrt{4+9-0} = \sqrt{13} = 3.6$

$r_1 + r_2 = 1 + 3.6 = 4.6$

$C_1\ C_2 = \sqrt{(1-2)^2 + (-1+3)^2 + (2)^2} = \sqrt{1+4+4} = 3$

We see that $r_1 + r_2 \neq c_1 c_2$

$\therefore$ both spheres donot touch each other

Now (1) – (2)

i .e. $S - S^1 \equiv 2x - 4y - 4z - 4$ represents a plane which contains all common points of the sphers S =0 and $S^1 = 0$.

But the section of plane with a sphere is a circle.

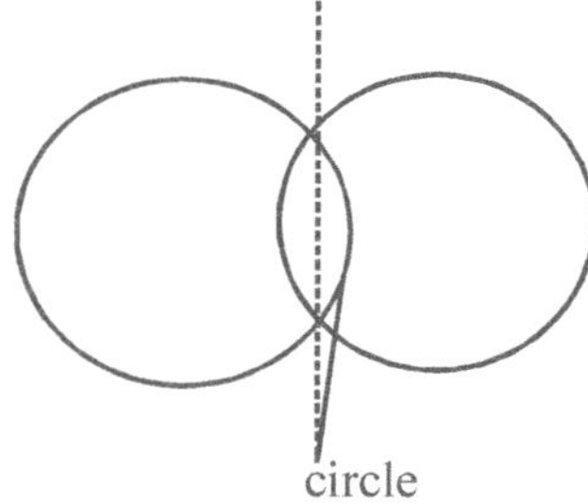

Hence the curve of intersection of two spheres is a circle, and the two equations to the sphers together represents a circle.

2. (a) Find the equation of the plane through the intersection of the planes x +2y – z +1 = 0 and 3x – y – 4z +3 = 0 and passing through

(1,1 ,1). $1\frac{1}{2}$

Ans. $S \equiv x + 2y - z + 1 = 0$ (plane)

$P \equiv 3x - y - 4z + 3 = 0$ (plane)

Equation of plane through intersection of S and P planes is $S + \lambda p = 0$

$\therefore\ (x+2y-z+1)+\lambda(3x-y-4z+3)=0$ ... (1)

(1) passes through (1, 1, 1)

$(1+2\times1-1+1)+\lambda(3\times1-1-4\times1+3)=0$

$3+\lambda(3-1-4+3)=0$

$3+\lambda=0$

$\therefore\ \lambda=-3$ put in (1) we get

$(x+2y-z+1)+(-3)(3x-y-4z+3)=0$

$(x-9x)+(2y+3y)-(z-12z)+(1-9)=0$

$-8x+5y+11z-8=0$

or $8x-5y-11z+8=0$ which is required equation of plane.

(b) Find the equation of the tangent plane to the conicoid

$3x^2 - 6y^2 + 9z^2 + 17 = 0$ at the point $(-1, 2, \frac{2}{3})$. 1

Ans. Equation of conicoid is

$3x^2-6y^2+9z^2+17=0$

or $3x^2-6y^2+9z^2=-17$

point is $(-1, 2, \frac{2}{3})$

$\therefore$ Equation of tangent plane is

$$3\times-1\times x+(-6)(2)y+9\left(\frac{2}{3}\right)z=-17$$

$-3x-12y+6z=-17$

or $3x+12y-6z=17$

or $3x+12y-6z-17=0$

(c) Find the nature of the planar section of the conicoid $2x^2 + 8y^2 - z^2 = 8$ by the plane

$2x - 4y - 2z = -3$. $2\frac{1}{2}$

Ans. Equations of the conicoid is

$$2x^2 + 8y^2 - z^2 = 8$$

or $$\frac{x^2}{4} + y^2 - \frac{z^2}{8} = 1 \qquad \dots (1)$$

Equation of plane is $2x - 4y - 2z = -3$ ... (2)

The equation of the cylinder passing through the section of the conicoid (1) by the plane (2) and having its generators parallel to z-axis is obtained by eliminating z between (1) and (2) and is therefore given by

$$\frac{1}{4}x^2 + y^2 + \left(-\frac{1}{8}\right)\{(-3 - 2x + 4y)/-2\}^2 = 1$$

$$\frac{1}{4}x^2 + y^2 - \frac{1}{8}\left\{\left(\frac{3 + 2x - 4y}{2}\right)^2\right\} = 1$$

$$\frac{1}{4}x^2 + y^2 - \frac{1}{32}\left\{9 + 4x^2 + 12x + 16y^2 - 2(3 + 2x)(4y)\right\} = 1$$

$$\frac{1}{4}x^2 + y^2 - \frac{1}{32}\left\{4x^2 + 12x + 16y^2 + 9 - 24y - 16xy\right\} = 1$$

$$\frac{1}{4}x^2 + y^2 - \frac{1}{32}\left\{4x^2 + 12x + 16y^2 - 24y - 16xy + 9\right\} = 0$$

$$\frac{x^2}{2} + \frac{y^2}{2} - \frac{3}{8}x + \frac{3}{4}y + \frac{1}{2}xy - \frac{9}{32} = 0 \qquad \dots (3)$$

The plane z = 0 being perpendicular to the generator of the cylinder (3) cuts it in the conic given by z =0,

$$\frac{1}{2}x^2 + \frac{1}{2}xy + \frac{1}{2}y^2 - \frac{3}{8}x + \frac{3}{4}y - \frac{9}{32} = 0 \qquad \dots (4)$$

which is a general equation of second degree, in which

$$a = \frac{1}{2},\ b = \frac{1}{2},\ h = \frac{1}{4},\ g = \frac{-3}{16},\ f = \frac{3}{8},\ c = \frac{-9}{32}$$

$$h^2 = \left(\frac{1}{4}\right)^2 = \frac{1}{16}$$

$$ab = \frac{1}{2} \times \frac{1}{2} = \frac{1}{4}$$

$$h^2 = ab = \frac{1}{16} - \frac{1}{4} = \frac{1-4}{16} = \frac{-3}{16} < 0$$

$\therefore$ the projection given by (4) and hence the given section is an ellipse.

3. (a) Roughly sketch the surface defined by

$$\frac{x^2}{16} - \frac{y^2}{9} - \frac{z^2}{9} = 1.$$

What are the curves formed by intersecting this with
(i) y = 3 ?
(ii) x = 4 ? **2**

Ans. The given curve is

$$\frac{x^2}{16} - \frac{y^2}{9} - \frac{z^2}{9} = 1 \qquad \text{... (1)}$$

from (1) $-\frac{x^2}{16} + \frac{y^2}{9} + \frac{z^2}{9} = -1$

$$a = \frac{1}{16},\ b =$$

We know that the general equation of hyperboloid of two sheet is

$$\frac{x^2}{a^2} - \frac{y^2}{b^2} - \frac{z^2}{c^2} = 1 \qquad \text{... (2)}$$

on comparing (1) with (2) we found that given curve is hyperboloid of two sheets in which $a^2 = 16$, $b^2 = 9$, $c^2 = 9$, $\therefore$ a=4, b=3, c=3

About hyperboloid of two shorts for tracing

(i) The origin is the centre of the surface (1)

(ii) The surface is symmetrical about the co-ordinate planes and these are principal planes of surface (1).

(iii) The surface (1) meets the x-axis in the points (4, 0, 0) and (–4, 0, 0). It does not intersect y-axis and z-axis.

Rough Sketch of the surface

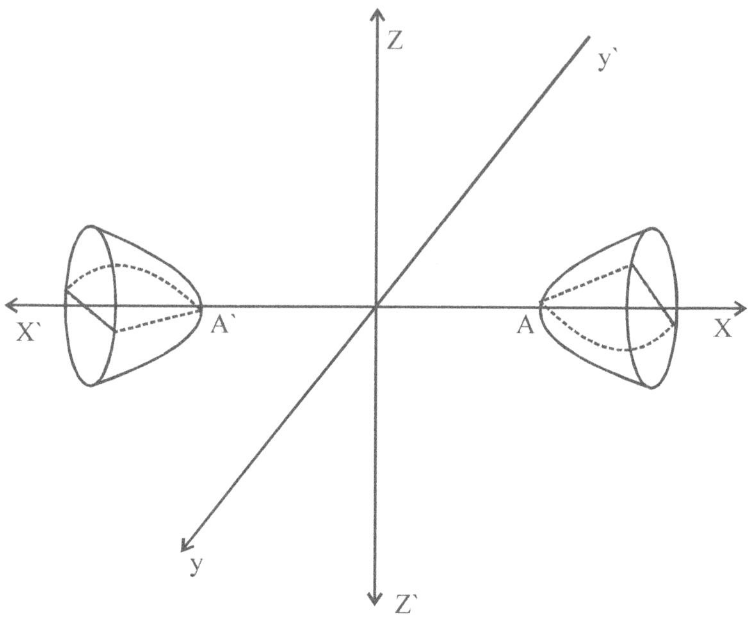

(i) When y=3, then the sections of the surface (1) is hyperbola.
(ii) When x = 4, then the section of the surface (1) be ellipse, given by

$$\frac{y^2}{9}+\frac{z^2}{9}=\frac{4^2}{16}=1$$

i.e $\frac{y^2}{9}+\frac{z^2}{9}=0$

Since the 4 = 4 (square root of a i.e. $\sqrt{16}=4$). Then the ellipse mode above be real.

(b) Reduce $x^2 + y^2 + 8xy + 3x + 2y - 1 = 0$ to standard form. Hence identify the object it represents. **3**

Ans. Refer to Study Material

4. (a) Define 'reciprocal cone'. Also obtain the reciprocal cone of $x^2 - 3y^2 + 4z^2 = 0$. **2**

Ans. Reciprocal cone : Two cones are reciprocal if each is the locus of the normal drawn through the vertex to the tangent planes of the other.

Cone is given by

$$ax^2 + by^2 + cz^2 + 2fyz + 2gzx + 2hxy = 0 \qquad \text{... (1)}$$

It's reciprocal cone is

$$Ax^2 + By^2 + Cz^2 + 2Fyz + 2Gzx + 2Hxy = 0 \qquad \text{... (2)}$$

where $A = bc - f^2$, $B = ca - g^2$, $C = ab - h^2$

$F = gh - af$, $G = hf - bg$, $H = fg - ch$

Give problem is

$x^2 - 3y^2 + 4z^2 = 0$

a=1, b=-3, c=4, g=0, f=0, h=0

$\therefore\ A = bc - f^2 = -3 \times 4 - 0 = -12$

$B = ca - g^2 = 4 \times 1 - 0 = 4$

$C = ab - h^2 = 1 \times -3 - 0 = -3$

$G = hf - bg \qquad = 0$

$H = fg - ch \qquad = 0$

$F = gh - af \qquad = 0$

put all values in (2)

$-12x^2 + 4y^2 - 3z^2 + 0 + 0 + 0 = 0$

or $12x^2 - 4y^2 + 3z^2 = 0$

Equation to the reciprocal cone.

(b) If $\cos\alpha, \cos\beta, \cos\gamma$ are the direction cosines of a line, then evaluate $\sin^2\alpha + \sin^2\beta + \sin^2\gamma$. **1**

Ans. Since, cosα, cosβ, and cosγ are d.c's of a line then we have

$\cos^2\alpha + \cos^2\beta + \cos^2\lambda = 1$

$1 - \sin^2\alpha + 1 - \sin^2\beta + 1 - \sin^2\gamma = 1$

$3 - (\sin^2\alpha + \sin^2\beta + \sin^2\gamma) = 1$

$\sin^2\alpha + \sin^2\beta + \sin^2\gamma = 2$

(c) Consider the conic given by $r = \dfrac{9}{4 - 2\cos\theta}$

Find

(i) its eccentricity

(ii) its focus/ foci in polar form. **2**

Ans. $r = \dfrac{9}{4 - 2\cos\theta} = \dfrac{9}{4(1 - \frac{2}{4}\cos\theta)} = \dfrac{9/4}{1 - \frac{1}{2}\cos\theta}$

$r = \dfrac{\frac{1}{2}.\frac{9}{2}}{1 - \frac{1}{2}\cos\theta}$ which is similar to equation of conic $r = \dfrac{ed}{1 - e\cos\theta}$, on

comparing both we get

$e = \dfrac{1}{2}$, $d = \dfrac{9}{2}$

$\because\ e = \dfrac{1}{2} < 1$

$\therefore$ conic is ellipse

$a = \dfrac{d}{2} = \dfrac{\frac{9}{2}}{2} = \dfrac{9}{4}$

$a = \dfrac{ed}{1 - e^2}$

$= \dfrac{\frac{9}{4}}{1 - \frac{1}{4}} = \dfrac{\frac{9}{4}}{\frac{3}{4}}$

$=3$

(i) Eccentricity $e = \dfrac{1}{2}$

(ii) Foci= (±ae, 0)= $\left(\pm 3\left(\dfrac{1}{2}\right),\ 0\right) = \left(\pm\dfrac{3}{2},\ 0\right)$

5. Are the following statements true or false? Give reasons for your answer. **10**

(i) The eccentricity of a pair of straight lines is less than one.

Ans. False

(ii) The direction rations of the line $\frac{x-5}{-2}$ = y, z = 4 are (–2, 1,0).

Ans. False

(iii) A line intersects a cone in at most 2 points.

Ans. Yes, cone is:-

$ax^2 + by^2 + cz^2 = 0$

line through (α, β, λ) is

$\frac{x-\alpha}{\ell} = \frac{y-\beta}{m} = \frac{z-\lambda}{n} = r$ (less)

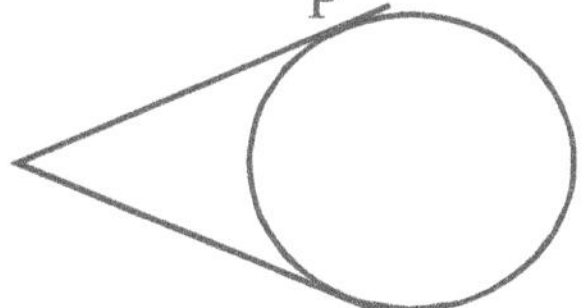

$(\alpha + r\ell, \beta + mr, \lambda + nr)$ lies on cone

∴ we get a quadratic equation in r hence which gives 2 values of r. Corresponding to which there will be two points in whcih line cut the cone.

(iv) Any section of a paraboloid will have two or more centres.

Ans. No, Because, A coincoid is a called a central if it has unique centre. If it has no centre or infinitely many centre, it is non central coinciod.

(v) Given any point on a sphere, there is one and only one tangent line at that point.

Ans. Yes

MTE-5 : ANALYTICAL GEOMETRY
June, 2007

Note : Question no. 5 is **compulsory.** Do any **three** questions out of questions no. 1 to 4. No calculators are allowed.

1. (a) Find the general equation of the conic passing through the points of intersection of

$$S \equiv \frac{x^2}{25} + \frac{y^2}{4} - 1 = 0 \text{ and}$$

$$S_1 \equiv \quad 4xy - 2x - 9 = 0.$$

Under what conditions will this equation represent
(i) an ellipse, (ii) a parabola? **3**

Ans. We have given that

$$S \equiv \frac{x^2}{25} + \frac{y^2}{4} - 1 \qquad \text{... (1)}$$

$$S_1 \equiv 4xy - 2x - 9 = 0 \qquad \text{... (2)}$$

Let $S + \lambda S_1$ be an surface represented by the equations (1) and (2)

$$\therefore \left(\frac{x^2}{25} + \frac{y^2}{4} - 1\right) + \lambda(4xy - 2x - 9) = 0$$

$$\frac{x^2}{25} + \frac{y^2}{4} + 4\lambda xy - 2x\lambda - 9\lambda = 0 \qquad \text{... (3)}$$

Comparing with general equation (4)
$ax^2 + by^2 + 2hxy + 2gx + 2fy + c = 0$

$$a = \frac{1}{25},\ b = \frac{1}{4},\ 2h = 4\lambda,\ 2g = -2\lambda,\ 2f = 0$$

$$h = 2\lambda,\ g = -\lambda,\ f = 0,\ c = -9\lambda$$

(i) Equation (3) represents an ellipse
If $\Delta \neq 0$ and $h^2 < ab$

where $\Delta = abc + 2fgh - af^2 - bg^2 - ch^2$
and $h^2 < ab$

i.e. $(2\lambda)^2 < \frac{1}{25} \times \frac{1}{4}$

$4\lambda^2 < \frac{1}{100}$

$\lambda^2 < \frac{1}{400}$

$\lambda < \frac{1}{20}$

$\lambda < \frac{1}{20}$ is the condition that the equations (1) and (2) represents an ellipse.

(ii) $h^2 = ab$, $\Delta \neq 0$ for parabola

$(2\lambda)^2 = \frac{1}{25} \times \frac{1}{4}$

$4\lambda^2 = \frac{1}{100}$

$\lambda^2 = \frac{1}{400}$

$\lambda = \pm\frac{1}{20}$

If $\lambda = \pm\frac{1}{20}$ then the equations (1) and (2) represents a parabola.

(b) Identify the objects obtained by taking the planar section of the conicoid $2y^2 + x^2 = 2z$ by the planes **2**

Ans. (i) $2x + y + z = 0$

$2y^2 + x^2 = 2z$ (Equation of conicoid) ... (1)

$2x + y + z = 0$ ... (2) (plane)

on homogenising the equation of sphere, we get

$(2y^2 + x^2) = 2z(2x + y + z)$

$2y^2 + x^2 = 4xz + 2yz + 2z^2$

$x^2 + 2y^2 - 2z^2 - 2yz - 4xz = 0$

This is second degree homogeneous equation in x, y and z. Hence it is required equation of cone.

(ii) 2x + y = 0

Ans. $2y^2 + x^2 = 2z$ ... (1)

$2x + y = 0$ ... (2)

$2y^2 + x^2 = 2z(2x + y)$

$2y^2 + x^2 = 4xz + 2yz$

$x^2 + 2y^2 - 2yz - 4xz = 0$ Equation of cone

2. (a) Find the equation of the plane through the points (2, 2, 1), (1, -2, 3) and parallel to the line joining the points (2, 61, -3) and (-1, 5, -8). 3

Ans. Equation to the plane through the point (2, 2, 1) is

$a(x - 2) + b(y - 2) + c(Z - 1) = 0$ ... (1)

If (1) passes through (1, –2, 3), we get

$a(1 - 2) + b(-2 - 2) + c(3 - 1) = 0$

$-a - 4b + 2c = 0$

or $a + 4b - 2c = 0$ ... (2)

Now, d.r. of st. line are $-1 - 2, 5 - 1, -8 - (-3)$

i.e. –3, 4, –5

∴ Equation of straight line passing through (2, 1, –3) and having d.r's –3, 4, –5 is

$$\frac{x-2}{-3} = \frac{y-1}{4} = \frac{z+3}{-5} \quad \text{... (3)}$$

Plane (2) is parallel to st. line (3). Therefore

$-3a + 4b - 5c = 0$ ... (4)

Solving (2) and (4)

$$\frac{a}{20 - 4 \times -2} = \frac{b}{1 \times -5 - (-2) \times (-3)} = \frac{c}{1 \times 4 - 4 \times -3} = k$$

$$\frac{a}{28} = \frac{b}{-11} = \frac{c}{16} = k$$

a = 28k, b = –11k, c = 16k put a, b, c in (1)

$$-3 \times 28k + 4 \times -11k - 5 \times 16k = 0$$

$$28k(x-2) + (-11k)(y-2) + 16k(z-1) = 0$$

$k \neq 0$,

$28x - 56 - 11y + 22 + 16z - 16 = 0$

$28x - 11y + 16z - 50 = 0$ Equation of required plane Ans.

(b) Show that the line 3y = 6x + 5 is tangent to $3y^2 = 4ax$. Also find the point of contact. 2

Ans. $y^2 = \frac{4}{3}ax$ (parabola) ... (1)

$y^2 = 4Ax$

$4A = \frac{4}{3}$

$A = \frac{1}{3}$

$3y = 6x + 5$

$y = \frac{6}{3}x + 5$

$y = 2x + 5$ ... (2)

$y = mx + c$

$m = 2, c = 5$

The line (2) touches (1) If $c = \frac{A}{m}$

$\frac{A}{m} = \frac{\frac{1}{3}}{2} = \frac{1}{6}$

$c = 5$

$\because c \neq \frac{A}{m}$

$\therefore$ line (2) does not touches the parabola

3. (a) Find the centre and radius of the sphere $2x^2 + 2y^2 + 2z^2 - 16x + 8y + 16z + 23 = 0$. Also determine whether the plane $2x - y + 5 = 0$ intersects this sphere in a real circle or not. **2**

Ans. Equation of sphere is

$2x^2 + 2y^2 + 2z^2 - 16x + 8y + 16z + 23 = 0$

or $x^2 + y^2 + z^2 - 8x + 4y + 8z + \frac{23}{2} = 0$ ... (1)

$u = -4, v = 2, w = 4, d = 23/2$

$\therefore$ centre $= (-u, -v, -w) = (4, -2, -4)$

radius $= \sqrt{u^2 + v^2 + w^2 - d}$

$$= \sqrt{(4)^2 + 2^2 + 4^2 - \frac{23}{2}}$$

$$= \sqrt{\frac{72 - 23}{2}}$$

$$= \sqrt{\frac{49}{2}}$$

$$= \frac{7}{\sqrt{2}}$$

Equation of plane is 2x – y + 5 = 0 ... (2)

Length of the perpendicular from centre of sphere to plane

$$= \frac{2 \times -4 - 2 + 5}{\sqrt{2^2 + (-1)^2}} = \frac{-8 - 2 + 5}{\sqrt{5}}$$

$$= \frac{-5}{\sqrt{5}}$$

$= -\sqrt{5}$ which is real

Therefore given sphere and plane intersects in a real circle. Ans.

(b) Show that the conicoid $3x^2 + 7y^2 + 3z^2 + 10yz - 2zx + 10xy + 4x - 12y - 4z + 1 = 0$ has a centre, and find the centre. Also find the new equation if the origin is shifted to the centre. **3**

Ans. Given equation is:

$F = 3x^2 + 7y^2 + 3z^2 + 10yz - 2zx + 10xy + 4x - 12y - 4z + 1 = 0$ ... (1)

a = 3, b = 7, c = 3, h = 5, g = –1, f = 5, u = 2, v = –6, w = –2, d = 1

$$\Delta = \begin{vmatrix} 3 & 5 & 7 \\ 5 & 7 & 5 \\ -1 & 5 & 3 \end{vmatrix} = 3(21-25) - 5(15+5) + 7(25+7)$$
$$= -12 - 100 + 224 = 112 \neq 0$$

$\because \Delta \neq 0$

$\therefore$ given equation (1) represents a central conicoid i.e. the conicoid has centre.

Now $\frac{\delta F}{\delta x} = 6x - 10z + 10y + 4$

$$\frac{\delta F}{\delta y} = 14y + 10z + 10x - 12$$

$$\frac{\delta F}{\delta y} = 6z + 10y - 2x - 4$$

For centre, $\frac{\delta F}{\delta x} = 0, \frac{\delta F}{\delta y} = 0, \frac{\delta F}{\delta z} = 0$

$\therefore$ 6x + 10y – 2z + 4 = 0

or 3x + 5y – z = –2 ... (2)

5x + 7y + 5z = 6 ... (3)

– x + 5y + 3z = 2 ... (4)

(2) × 5 + (3)

$$\begin{array}{l} 15x + 25y - 5z = -10 \\ \underline{5x + 7y + 5z = 6} \\ 20x + 32y = -4 \end{array} \quad \text{... (5)}$$

(3) × 3 – (4) × 5

$$\begin{array}{l} 15x + 21y + 15z = 18 \\ -5x + 25y + 15z = 10 \\ \underline{+ \quad - \quad -} \\ 20x - 4y = 8 \end{array} \quad \text{.. (6)}$$

(5) – (6) 36y = – 12 $\therefore \boxed{y = -\frac{1}{3}}$ put in (5)

$$20x + 32 \times -\frac{1}{3} = -4$$

$$20x = -4 + \frac{32}{3} = \frac{-12 + 32}{3} = \frac{20}{3}$$

$$\therefore \boxed{x = \frac{1}{3}}$$

put x, y in (2)

$$3 \times \frac{1}{3} + 5 \times -\frac{1}{3} - z = -2$$

$$-z=-2+\frac{5}{3}-1=-3+\frac{5}{3}=-\frac{4}{3} \quad \therefore \boxed{z=\frac{4}{3}}$$

Hence centre $=\left(\frac{1}{3},-\frac{1}{3},\frac{4}{3}\right)$

If the origin is shifted to the centre $\left(\frac{1}{3},-\frac{1}{3},\frac{4}{3}\right)$. Then transformed equations are: $x=x'+\frac{1}{2}, y=y'-\frac{1}{3}, z=z'+\frac{4}{3}$ put this in (1) we get

$$3\left(x'+\frac{1}{2}\right)^2+7\left(y'-\frac{1}{3}\right)^2+3\left(z+\frac{4}{3}\right)^2+10\left(y'-\frac{1}{3}\right)\left(z'+\frac{4}{3}\right)$$

$$-2\left(z'+\frac{4}{3}\right)\left(x'+\frac{1}{2}\right)+10\left(x'+\frac{1}{2}\right)\left(y'-\frac{1}{3}\right)$$

$$+4\left(x'+\frac{1}{2}\right)-12\left(y'-\frac{1}{3}\right)-4\left(z'+\frac{4}{3}\right)+1=0$$

$$3x'^2+\frac{3}{4}+3x'+7y'^2+\frac{7}{9}-\frac{14y'}{3}+3z'^2+\frac{16}{3}+8z'$$

$$+10x'y'-\frac{10}{3}x'+5y'-\frac{5}{3}+4x'+2-12y'+4-4z'-\frac{16}{3}+1$$

$$+10y'z'+\frac{40}{3}y'-\frac{10}{3}z'-\frac{40}{9}-23x'-z'-\frac{8}{3}x'-\frac{4}{3}=0$$

$$3x'^2+7y'^2+3z'^2+10x'y'+10y'z'-2z'x'+x'+\frac{19}{3}y'-z+\frac{97}{4}=0 \text{ Ans.}$$

4. (a) Find the equation of the cone, whose vertex is at the origin and which passes through the curve of intersection of $3x^2 + 2y^2 + 5z^2 = 1$ and $x^2 - y^2 = 2z$. **2**

Ans. We have given

$3x^2 + 2y^2 + 5z^2 = 1$ ... (1)

$x^2 - y^2 = 2z$ ... (2)

Combined equations are

$3x^2 + 2y^2 + 5z^2 - 1 = 0 = x^2 - y^2 - 2z$

Let any generator through (0, 0, 0) be

$$\frac{x}{l}=\frac{y}{m}=\frac{z}{n}=r \text{ (say)} \qquad \ldots (3)$$

$\therefore$ any point P on (1) is (rl, rm, rn). Let this point where (3) meets the guiding curve

$3x^2 + 2y^2 + 5z^2 - 1 = 0 = x^2 - y^2 - 2z$ ... (4)

Hence co-ordinate P will satisfy (4)

$\therefore 3(rl)^2 + 2(rm)^2 + 5(rn)^2 - 1 = 0$

$3r^2l^2 + 2r^2m^2 + 5r^2n^2 = 1$

$r^2 (3l^2 + 2m^2 + 5n^2) = 1$ ... (5)

and $(rl)^2 - (mn)^2 - 2(rn) = 0$

$r^2l^2 - r^2m^2 - 2rn = 0$

$r(rl^2 - rm^2 - 2n) = 0$

r.r $\neq 0$, r(l – m) = 2n

$$r = \frac{2n}{l^2 - m^2} \qquad \ldots (6)$$

$$r^2 = \frac{4n^2}{\left(l^2 - m^2\right)^2} \qquad \ldots (7)$$

put r^2 in (5)

$$\frac{4n^2}{\left(l^2 - m^2\right)^2}(3l^2 + 2m^2 + 5n^2) = 1$$

$4n^2 (3l^2 + 2m^2 + 5n^2) = (l^2 - m^2)^2$ (8)

Replacing l, m, n in (8) by x, y, z we get

$4z^2 (3x^2 + 2y^2 + 5z^2) = (x^2 - y^2)^2$. This is required equation of the cone.

(b) Reduce the equation $x^2 + 2xy + y^2 - 10x + 2y - 5 = 0$ to standard form. Also give a rough sketch of it. **3**

Ans. Given equation is

$x^2 + 2xy + y^2 - 10x + 2y - 5 = 0$ ... (1)

a = 1, b = 1, h = 1, g = –5, f = 1, c = –5

$$\Delta = abc + 2fgh - af^2 - bg^2 - ch^2$$

$$= 1\times1\times1 + 2\times1\times-5\times1 - 1\times1^2 - 1\times(-5)^2 - (-5)1^2$$

$$= 1 - 10 - 1 - 25 - 25$$

$$= -60(\neq 0)$$

$\boxed{\Delta \neq 0}$

$h^2 - ab = 1^2 - 1 \times 1 = 0$

$\because h^2 - ab = 0$ it means $\boxed{h^2 = ab}$ i.e. given equation represents parabola.

Now the second degree terms form a perfect square which is equal to $(x + y)^2$ and so equation (1) may written as:

$(x + y)^2 = 10x - 2y + 5$

we introduce λ,

$$(x + y + \lambda)^2 = (10x - 2y + 5) + \lambda^2 + 2\lambda(x + y)$$

$$= 2x(5 + \lambda) + 2y(\lambda - 1) + \lambda^2 + 5 \qquad \text{... (2)}$$

Choose λ such that the straight lines $(x + y + \lambda) = 0$ and

$2x(5 + \lambda) + 2y(\lambda - 1) + \lambda^2 + 5 = 0$ may be at right angles to each other. This will be so, when $m_1 \times m_2 = -1$

i.e.

$$-1 \times -\frac{(5 + \lambda)}{(\lambda - 1)} = -1 \qquad \left(\begin{aligned} &\text{where } m_1 = -1 \\ &m_2 = -\left(\frac{5 + \lambda}{\lambda - 1}\right) \end{aligned}\right)$$

$$5 + \lambda = -\lambda + 1$$

$2\lambda = -4$ $\qquad \therefore \boxed{\lambda = -2}$ put this in (2)

$(x + y - 2)^2 = 2x(5 - 2) + 2y(-2 - 1) + (-2)^2 + 5$

$(x + y - 2)^2 = 6x - 6y + 9$

$$2\left(\frac{x + y - 2}{\sqrt{2}}\right)^2 = 2\left(\frac{6x - 6y + 9}{2}\right)$$

$$\therefore \left(\frac{x + y - 2}{\sqrt{2}}\right)^2 = \left(\frac{6x - 6y + 9}{2}\right) \qquad \text{... (3)}$$

We compare this (3) with general equation

$y^2 = 4ax \qquad \therefore y = x + y - 2$

$\therefore \qquad x = 6x - 6y + 9$

Axis of parabola is y = 0, x + y - 2 = 0 ... (4)

and tangent at the vertex is x = 0, i.e. 6x – 6y + 9 = 0 ... (5)

Also latus rectum of the parabola = 4a

$4a = \frac{1}{2}$ $\quad\quad \therefore \boxed{a = \frac{1}{8}}$

We take (4) and (5)

$12x = 3 \quad\quad \therefore x = \frac{1}{4} \quad\quad (4) + (5)$

$y = \frac{7}{4}$

$\therefore$ vertex is $\left(\frac{1}{4}, \frac{7}{4}\right)$

Focus : Focus is the point of intersection of the lines y = 0, and x = a
$\therefore$ from (4) x + y – 2 = 0 i.e. x + y = 2 ... (6)

and from (5) $6x - 6y + 9 = \frac{1}{8}$ i.e $6x - 6y = \frac{1}{8} - 9 = \frac{71}{8}$ ... (7)

eqn. (6) $\times$ 6 + eqn. (7)

$$\begin{array}{l} 6x + 6y = 12 \\ _{+}6x \;_{-}{-6y} = _{-}{-\frac{71}{8}} \\ \hline 12x = 12 - \frac{71}{8} = \frac{25}{8} \end{array}$$

$x = \frac{25}{96}$

$\therefore$ from (6) $y = 2 - x = 2 - \frac{25}{96} = \frac{192 - 25}{96} = \frac{167}{96}$

$y = \frac{167}{96}$

$\therefore$ focus $= \left(\frac{25}{96}, \frac{167}{96}\right)$

Directrix : The equation to the directrix is
x + a = 0
i.e. x = – a

$$6x - 6y + 9 = -\frac{1}{8}$$

$$6x - 6y + 9 + \frac{1}{8} = 0$$

$$6x - 6y + \frac{73}{8} = 0$$

$$\boxed{48x - 48y + 73 = 0}$$

Rough Sketch of Parabola

The curve meets the x-axis where y = 0 therefore putting y = 0 in (1)

$x^2 - 10x - 5 = 0$

$$x = \frac{-(-10) \pm \sqrt{100 - 4 \times 1 \times -5}}{2}$$

$$= \frac{10 \pm \sqrt{120}}{2} = \frac{10 \pm 10.95}{2}$$

taken (+ve) taken (-ve)

$$x_1 = \frac{20.95}{2} \qquad x_2 = \frac{.95}{2}$$

$$= 10.47 \qquad x_2 = .47$$

$$= 10.5 \qquad x_2 = .5$$

$\therefore$ Point on x axis are $_P(10.5, 0)$, and $_Q(0.5, 0)$

Since the curve meets at y axis $\therefore$ put x = 0 in (1)

$y^2 + 2y - 5 = 0$

$$y = \frac{-2 \pm \sqrt{2^2 = 4 \times 1 \times -5}}{2} = \frac{-2 \pm \sqrt{4 + 20}}{2} = \frac{2 \pm \sqrt{24}}{2}$$

$$= \frac{-2 \pm 4.89}{2} = \frac{-2 \pm 4.9}{2}$$

taken (+ve) taken (-ve)

$$y_1 = \frac{-2 + 4.9}{2} \qquad y_2 = \frac{-2 - 4.9}{2}$$

$$y_1 = 1.4 \qquad y_2 = -3.5$$

$\therefore$ points on y axis are R(0, 1.4) and S(0, – 3.5)

Now plot the vertex A $\left(\frac{1}{4}, \frac{7}{4}\right)$. Through A draw the line MAM' inclined at an angle $\left(m = -1 \text{ i.e.} \theta = \tan^{-1}(-1) \text{ i.e.} \theta = 135^\circ\right)$ to the x-axis. Draw an other line LAL' through a perpendicular to MAM'. Mark the point P(10.5, 0), Q(0.5, 0) R(0, 1.4) and S(0, -3.5) and draw the parabola shown in figure.

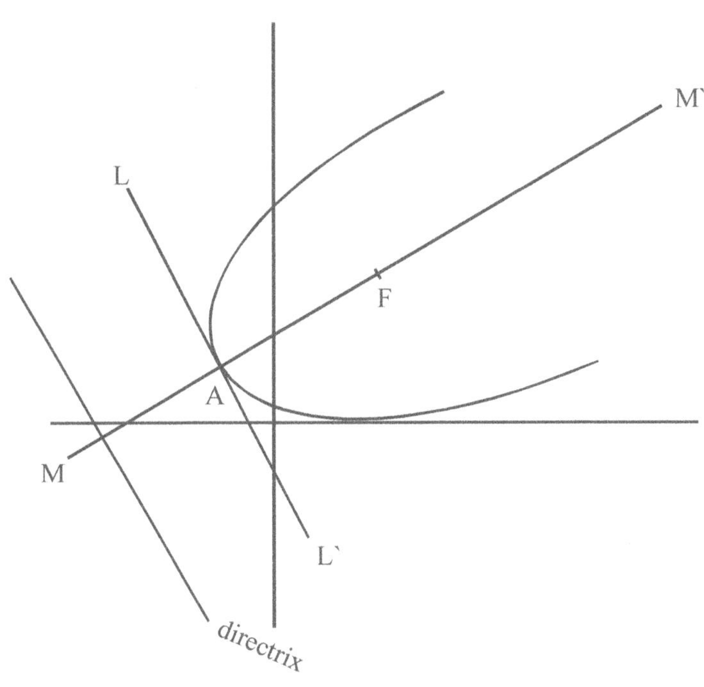

Parabola

5. Which of the following statements are true? Justify your answers with valid reasons. **10**

(i) A pair of straight lines is a conic section.

Ans. True

General equation of second degree is, $ax^2 + 2hxy + by^2 + 2gx + 2fy + c = 0$.
It represents pair of straight line. If $\Delta = abc + 2fgh - af^2 - bg^2 - ch^2 = 0$

(ii) A unique plane passes through any three points.

Ans. True

(iii) All planar sections of an ellipsoid are ellipses.

Ans. True

Ellipsoid $\frac{x^2}{a^2}+\frac{y^2}{b^2}+\frac{z^2}{c^2}=1$ is the surface by planes parallel to the co-ordinate axis are ellipses.

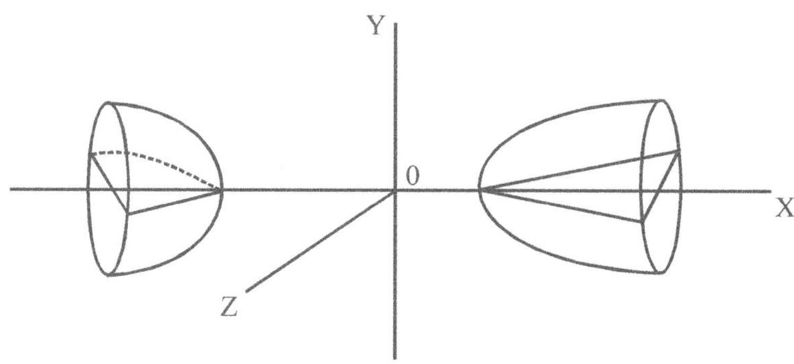

(iv) 3x – y = 5 + z represents a line.

Ans. True

(v) If a curve in a plane is symmetric with respect to the origin, then it is symmetric with respect to the x-axis.

Ans. True

MTE-5 : ANALYTICAL GEOMETRY
December, 2007

Note : Question no. 5 is **compulsory.** Do any **three** questions out of questions no. 1 to 4. No calculators are allowed.

Q1. (a) If by = 4x + 5 touches $3y^2 = 8x + 1$ at a point P, find b and the coordinates of P. Also find the equation of the normal at P. **3**

(b) If the sphere $S_1 \equiv x^2 + y^2 + z^2 - 9 = 0$ **cuts the sphere** $S_2 \equiv x^2 + y^2 + z^2 - 2x + 2y - 2z - k = 0$ **in a great circle of** $S_2 \equiv 0$**, find k.** **2**

Q2. (a) Find the equation of the right circular cone which passes through the point (1, 1, 2), has its vertex at the origin and axis is the line.

$$\frac{x}{2} = \frac{y}{-4} = \frac{z}{3}.$$ **3**

(b) Roughly sketch the surface defined by

$$y^2 = 1 + \frac{x^2}{16} + \frac{z^2}{9}.$$

Further, identify the conics formed by intersecting this surface with (i) y = 1; (ii) z = 3. **2**

Q3. (a) Reduce the equation
$9x^2 + 4y^2 + 4z^2 + 4x + y + 10z + 1 = 0$
to standard form, and *hence* identify the object it represents. **2½**

(b) If the length of the normal at an extremely of the latus rectum of the parabola $y^2 = 4ax$, a > 0, intercepted by the parabola, is 4 units, find a. **2½**

Q4. (a) Find the equation of the right circular cylinder of radius 2 whose axis passes through the point (1, 2, 3) and has direction ratios 2, -3, 6. **1½**

(b) Under what conditions on k will

$\frac{x-4}{1}=\frac{y+k}{-4}=\frac{z+1}{7}$ **and**

$\frac{x-1}{2}=\frac{y+1}{-k}=\frac{z+10}{8}$ **intersect?** **2**

(c) The projection of a line segment on the coordinate axes are 2, 1, 5 respectively. Find the length of the segment and the direction cosines of the line. **1½**

Q5. Are the following statements are *true* of *false*? Give reasons in support of your answers. **10**

(i) The equation $r = 2\cos\theta + 3\sin\theta$ **represents a straight line.**

(ii) The coordinates of the foci of the conic

$\frac{x^2}{9}-\frac{y^2}{4}=-1$ **are** $\left(\pm\sqrt{13},0\right)$**.**

(iii) The equation of the plane passing through the line of intersection of the planes $2x - y = 0$ and $3z - y = 0$ and perpendicular to the plane $4x + 5y + 3z = 8$ is $8x - y - 9z = 0$.

(iv) Any section of a paraboloid will have two or more centers.

(v) The equation of the reciprocal cone of

$x^2 - 3y^2 + 4z^2 = 0$ is $\frac{1}{x^2}-\frac{3}{y^2}+\frac{4}{z^2}=0.$

MTE-5 : ANALYTICAL GEOMETRY
June, 2008

Note : Question no. 5 is **compulsory.** Do any **three** questions out of questions no. 1 to 4. No calculators are allowed.

Q1. (a) Find the equation of the right circular cone whose wertex is (1, 1, 1), axis is $\frac{x-1}{2}=\frac{y-1}{2}=z-1$ and the semiverticla angle is 60^0. Further, find the conic obtained by intersecting the cone with the plane z = 0.

(b) Find the eccentricity, foci and the length of the chord through a focus and perpendicular to the major axis of the ellipse $4x^2+18y^2=36$.

Q2. (a) Obtain the equation of the sphere having the circle $x^2+y^2+z^2+10y-4z-8=0, x+y+z=3$ as a great circle.

(b) Find the standard equation of the conicoid

$3x^2+5y^2+3z^2+2x+12y+10z+20=0$

Q3. (a) Check whether the plane 16x-6y-z=5 touches the paraboloid $2x^2-\frac{y^2}{3}=z$ or not. Also find the point of contact.

(b) Write the equation of the pair of straight lines through the points of intersection of $4x^2+9y^2=36$ and 4xy=9 + 2x.

Q4. (a) Find the projection of the line segment AB on the line CD and the y-axis, where the coordinates of A, B, C, D are (-1, 2, 1), $(o, \frac{1}{2}, 0)$, $(-1, 3, 5)$ and $(0, -1, -2)$, respectively.

(b) Reduce $x^2+y^2-2xy-8x-4y+10=0$ to standard form. Hence identify the conic it represents. Further, roughly sketch the standard form.

Q5. Are the following statements true or false? Give reasons for your answer.

(i) A hyperboloid of two sheets has only hyperbolas as planar sections.

(ii) A tangent plane to a cone intersects the cone in only one point.

(iii) The curve $(x-1)^2 = y+1$ **is symmetric about the line** $x=1$.

(iv) Any two cylinders intersect in a circle.

(v) $x+3y=2z$ **represent a line in 3-dimensional space.**

MTE-5 : ANALYTICAL GEOMETRY
December, 2008

Note : Question no. 5 is **compulsory.** Do any **three** questions out of questions no. 1 to 4. No calculators are allowed.

Q1. (a) A circle cuts the parabola $y^2 = 4ax$ at four points (x_1, y_1), $i = 1,2,3,4$. Prove that $y_1 + y_2 + y_3 + y_4 = 0$.

(b) Prove that the spheres $x^2 + y^2 + z^2 = 64$ and $x^2 + y^2 + z^2 - 12x + 4y - 6z + 48 = 0$ touch, and find the point of contact.

Q2. (a) Find c such that the plane $2x+3y+cz=0$ cuts cone $yz+zx+xy=0$ in perpendicular lines.

(b) Find the standard equation C of the conicoid $5x^2 + 3y^2 + 3z^2 - 2xy + 2yz - 2zx - 1 = 0$, by rotating the axes so that the direction ratios of the new axes are 0, 1, -1; 1, 1, 1; -2, 1, 1. Further, give two planes P_1 and P_2 such that the intersection of C with P_1 is a real conic, and $C \cap P_2$ is an imaginary conic.

Q3. (a) Reduce the equation $x^2 + 2y^2 - 3z^2 - 4x - 12y + x + 1 = 0$ to standard form, and hence identify the object it represents.

(b) Prove that the line $lx+my+n=0$ is a moral to the ellipse $\frac{x^2}{a^2} + \frac{y^2}{b^2} = 1$ if

$$\frac{a^2}{l^2} + \frac{b^2}{m^2} = \frac{(a^2 - b^2)^2}{n^2}.$$

Q4. (a) Find the distance of the point (1, -2, 3) from the plane $2x + 3y - 4z = 16$, measured along the straight line with direction ratios 1, -2, -3.

(b) Find the equation of the right circular cylinder whose base curve is the circle $x^2 + y^2 + z^2 - 16 = 0,\ x + y - z - 3 = 0$.

Q5. Which of the following statements are true? Give reasons in support of your answer.

(i) The equation $r(3\cos\theta + 4\sin\theta + 5) = 12$ **represents a parabola.**

(ii) The coordinates of the vertices and the eccentricity of the conic $4x^2 - 25y^2 + 100 = 0$ **are, respectively,** $(\pm 5, 0)$ and $\frac{\sqrt{29}}{5}$.

(iii) $x^2 + y^2 = 4$ **represents a circle in 3-dimensional space.**

(iv) The intersection of $x^2 - y^2 + z^2 = 4$ **with a plane parallel to the xz-plane is a hyperbola.**

(v) A plane is uniquely determined by any three given points.

MTE-5 : ANALYTICAL GEOMETRY
June, 2009

Note : Question no. 5 is **compulsory.** Do any **three** questions out of questions no. 1 to 4. No calculators are allowed.

Q1. (a) If $y = x + c$ is a normal to the parabola $y^2 = 8x$, find the value of c. Also find the coordinates of the point where it is normal.

(b) find the equation of the right circular cone whose axis is the x-axis, vertex is the origin and semi-vertical angle is $\frac{\pi}{6}$.

Q2. (a) Identify the conic represented by $36x^2 + 24xy + 29y^2 - 72x + 126y + 81 = 0$. If it is central, find its latus rectum.

(b) Find the centre of the conicoid represented by $x^2 + y^2 + z^2 - 6yz - 2zx - 2xy - 6x - 2y - 2z + 2 = 0$. What will its equation be when the origin is translated to its centre?

Q3. (a) Find the equation of the plane passing through the line $2x - y = 0 = 3z - y$ and perpendicular to the plane $4x + 5y + 3z = 8$.

(b) Sketch the surface $\frac{x^2}{10} - \frac{y^2}{9} - \frac{z^2}{9} = 1$. What is the curve obtained when this surface is intersected by

(i) $y = 3$?

(ii) $x = 4$?

Q4. (a) Find the centre and radius of the circle $x^2 + y^2 + z^2 + x + y + z - 4 = 0, x + y + z = 0.$

(b) Show that the plane $20x - 12y - 7z = 14$ touches the paraboloid $5x^2 - 6y^2 = 7z$. Also find the point of contact.

Q5. Are the following statements true or false? Give reasons in support of your answers.

(a) The equation, $\frac{2}{r}=3\cos\left(\theta-\frac{\pi}{4}\right)+2\sin\left(\theta+\frac{\pi}{4}\right)$ **represents a straight line.**

(b) The points of intersect of the circle $x^2+y^2-6x+1=0$ **and the parabola** $y^2=4x$ **lie on the line** $x=1$.

(c) The projection of the line segment joining the points P(1, 2, 3) and Q(-2, 1, 4) on the line $\frac{x}{3}=\frac{y}{4}=\frac{z}{5}$ **is 8.**

(d) The equation, $x^2+y^2+z^2+4x+6y+8z+30=0$ **represents a real sphere.**

(e) The equation $x^2-y^2-2z^2+3=0$ **represents a hyperboloid of two sheets.**

MTE-5 : ANALYTICAL GEOMETRY

December, 2009

Note : Question no. 5 is **compulsory.** Do any **three** questions out of questions no. 1 to 4. No calculators are allowed.

Q1. (a) Show that for all values of α , the line x cos α +y sin α +asin α tan α = 0 touches the parabola y2 = 4ax. Also find the point of contact.

(b) Find the centre of the conicoid
$3x^2+5y^2+3z^2+2yz+2zx+2xy-4x-8z+5=0$.
What will its equation be when the origin is translated to its centre ?

Q2. (a) Find the distance from the origin to the point

of intersection of the line $\frac{x-1}{2}=\frac{y+2}{3}=\frac{z-3}{-6}$ **and the plane x-y+z=13**

(b) Find the equations of those tangent planes to the conicoid $x^2+2y^2+z^2=4$ which pass through the line
$x + y + z + 1=0 = 2x + 3y + 2z — 3$.

Q3. (a) What is the eccentricity of a parabola? Find the equation of the parabola whose focus is the point (2, 3) and whose directrix has the equation $3x + 4y-1 = 0$.

(b) Reduce the equation
$x^2+2y^2-3z^2+4x-12y-24z-34=0$ to the standard form. Hence identify the object it represents.

Q4. (a) If the angle between the two lines in which the plane ax + by + cz =0 intersects the cone

$7x^2+z^2 = 6zx -2yz$ is $\frac{\pi}{4}$, obtain an equation satisfied by (a, b, c).

(b) Find the centre and radius of the sphere $x^2+y^2+z^2-2y-4z-11=0$. Also determine whether the plane x + 2y + 2z =15 intersects the sphere in a real circle or not.

Q5. Are the following statements true or false? Give reasons in support of your answers.

(a) The equation r =2 cos $(\theta - \frac{\pi}{3})$ **represents a circle.**

(b) If a curve is symmetric about the origin, then it is symmetric about the y-axis.

(c) The eccentricity of a rectangular hyperbola is $\sqrt{2}$.

(d) $x^2+y^2+2x+4z+1=0$ **represents a circle.**

(e) If a plane cuts a conicoid in a pair of intersecting lines, then the conicoid must be a cone.

Whatever you do, do with determination. You have one life to live; do your work with passion and give your best. Whether you want to be a chef, doctor, actor, or a mother, be passionate to get the best result.

MTE-5 : ANALYTICAL GEOMETRY
June, 2010

Note : Question no. 5 is **compulsory.** Do any **three** questions out of questions no. 1 to 4. No calculators are allowed.

Q1. (a) Find the equations of the tangent and normal, at the point $(a \sec\theta, b \tan\theta)$, to the hyperbola $\frac{x^2}{a^2} - \frac{y^2}{b^2} = 1$.

(b) Prove that $3x + 5y = z$ touches the cone $ax^2 + by^2 + cz^2 = 0$, if and only if $\frac{9}{a} + \frac{25}{b} + \frac{1}{c} = 0$, where a, b, c are non-zero real numbers.

Q2. (a) Identify the conic represented by, $14x^2 - 4xy + 11y^2 - 44x - 58y + 71 = 0$. If it is central, find its centre and its equation when the origin is shifted to the centre. If it is not central, find its latus rectum.

(b) Sketch the surface given by $\frac{y^2}{4} - \frac{x^2}{9} - z^2 = 1$. Check whether the coordinate planes intersect the surface. If so, what are the objects represented by the curves of intersection?

Q3. (a) Find the distance of the point (–1, –5, –10) from the point of intersection of the line $\frac{x-2}{3} = \frac{y+1}{4} = \frac{z-2}{12}$ and the plane $x - y + z = 5$.

(b) Show that the equation, $4y^2 - 4z^2 - 2x - 14y - 22z + 33 = 0$ represents a paraboloid. Is it elliptic or hyperbolic? Give reasons for your answer.

Q4. (a) Prove that the plane $x + 2y - z = 4$ cuts the sphere $x^2 + y^2 + z^2 - x + z = 2$ in a circle of radius 1. Also find the centre of the circle.

(b) Find the equations to the tangent planes to $7x^2 - 3y^2 - z^2 + 21 = 0$ which pass through the line $7x - 6y + 9 = 0$, $z = 3$.

Q5. Are the following statements true or false? Give reasons in support of your answers.

(a) The equation $r = 2a\cos(\theta - \alpha)$ represents hyperbola.

(b) The circle $x^2 + y^2 = 1$ intersects the parabola $y^2 = 4(x-1)$ in two distinct real points.

(c) If a conicoid is such that it has some planar sections which are ellipses, then it must be an ellipsoid.

(d) A right circular cylinder has infinitely many centres.

(e) The projection of the line segment joining the points (1, 3, –1) and (2, –1, 4) on the line with direction ratios 3, 5, 4 is 3.

MTE-5 : ANALYTICAL GEOMETRY
December, 2010

Note : Question no. 5 is **compulsory.** Do any **three** questions out of questions no. 1 to 4. No calculators are allowed.

Q1. (a) Find the equation of the normal to the ellipse $\frac{x^2}{a^2}+\frac{y^2}{b^2}=1$ at the point $(a\cos\theta, b\sin\theta)$.

(b) Find the equation of the tangent plane to the cone $2x^2+3y^2+4z^2-6yz-xy-4xz=0$ at the point (1, 2, 3), and write the direction cosines of its normal.

Q2. (a) Let $S\equiv 4x^2-9y^2-36=0$ and $S^1\equiv y^2-4x=0$ be two conics. Under what conditions on k, will the conic $S+kS^1=0$ represent:
(i) an ellipse?
(ii) a hyperbola?

(b) Find the condition that the plane $lx + my + nz = p$ touches the conicoid $2x^2-3y^2+4z^2=24$. Hence obtain the values of a for which the plane $ax - 3y + z = 1$ touches the given conicoid.

Q3. (a) Prove that the planes $7x + 4y - 4z + 30 = 0$, $36x - 51y + 12z + 17 = 0$, $14x + 8y - 8z - 12 = 0$ and $12x - 17y + 4z - 3 = 0$, form the four faces of a cuboid.

(b) Reduce the equation. $4x^2-y^2+9z^2-12x+24z=0$ to standard form. Hence identify the surface it represents. Further, identify the curves obtained when this surface intersects with the plane (i) $2x = 3$, (ii) $y = 0$.

Q4. (a) The plane $\frac{x}{a}+\frac{y}{b}+\frac{z}{c}=1$ meets the coordinate axes in A, B and C. Find the equation of the sphere through O, A, B and C, where O is the origin.

(b) Prove that the path traced by the foot of the perpendicular from the focus of a parabola on any tangent to the parabola is the tangent at its vertex.

Q5. Are the following statements true or false? Give reasons in support of your answers.

(a) The equation $\frac{3}{r} = 2 + \cos\theta$ represents an ellipse.

(b) The angle between two lines with direction ratios $\frac{1}{2}, \frac{1}{\sqrt{2}}, \frac{1}{2}$ and 2, 1, –2 is $\frac{\pi}{4}$.

(c) There is a unique conic that gives a cylinder if it is rotated about the x-axis.

(d) All planar sections of a hyperboloid are hyperbolas.

(e) The projection of a line segment AB on a line perpendicular to it is zero.

MTE-5 : ANALYTICAL GEOMETRY
June, 2011

Note : Question no. 5 is **compulsory.** Do any **three** questions out of questions no. 1 to 4. No calculators are allowed.

Q1. (a) Find the equation of the normal to the parabola $y^2 + 4x = 0$ at the point where the line y = x + c touches it.

(b) Prove that the plane 2x – 3y + 6z = 6 touches the conicoid $4x^2 - 9y^2 + 36z^2 = 36$, and find the point of contact.

Q2. (a) Obtain the equation of the conic, a focus of which lies at (2, 1), the directrix of which is x + y = 0 and which passes through (1, 4). Also identify the conic.

(b) Find the equation of the spheres which pass through the circle $x^2 + y^2 + z^2 = 9$, 2x + 2y – 7 = 0 and the touch the plane x – y + z + 3 = 0.

Q3. (a) Find the distance of the point of intersection of the line $\frac{x-2}{1} = \frac{y+3}{-1} = \frac{z}{3}$ and the plane 2x – 3y + 4z + 4 = 0 from the origin.

(b) Reduce the equation $2x^2 + 3y^2 + 4z^2 - 4x + 12y - 24z + 38 = 0$ to the standard form. Hence identify the surface it represents. Also identify the curve represented by the intersection of this surface and the plane y + 2=0.

Q4. (a) Find the equation of the normal to the paraboloid $3x^2 + 4z^2 + 4y = 0$ at the point (2, – 4, 1). Also find the point where this line again intersects the paraboloid.

(b) Find the equation of the right circular cone whose axis is x-axis, vertex is the origin and the semi - vertical angle is $\frac{\pi}{3}$.

Q5. Are the following statements true or false? Give reasons in support of your answers.

(a) The equation $r = a\cos(\theta+\alpha) + b\sin(\theta+\alpha)$ represents a circle.

(b) The direction ratios of $x - 5 = 5 - y, z = 5$ are (1, 1, 5).

(c) The intersection of a plane and a cone can be a pair of lines.

(d) The equations $2x^2 + y^2 + 3z^2 + 4x + 4y + 18z + 34 = 0$, $2x^2 - y^2 = 4y - 4x$ represents a real conic.

(e) $4x^2 - 9y^2 + z^2 + 36 = 0$ represents a hyperboloid of one sheet.

MTE-5 : ANALYTICAL GEOMETRY
December, 2011

Note : Question no. 5 is **compulsory.** Do any **three** questions out of questions no. 1 to 4. No calculators are allowed.

Q1. (a) Find the Cartesian form of the equation $r = a(1-\sin\theta)$ where a is a constant.

(b) Find the equations of the planes which contain the line 7x + 10y – 30 = 0, 5y – 3z = 0 and touch the ellipsoid $7x^2 + 5y^2 + 3z^2 = 60$.

Q2. (a) Find the equation to the plane passing through the point (1, 2, 3) and parallel to 6x – 5y + 3z = 0.

(b) Find the radius of the circle $x^2 + y^2 + z^2 + x - 2y + 2z = 0,\ 2x + y + 2z = 1$.

Q3. (a) Obtain the equation of the cylinder whose axis is 2x = y = – z and radius is 3.

(b) Find the centre of the conicoid $14x^2 + 14y^2 + 8z^2 - 4yz - 4zx - 8xy + 18x - 18y + 5 = 0$ what will be its new equation if the origin is shifted to the centre?

Q4. (a) Under what condition on k will $S + kS_1 = 0$ be a hyperbola where $S \equiv \frac{x^2}{4} + \frac{y^2}{9} - 1 = 0$ and $S_1 \equiv xy - 15 = 0$?

(b) The intersection with any plane parallel to the xy-plane of the paraboloid $x^2 + 2y^2 = 6z$ will be a conic. Identify the conic and give a rough sketch of it.

Q5. Are the following statements true or false? Give reasons for your answers.

(a) Any two spheres intersect in four real points.

(b) The point (4, – 3) lies inside the ellipse $5x^2 + 7y^2 = 11$.

(c) At each point of a cone we can draw infinitely many tangents to the cone.

(d) The vertical cross-section of the hyperboloid of one sheet $x^2 + y^2 + z^2 - 1 = 0$ by the plane x = 0 is a parabola.

(e) $\frac{x-3}{7} = \frac{y-5}{-2}$ represents a plane in 3-dimensional space.

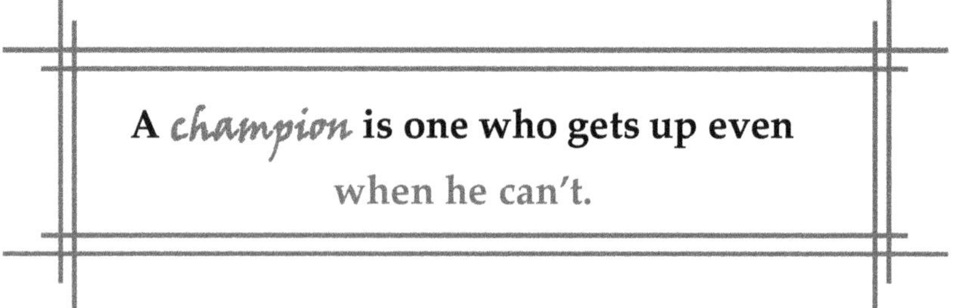

MTE-5 : ANALYTICAL GEOMETRY
June, 2012

Note : Question no. 5 is **compulsory.** Do any **three** questions out of questions no. 1 to 4. No calculators are allowed.

Q1. (a) Draw an ellipse with eccentricity $\frac{1}{2}$ and a string of length 8 units. What will be the co-ordinates of its vertices and foci?

(b) Under what conditions on a and b will the asymptotes of the hyperbola $\frac{x^2}{a^2}-\frac{y^2}{b^2}=1$ be perpendicular to each other?

(c) Obtain the equation of the tangent plane to the conicoid $2x^2-6y^2+3z^2=5$ at (1, –1, 1).

Q2. (a) Is the conic $3x^2+7xy+2y^2+5x+5y+2=0$ central? If yes, find its centre.

(b) Check whether the cones $2x^2+3y^2+4z^2=0$ and $\frac{x^2}{2}+\frac{y^2}{3}+\frac{z^2}{4}=0$ are reciprocal or not.

Q3. (a) Find the equation of a right Circular Cylinder of radius 3 and axis $2x=y=-z$.

(b) Find the angle of intersection of the spheres $x^2+y^2+z^2-2x+2y-4z+2=0$ and $x^2+y^2+z^2=4$

(c) Find the intersection of plane y = 2 with the ellipsoid $\frac{x^2}{9}+\frac{y^2}{9}+\frac{z^2}{16}=1$ What is the name of the conic to obtained?

Q4. (a) Give a rough sketch of the Conicoid represented by $3x^2-5y^2+7z^2=1$. Also list 2 properties that you used for sketching it.

(b) Show that the four points (2, 0, 0), (0, –1, 0), (0, 0, 5) and (2, 1, 5) are coplanar.

(c) Identify the type of conicoids that are represented by the following equations:

(i) $4x^2 + 3y^2 - 6z^2 = -10$

(ii) $2z^2 + x^2 = 4y$

Q5. Are the following statements true or false? Give reasons for your answers.

(a) All the planar sections of a paraboloid are parabolas

(b) The direction ratios of the line $\frac{x-1}{2} = \frac{y+3}{1}, z = 2$ **are 1, – 3, 1.**

(c) Any tangent plane to a cone intersects the cone in only one point.

(d) $y^2 + z^2 = 16$ **represents a circle in 3-dimensional space.**

(e) If the projection of a line segment AB on another line is the line segment of CD, then $|AB| = |CD|$.

"Don't aim for success if you want it; just do what you love and believe in, and it will come naturally."

MTE-5 : ANALYTICAL GEOMETRY
December, 2012

Note : Question no. 5 is **compulsory.** Do any **three** questions out of questions no. 1 to 4. No calculators are allowed.

Q1. (a) In a parabola show that the tangent at any point makes equal angles with the focal radius of the point and the line parallel to the axis through the point.

(b) Show that the plane $x + 2y + 2z = 9$ touches the sphere $x^2 + y^2 + z^2 = 9$. Find the point of contact.

Q2. (a) Find the length of the major axis of the ellipse $r = \frac{2e}{1+e\cos\theta}$.

(b) Find the equation of right circular cone whose axis is the y-axis, vertex is the origin and semi vertical angle is $\pi/6$.

Q3. (a) Prove that the equations of line of intersection of planes $4x+4y-5z=12$ and $8x + 12y - 13z = 32$ can be written as: $\frac{x-1}{2} = \frac{y-2}{3} = \frac{z}{4}$.

(b) Check whether the conicoid.
$x^2+y^2+z^2-6yz-2zx-2xy-6x-2y-2z+1=0$ has a centre or not. If so find the centre.

Q4. (a) Find the equation of tangent planes to $7x^2-3y^2-z^2+21=0$ which pass through the line $7x - 6y + 9 = 0$, $z = 3$.

(b) For the hyperbola $9x^2-4y^2=36$, find the vertices eccentricity, foci and equations of asymptotes.

Q5. Are the following statements true or false? Give reasons in support of your answers.
(a) All planar sections of an ellipsoid are ellipses.

(b) $5x - 2y = 5 + 2z$ represents a line.

(c) The projection of the line segment joining the points P(1, 2, 3) and Q(– 2, 1, 4) on x- axis is 5.

(d) The length of the perpendicular from any point on the cylinder $x^2 + y^2 = 9$ to its axis is 4.

(e) The equation. $\frac{2}{r} = 3\cos\left(\theta - \frac{\pi}{4}\right) + 2\sin\left(\theta + \frac{\pi}{4}\right)$ represents a straight line.

MTE-5 : ANALYTICAL GEOMETRY
June, 2013

Note : Question no. 5 is **compulsory.** Do any **three** questions from question numbers 1 to 4. Calculators are not allowed.

Q1. (a) If normal at one extremity of latus rectum of an ellipse passes through one extremity of minor axis, prove that the eccentricity e is given by $e^4 + e^2 - 1 = 0$.

(b) Find the equation of the sphere which has (–1, 1, 0) and (3, –1, 2) as ends of a diameter.

Q2. (a) Find the eccentricity and equations of the asymptotes of the hyperbola $4x^2 - 9y^2 = 9$.

(b) Find the equation of the cone with vertex at the origin and base curve as $\frac{x^2}{3} + \frac{y^2}{5} = 1, z = 2$.

Q3. (a) Find the equation of the plane through the points (–1, 1, 1) and (1, –1, 1) and perpendicular to the plane $x + 2y + 2z = 5$.

(b) Find the standard equation of the conicoid $3x^2 + 5y^2 + 3z^2 - 2yz + 2zx - 2xy + 2x + 12y + 10z + 20 = 0$ by shifting the origin to the centre $\left(-\frac{1}{6}, \frac{5}{3}, -\frac{13}{6}\right)$ and then for rotating the coordinates axes so that direction ratios of the new axes are –1, 0, 1; 1, 1, 1; 1, 2, 1 respectively.

Q4. (a) Find the equations of tangent planes to the conicoid $x^2 + 2y^2 + z^2 = 4$ which pass through the line $x + y + z + 1 = 0, 2x + 3y + 2z - 3 = 0$.

(b) Find the equation of normal to the parabola $y^2 = 4ax$ at the point of contact of the tangent $x + my + am^2 = 0$.

Q5. Are the following statements true or false? Give reasons in support of your answers.

(a) The equation $x^2+y^2+z^2+4x+6y+8z+30=0$ represents a real sphere.

(b) The equation $y^2+z^2=a^2$ represents a circle in 3-dimensional space.

(c) The conic $3x^2+7xy+2y^2+5x+5y+2=0$ represents a hyperbola.

(d) if a curve in a plane is symmetric with respect to the origin, then it is symmetric with respect to the x-axis.

(e) The section of the conicoid $x^2+2y^2+z^2=9$ with the plane $y=2$ is a circle.

MTE-5 : ANALYTICAL GEOMETRY
December, 2013

Note : Question no. 5 is **compulsory.** Do any **three** questions from question numbers 1 to 4. Calculators are not allowed.

Q1. (a) Show that the difference of focal distances of any point on a hyperbola is equal to the length of its transverse axis.

(b) Check whether the points (1, 0, 1), (3, 4, 0), (5, 9, –1) and (0, 8, 7) are coplanar or not.

Q2. (a) Find the new equation of the plane x + 2y + z = 1 under the transformations given by the following table

	x	y	z
x'	$\frac{1}{\sqrt{14}}$	$\frac{2}{\sqrt{14}}$	$\frac{3}{\sqrt{14}}$
y'	$\frac{-2}{\sqrt{5}}$	$\frac{1}{\sqrt{5}}$	0
z'	$\frac{1}{4}$	$\frac{1}{2}$	$\frac{-5}{12}$

(b) When does the spheres $x^2 + y^2 + z^2 - 2x - 4y - 4z = 0$ and $x^2 + y^2 + z^2 + 10x + 2z + c = 0$ touch each other?

Q3. (a) What is the slope of the line passing through (1, 4) and (–4, 2)? Write the equation of this line.

(b) Does the conicoid $2x^2 - 7y^2 + 2z^2 - 10yz - 8zx - 10xy + 6x + 12y - 6z + 2 = 0$ have a centre? If so find it.

Q4. (a) Identify the conicoids from the following equations.

(i) $3x^2 + 6y^2 - 9z^2 + 1 = 0$

(ii) $3(x-1)^2 + 2(y+1)^2 + 6(z+2)^2 = 6$

(b) Trace the conic $x^2 - 2xy + y^2 - 2x - 2y + 3 = 0$ and find its focus.

Q5. Are the following statements true or false? Give reasons for your answers.
(a) The curve xy =1 is symmetric with respect to the origin.

(b) In two dimensional space the line passing through origin and equally inclined to the coordinate axis is $\alpha x - \beta y = 0$ where $\alpha \neq \beta$.

(c) Two spheres with centres C_1, C_2 and radii r_1, r_2 respectively will not intersect if $C_1C_2 < r_1 + r_2$.

(d) A tangent plane to a cone touches it at only one point.

(e) The plane $ux + vy + wz = p$ is a tangent plane to the ellipsoid $\frac{x^2}{a^2} + \frac{y^2}{b^2} + \frac{z^2}{c^2} = 1$ if $a^2u^2 + b^2v^2 + c^2w^2 = p^2$.

MTE-5 : ANALYTICAL GEOMETRY
June, 2014

Note : Question no. 5 is **compulsory.** Do any **3** questions from question no. 1 to 4. Calculators are not allowed.

Q1. (a) Identify the conic $9x^2 - 6xy + y^2 + 60x - 20y + 75 = 0$ and trace it.

(b) Find the radius and the centre of the circle $x^2 + y^2 + z^2 - x + z - 2 = 0$, $x + 2y - z = 4$.

Q2. (a) Show that the sum of focal distances of any point on an ellipse is equal to the length of its major axis.

(b) Find the angle between the lines of intersection of $x + y - z = 0$ and $yz + 6zx - 12xy = 0$.

Q3. (a) Find the centre of the conicoid $3x^2 + 5y^2 + 3z^2 + 2yz + 2zx + 2xy - 4x - 8z + 5 = 0$. What will be its new equation, if the origin is shifted to this point?

(b) Find the equation of the cylinder whose base is the circle $x^2 + y^2 = 9, z = 0$ and the axis is $\frac{x}{4} = \frac{y}{3} = \frac{z}{5}$.

Q4. (a) Trace roughly the conicoid $3(x-1)^2 + 2(y+1)^2 + 6(z+2)^2 = 6$. What is the section of this conicoid by the plane $z = -2$?

(b) Find the equations of tangents to the conic $x^2 + 4xy + 3y^2 - 5x - 6y + 3 = 0$ which are parallel to the line $x + 4y = 0$.

Q5. Which of the following statements are true and which are false? Give reasons for your answers.

(i) The line $y = x$ is a tangent to the conic $\frac{x^2}{9} - \frac{y^2}{4} = 1$

(ii) The angle between the planes $x + 2y + 2z = 5$ and $2x + 2y + 3 = 0$ is 60°.

(iii) Every section of a paraboloid by a plane is a central conic.

(iv) $S = \{(x, y, z) \in R^3 \mid y^2 + z^2 = 1\}$ represents a circle.

(v) The projection of the line segment joining (1, 5, 0) and (-2, 4, 1) on the line with direction ratios 3, –1, 8 is 0.

MTE-5 : ANALYTICAL GEOMETRY
December, 2014

Note : Question no. 5 is **compulsory.** Answer any **three** questions from question no. 1 to 4. Use of calculators is not allowed.

Q1. (a) Find the equation of the conic section with eccentricity 1, (1, 0) as its focus and y = x as its directrix.

(b) Trace the surface $\frac{x^2}{9}+\frac{y^2}{25}+\frac{z^2}{4}=1$. Describe its sections by the planes $z=\pm 4$.

Q2. (a) A circle cuts the parabola $y^2=4ax$ in the points $\left(at_i^2, 2at_i\right)$ for $i=1,2,$ 3, 4. Prove that $t_1+t_2+t_3+t_4=0$.

(b) Show that if the sum of the squares of the distances of (a, b, c) from the planes x + y + z = 0, x = z and x + z = 2y is 3, then $a^2+b^2+c^2=3$.

Q3. (a) Find the equation of the cylinder whose axis is x = y = – z and radius is 2.

(b) Find the equation of the line parallel to y + x + 1 = 0 and passing through (1, 1). What is the angle between the line obtained and 2x = y?

Q4. (a) Show that the conicoid $3x^2+7y^2+3z^2+10yz-2zx+10xy+4x-12y-4z+1=0$ has a centre, and find the centre.

(b) Find the equation of a right circular cone with vertex at O, axis at OX and semi-vertical angle $\frac{\pi}{3}$. What will be its new equation when the origin is shifted to (0, 1, -1)?

Q5. Are the following statements true or false? Justify your answer.
(a) The relation between the cartesian and the polar co-ordinates is $x=r\sin\theta, y=r\cos\theta$ and $\theta=\tan^{-1}\frac{y}{x}$.

(b) The conditions on m and c, so that y = mx + c will be a tangent to $x^2 = 4ay$ are $m \neq \tan\frac{\pi}{2}$ and $c = -am^2$.

(c) The line $\frac{x}{2} = y = \frac{z}{3}$ is parallel to the x-axis.

(d) If $s \equiv \frac{x^2}{9} + \frac{y^2}{4} - 1 = 0$ and $s_1 \equiv xy - 9 = 0$, then the condition on k for which $s + ks_1 = 0$ will be an ellipse is $k^2 < \frac{1}{9}$.

(e) The condition for a line with direction ratios α, β, γ to be a tangent to the central conicoid $ax^2 + by^2 = 2z$ at (x_0, y_0, z_0) is $ax_0\alpha - by_0\beta = \gamma$.

MTE-5 : ANALYTICAL GEOMETRY
June, 2015

Note : Question no. 5 is **compulsory.** Answer any **three** questions from question no. 1 to 4. Use of calculators is not allowed.

Q1. (a) Find the focus and equation of the latus rectum of $x^2 + ky = 0$, where $k > 0$.

(b) Find the equation of a plane passing through the line of intersection of the planes $2x - 4y + 2z + 8 = 0$ and $3x + 5y - 3z + 15 = 0$. Find the condition of such plane to be perpendicular to $2x - y + z + 3 = 0$.

Q2. (a) Test whether $2x - y - 2z = 16$ touches the sphere $x^2 + y^2 + z^2 - 4x + 2y + 2z - 3 = 0$ or not.

(b) Find the equation of the tangent plane to the given conicoid $x^2 + y^2 = 6z$ at $(1, -2, 3)$.

Q3. (a) Write the resultant transformation of the straight line $x + y = 1$, when the axes are rotated through 30° and the origin is shifted to (1, 1).

(b) Reduce the equation $x^2 + 2xy + y^2 - 10x + 2y - 5 = 0$ to standard form.

Q4. (a) Find the equation of the cone with the axes as generator.

(b) Find the equation of the tangent planes to $7x^2 - 3y^2 - z^2 + 21 = 0$ which pass through the line $7x - 6y + 9 = 0, z = 3$.

Q5. Are the following statements true or false? Justify your answer.

(a) The projection of the line segment joining (1, 2, 2) and (–1, 4, 3) on the line with direction cosines $\frac{1}{2}, \frac{1}{2}, \frac{1}{\sqrt{2}}$ is 8.

(b) The conic $3x^2 + 7xy + 2y^2 + 5x + 5y + 2 = 0$ is central.

(c) The line $\frac{x}{2} = y = \frac{z}{3}$ is parallel to the y-axis.

(d) The more eccentric is a hyperbola, the more its branches open out from its transverse axis.

(e) $x^2 - 4y^2 + z^2 = 1$ represents a hyperboloid of two sheets.

MTE-5 : ANALYTICAL GEOMETRY
December, 2015

Note : Question no. 5 is **compulsory.** Answer any **three** questions from question no. 1 to 4. Use of calculators is not allowed.

Q1. (a) Let $y^2 = 4ax$ be a parabola and P be a point on it. Let the normal at P intersect the x-axis at Q. Draw a line at Q perpendicular to the above normal. Show that this line intersects the parabola $y^2 + 4a(x-2a) = 0$.

(b) Show that the coplanar points A(2, 3, 2,), B(4, 7, 6,), C(1, 2, 3), D(–1, –2, –1) form a parallelogram.

Q2. (a) Show that the point $\left(0,\ 3+\sqrt{5}\right)$ lies on the ellipse with foci (2, 3) and (–2, 3) and semi-major axis 3.

(b) Show that the cone whose vertex is at the origin and which passes through the curve of intersection of the sphere $x^2 + y^2 + z^2 = 3p^2$ and any plane which is at a distance 'p' from the origin has mutually perpendicular generators.

Q3. (a) Find the equations of the spheres which pass through the circle $x^2 + y^2 + z^2 - 6x + z + 6 = 0, x - y = 0$ and touch the plane $z = 0$.

(b) Identify the conicoid $1 + 2x^2 + 9y^2 = 3z^2$. Does the xy-plane intersect with it? Justify your answer.

Q4. (a) Find the new equation of straight line $2x + y = 5$ after rotating the axes through 45°.

(b) Show that the conicoid $x^2 + 2y^2 + 2yz + 2x + 4y + 8z + 1 = 0$ is central. Find the new equation of the conicoid if the origin is shifted to its centre.

Q5. State whether the following statements are *true* or *false*. Justify your answer with a short-explanation or a counter-example.

(a) The plane making intercept 1 at the z-axis and parallel to the xy-plane intersects the cone $x^2 + y^2 = z^2 \tan^2\theta$ in a circle.

(b) There exists no line with $\frac{1}{\sqrt{3}}, \frac{1}{\sqrt{2}}, \frac{1}{\sqrt{6}}$ as direction cosines.

(c) The curve $xy^2 + yx^2 = 0$ is symmetric about the origin.

(d) The plane $3x + 4y + 2z = 1$ touches the conicoid $3x^2 + 2y^2 + z^2 = 1$.

(e) Non-degenerate conics are non-central.

MTE-5 : ANALYTICAL GEOMETRY
June, 2016

Note : Question no. 5 is **compulsory.** Answer any **three** questions from question no. 1 to 4. Use of calculators is not allowed.

Q1. (a) If the tangents at two points of a parabola are at right angles, then show that they intersect at a point on the directrix.
(b) Show that the points (2, 0, 1), (0, 4, –3) and (–2, 5, 0) are non-collinear. Hence find the equation of plane passing through them.

Q2. (a) Identify the type of the conic $4(x-2y+1)^2+9(2x+y+2)^2=25$.

(b) What surface is represented by $x^2+y^2=9z$? Give a rough sketch of it. Obtain the section of this surface by the plane y = 0.

Q3. (a) Find the equation of the right circular cone when the straight line 2y + 3z = 6, x = 0 revolves about the z-axis.

(b) Does the equation $\frac{2}{r}=3\cos\left(\theta-\frac{\pi}{4}\right)+2\sin\left(\theta+\frac{\pi}{4}\right)$ represent a straight line? Justify your answer.

Q4. (a) Find the equations of the tangent planes to the conicoid $7x^2-3y^2-z^2+21=0$, which pass through the line 7x – 6y + 9 = 0, z = 3.
(b) Find the new equation of the curve $(x-2)^2=y(y-1)^2$ by transforming to parallel axes through the point (2, 1).

Q5. State whether the following statements are true or false. Justify your answer with a brief explanation or with a counter-example.
(a) The curve $x^4+y^4=4a^2xy$ is symmetric with respect to the origin.
(b) The direction cosines of the line x = –y, z = 0 are $\frac{1}{\sqrt{2}},-\frac{1}{\sqrt{2}},0$.
(c) The section of $2x^2+y^2=2(1-z^2)$ by the plane x + 2 = 0 is a hyperbola.
(d) The xy-plane intersects the sphere $x^2+y^2+z^2+2x+2y-z=2$ in a great circle.
(e) If the projection of a line segment AB on another line is the line segment CD, then $|AB|=|CD|$.

MTE-5 : ANALYTICAL GEOMETRY
December, 2016

Note : Question no. 5 is **compulsory.** Attempt any **three** questions from question no. 1 to 4. Use of calculators is not allowed.

Q1. (a) Find the equation of the parabola with focus (3, – 4) and directrix x + y = 2.

Ans. Let p (x, y) be a variable point on parabola, lx + my + n = 0 is directrix and S (h, k) be the focus, then standard equation of the parabola is given by:

$(mx - ly)^2 = -2(gx + fy) - c$

where $g = 2\{h(l^2 + m^2) + lm\}$, $f = -k\{(l^2 + m^2) + mn\}$

and $c = (l^2 + m^2)(h^2 + k^2) - n^2$

Now, S (h, k) = (3, –4)

and lx + my + n = x + y – 2

giving h = 3, k = –4, l = 1, m = 1, n = –2

$\therefore g = 2\{3(1+1)+1\} = 14$

$f = -(-4)\{(1+1)+(-2)\} = 0$

$c = (1+1)(9+16)-(4) = 46$

$\therefore$ equation of the parabola is

$(x-y)^2 = -2(14x + 0.y) - 46$

or $(x-y)^2 = -2x - 46$

or $x^2 + y^2 - 2xy + 2x + 46 = 0$

(b) Find the equation of the plane which passes through the line of intersection of the planes 2x – 3y + z – 4 = 0 and x – y + z + 1 = 0 and which is perpendicular to the plane x + 2y – 3z + 6 = 0.

Ans. Same as Chapter-4, Q.No.-9 (Solved Examples)

Q2. (a) Find the new equation of the conic $x^2 + y^2 + 4x - 2y + 4 = 0$ after shifting the origin to (– 2, 1) and then rotating the axes through 45°.

Ans. Same as Chapter-1, Q.No.-8 (Solved Examples)

(b) Find the centre and radius of the sphere $2x^2 + 2y^2 + 2z^2 - 16x + 8y + 16z + 23 = 0$. Hence, determine whether the point (1, 4, 2) lies inside or outside the sphere.

Ans. Same as Chapter-4, Q.No.-24 (Solved Examples)

Q3. (a) Find the centre of the conicoid $9x^2 + 4y^2 + 4z^2 + 4x + y + 10z + 1 = 0$. Hence reduce it to standard form. Also identify the type of the conicoid.

Ans. Same as Chapter-6, Q.No.-1 (Solved Examples)

Since a, b, c all are positives, so this is an

(i) ellipsoid, if $d \neq 0$

(ii) cone, if $d = 0$

(b) Reduce the following equations to cartesian form and identify the curves they represent:

(i) $r \cos\left(\theta - \frac{\pi}{4}\right) = \sqrt{2}$

(ii) $r^2 = 3r \sin\theta$

Ans. Same as Chapter-2, Q.No.-25 (Solved Examples)

Q4. (a) Find the equation of the right circular cone whose vertex is (1, 1, 0), axis is $\frac{x-1}{2} = \frac{y-1}{2} = z$ and semi-vertical angle is $60°$. Further, find the section of the cone with the plane $x = 2$.

Ans. Same as Chapter-5, Q.No.-25 (Solved Examples) and Chapter-6, Q.No.-16 (Solved Examples)

(b) Find the section of the conicoid $y^2 - 3z^2 = x$ by the plane $y = 2$. Identify the curve represented by the section.

Ans. Same as Chapter-6, Q.No.-16 (Solved Examples)

Q5. Which of the following statements are true and which ones are false? Give reasons for your answers.

(a) The equation $x + 3y = 0$ represents a line in 3-dimensional space.

Ans. False.

Explanation: The equation $x + 3y = 0$ is given in 3-D space.

Since, in 2-D space a linear equation represents a line, while in 3-D space a linear equation represents a plane. This is a linear equation in 3-D space, so this equation represents a plane, not a line.

(b) The conics $y^2 = 2x$ and $y^2 - x^2 = 1$ do not intersect.

Ans. False.

Explanation: If (x_1, y_1) is a point of intersection,

then $y_1^2 = 2x, \ y_1^2 - x_1^2 = 1$

Eliminating y, from the equations, we get

$2x_1 - x_1^2 = 1 \ \Rightarrow x_1^2 - 2x_1 + 1 = 0$

$\Rightarrow (x_1 - 1)^2 = 0, \text{ so } x_1 = 1$

Then $y_1^2 = 2x_1$, gives us

$y_1^2 = 2(1)$

or $y_1^2 = 2$

or $y_1 = \pm 2$

Thus, therefore two points of intersection, namely:
(1, 2) and (1, – 2).
Hence the two conics will intersect.

(c) The plane x + y + z = 0 touches the cone $x^2 + y^2 + z^2 + 2yz + 2zx + 2xy = 0$.
Ans. True.
Explanation: x + y + z = 0
gives u =1, v = 1, w = 1
and $x^2 + y^2 + z^2 + 2yz + 2zx + 2xy = 0$
gives a = 1, b = 1, c = 1, h = 1, g = 1, f = 1
Now,

$$\begin{vmatrix} a & h & g & u \\ h & b & f & v \\ g & f & c & w \\ u & v & w & o \end{vmatrix} = \begin{vmatrix} 1 & 1 & 1 & 1 \\ 1 & 1 & 1 & 1 \\ 1 & 1 & 1 & 1 \\ 1 & 1 & 1 & 1 \end{vmatrix} = 0$$

which shows that the plane touches the cone.

(d) Every planar section of a paraboloid is a parabola.
Ans. False.
Explanation: Planer section of a paraboloid is always a parabola if and only, w = 0, otherwise it can be a hyperbola or a parabola or an ellipse.

(e) A curve which is symmetric about the origin is symmetric about both the coordinate axes.
Ans. False.
Explanation: A curve which is symmetric about the origin is not necessary to be symmetric about both the coordinate axis. e.g. the line y = x is not symmetric about any of the axes, but it is symmetric about the origin.

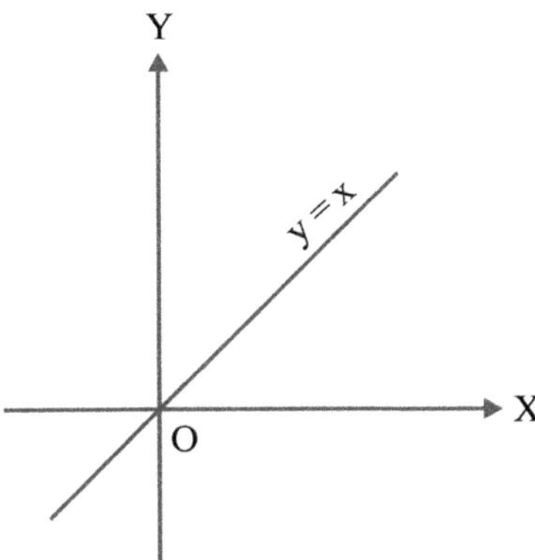

Fig.: Graph for line y = x

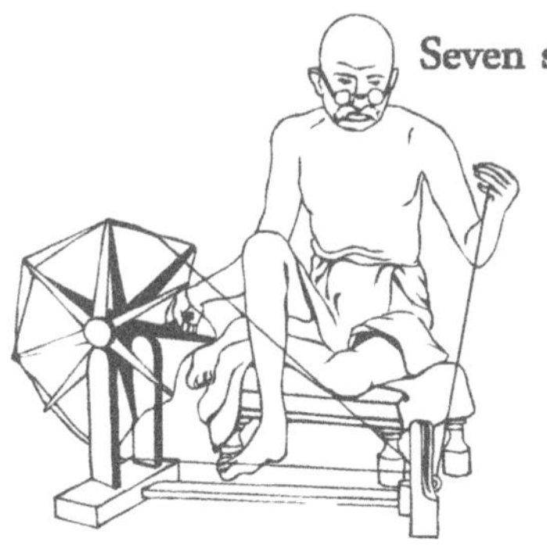

Seven social sins: Politics without principles,

wealth without work,

pleasure without conscience,

knowledge without character,

commerce without morality,

science without humanity,

and worship without sacrifice.

MTE-5 : ANALYTICAL GEOMETRY

June, 2017

Note : Question no. 5 is **compulsory.** Answer any **three** questions from question no. 1 to 4. Use of calculators is not allowed.

Q1. (a) Find the eccentricity, foci and centre of the conic $4x^2+9y^2=36$. Draw a rough sketch of it.

(b) Show that the plane $2x-4y-z+9=0$ touches the sphere which passes through (1, 1, 6) and whose centre is (2, –3, 4). Also, find the point of contact.

Q2. (a) Find the equation of the cone whose vertex is at the origin and base is the circle $x=a,\ y^2+z^2=b^2$.

(b) Find the equation of the line which is parallel to the line 3x + 4y = 1 and which passes through the mid-point of the line segment joining (1, 2) and (–2, 1). Find the distance of this line from the given line.

Q3. (a) Check whether the following equations represent a paraboloid or not. For those that do classify them as elliptic or hyperbolic paraboloid.

(i) $x^2+y^2+z^2-2x+4y=1$

(ii) $4y^2-4z^2-x-10y-6z-3=0$

(b) Find the angle between the lines

$$\frac{x+1}{-3}=\frac{y-3}{2}=z+2 \text{ and } x=\frac{y-7}{-3}=\frac{z+7}{2}.$$

Q4. (a) Find the sections of the conicoid

$$\frac{x^2}{36}+\frac{y^2}{9}-\frac{z^2}{4}=x^2-1$$

by the coordinate planes and identify them.

(b) Find the equation of the cylinder whose base is the circle $x^2+y^2+z^2=4,\ x+y+2z=3$

Q5. Which of the following statements are true and which are false? Justify your answer.

(a) The line x + 1 = 1 – y = –5z lies in the plane 2x + 3y – 5z = 1.

(b) The line $x = y = z - 1$ intersects the cone $x^2 + y^2 + z^2 + 2yz + 2zx + 2xy = 0$ at exactly one point.

(c) The section of the conicoid $3x^2 - y^2 + z^2 = 1$ by the plane $y + 2z = 4$ is an ellipse.

(d) The projection of the line segment joining (1, 2, –1) and (4, 2, 1) on the line $\frac{x}{2} = -y = z$ is 7/2.

(e) The equation $x^2 + y^2 - 2xy + 2x + 1 = 0$ represents a parabola.

MTE-5 : ANALYTICAL GEOMETRY
December, 2017

Note : Question no. 5 is **compulsory.** Attempt any **three** questions from question no. 1 to 4. Use of calculators is not allowed.

Q1. (a) Find the equation of the plane passing through the points (1, 0, 1) , (2, 1, –1) and (0, 1, 0).
Ans. Same as Chapter-4, Q.No.-3 (Solved Examples)

(b) Obtain the equation of the conic, a focus of which lies at (2, 1), the directrix of which is x + y = 0 and which passes through (1, 4). Also identify the conic.
Ans. Same as Chapter-2, Q.No.-1 (Solved Examples)

Q2. (a) Find the equation of the right circular cylinder whose base curve is $x^2 + y^2 + z^2 = 16, x - y + z = 6$.
Ans. Same as Chapter-5, Q.No.-19 (Solved Examples)

(b) Find the new equation of the curve $x^2 + y^2 - 6x + 2y + 1 = 0$ **by shifting the origin to (3, –1) without changing the direction of the axes.**
Ans. Same as Chapter-1, Q.No.-17

Q3. (a) Find the equation of the right circular cone whose vertex is (1, –1, 2), the axis is
$\frac{x-1}{2} = \frac{y+1}{1} = \frac{z-2}{-2}$ **and the semi-vertical angle is** 45°.
Ans. Same as Chapter-5, Q.No.-25 (Solved Examples)

(b) Trace the conic obtained by the intersection of yz-plane with the conicoid $\frac{x^2}{4} + \frac{y^2}{9} - \frac{z^2}{16} = -1$.
Ans. Same as Chapter-6, Q.No.-11 (Solved Examples)

Q4. (a) Show that if ux + vy + wz = p is a tangent plane to the paraboloid $ax^2 + by^2 = 2z$, **then** $\frac{u^2}{a} + \frac{v^2}{b} + 2pw = 0$.
Ans. Same as Chapter-6, Page No.-142-143
(b) Reduce the following equations to Cartesian form:

(i) $2r^2(1-\sin 2\theta)+r\cos\theta=0$

(ii) $r^2=\dfrac{4}{2-\sin 2\theta}$

Ans. Same as Chapter-2, Q.No.-25 (Solved Examples)

Q5. Which of the following statements are true and which are false? Justify your answers.

(a) The angle between the line x = y = z and the plane 2x – y + z = 1 is $\sin^{-1}\left(\dfrac{\sqrt{2}}{3}\right)$.

Ans. Same as Chapter-3, Q.No.-1 (Solved Examples)

(b) The projection of the line segment joining (2, –1, 3) and (4, 1, 0) on the x-axis is 2.

Ans. False

(c) The equation $x^2+2xy+yz+1=0$ **represents a central conicoid.**

Ans. False

(d) The line x –1 = y = z is a tangent to the sphere $x^2+y^2+z^2=1$

Ans. True, because, a line intersects a sphere at most two points. It is a tangent of the sphere. If it intersects the sphere at only two point.

(e) The eccentricity of $x^2-y^2=9$ **is 3.**

Ans. True.

MTE-5 : ANALYTICAL GEOMETRY
June, 2018

Note : Question no. 1 is **compulsory.** Do any **three** questions from questions no. 2 to 5. Use of calculators is not allowed.

Q1. Are the following statements true or false? Justify your answer with a short proof or a counter-example.

(a) The line ax + by = 0 is tangent to the conic $x^2 + y^2 + 2ax + 2by = 1$, where a and b are non-zero constants.

Ans. False.

Given line is

$ax + by = 0$

comparing this line with $px + qy + r = 0$, then we have

$p = a, q = b, r = 0$

Given conic is

$x^2 + y^2 + 2ax + 2by = 1$

comparing this conic with

$ax^2 + 2hxy + by^2 + 2gx + 2fy + c = 0,$

we have

$a = 1, h = 0, b = 1, g = a, f = b, c = -1$

Now, we have the following determinant

$$\begin{vmatrix} a & h & g & p \\ h & b & f & q \\ g & f & c & r \\ p & q & r & 0 \end{vmatrix} = \begin{vmatrix} 1 & 0 & a & a \\ 0 & 1 & b & b \\ a & b & -1 & 0 \\ a & b & 0 & 0 \end{vmatrix} = (-1)^{4+1} a \begin{vmatrix} 0 & a & a \\ 1 & b & b \\ b & -1 & 0 \end{vmatrix} + (-1)^{4+2} b \begin{vmatrix} 1 & a & a \\ 0 & b & b \\ a & -1 & 0 \end{vmatrix}$$

$$= -a\left[-a\left(0 - b^2\right) + a\left(-1 - b^2\right)\right] + b\left[1(0 + b) - a(0 - ab) + a(0 - ab)\right]$$

$$= -a\left[ab^2 - a - ab^2\right] + b\left[b + a^2b - a^2 b\right]$$

$$= a^2 + b^2 \neq 0$$

Therefore, Given line is not a tangent of given conic.

(b) The equation $x^2 + xy + \lambda(x + y) = 0$ represents a pair of straight lines for all $\lambda \in R$.

Ans. True.

Given equation is

$x^2 + xy + \lambda(x + y) = 0$

comparing this equation with

$ax^2 + 2hxy + by^2 + 2gx + 2fy + c = 0,$

we have

$a = 1,\ h = 1/2,\ b = 0,\ 2g = \lambda \Rightarrow g = \frac{\lambda}{2}$

$2f = \lambda \Rightarrow f = \frac{\lambda}{2},\ c = 0$

Now, we have the following determinant:

$$\begin{vmatrix} a & h & g \\ h & b & f \\ g & f & c \end{vmatrix} = \begin{vmatrix} 1 & 1/2 & \frac{\lambda}{2} \\ \frac{1}{2} & 0 & \frac{\lambda}{2} \\ \frac{\lambda}{2} & \frac{\lambda}{2} & 0 \end{vmatrix}$$

$$= 1\left(0 - \frac{\lambda^2}{2}\right) \frac{-1}{2}\left(0 - \frac{\lambda^2}{4}\right) + \frac{\lambda}{2}\left(\frac{\lambda}{4} - 0\right)$$

$$= -\frac{\lambda^2}{4} + \frac{1}{2}\frac{\lambda^2}{4} + \frac{1}{2}\frac{\lambda^2}{4}$$

$$= -\frac{\lambda^2}{4} + \frac{\lambda^2}{4} = 0$$

Therefore, the equation $x^2 + xy + \lambda(x + y) = 0$ represents a pair of straight lines for all $\lambda \in \mathbf{R}$.

(c) The planes x + y – z + 1 = 0 and 3x + 3y – 3z = 0 are parallel.

Ans. True.

Given planes are $x + y - z + 1 = 0$

and $3x + 3y - 3z = 0$

Here, $\frac{a_1}{a_2} = \frac{1}{3},\ \frac{b_1}{b_2} = \frac{1}{3},\ \frac{c_1}{c_2} = \frac{1}{3}$

$\Rightarrow \frac{a_1}{a_2} = \frac{b_1}{b_2} = \frac{c_1}{c_2}$

Therefore, given planes are parallel.

(d) The xy-plane intersects the sphere $x^2 + y^2 + z^2 - 2x - 2y + 1 = 0$ in a great circle.

Ans. Same as Chapter-4, Q.No.-43 (Pg. No.-110)

(e) The section of a paraboloid by a plane is a parabola.

Ans. False.

For example, the conic section formed by taking the planar section of the paraboloid $\frac{x^2}{2} - \frac{y^2}{3} = z$ by the plane 3 (x – y) + 4z + 2 = 0 is hyperbola.

Q2. (a) Find the points of intersection of the conics $a^2x^2 - b^2y^2 = 1$ and $b^2x^2 + a^2y^2 = 1$.

Ans. Same as Chapter-3, Q.No.-7 (Pg. No.-61)

(b) Find the centre and radius of the sphere passing through (1, 0, 0), (0, 1, 1), (0, 0, 1) and $\left(\frac{1}{\sqrt{2}}, \frac{1}{\sqrt{2}}, \frac{1}{\sqrt{2}}\right)$.

Ans. Same as Chapter-4, Q.No.-12 and Q.No.-24 (Pg. No.-90, 97)

Q3. (a) Identify and trace the conic $x^2 - 2y^2 + 2x + 4y - 3 = 0$.

Ans. Same as Chapter-3, Q.No.-15 and Q.No.-19 (Pg. No.-67, 73)

(b) Find the equation of the plane passing through the line $\frac{x}{2} = \frac{y-2}{4} = \frac{z-1}{3}$ and the point (–1, –1, –1).

Ans. Same as Chapter-4, Q.No.-6 (Pg. No.-88)

Q4. (a) Check whether the surface represented by $x^2 + y^2 = 2(z+1)$ is symmetric about the YZ-plane, ZX-plane and XY-plane. Do the coordinate axes intersect the surface?

Ans. Given surface is

$x^2+y^2=2(z+1)=f(x,y,z)$ [Let]

Transform $z \longrightarrow -z$, we have

$x^2+y^2=2(-z+1)$

Therefore, $f(x, y, -z) \neq f(x, y, z)$

So, given surface is not symmetrical about XY-plane.

Now transform $x \longrightarrow -x$, we have

$(-x)^2+y^2=2(z+1)$

$\Rightarrow x^2+y^2=2(z+1)$

$\Rightarrow f(-x,y,z)=f(x,y,z)$

so, surface is symmetrical about YZ-plane. Similarly, transforming $y \longrightarrow -y$, we have

$x^2+(-y)^2=2(z+1)$

$x^2+y^2=2(z+1)$

$\Rightarrow f(x,-y,z)=f(x,y,z)$

so, surface is symmetrical about XZ-plane.

Now, putting $x = y = 0$ in given surface, we get

$0 + 0 = 2z + 2$

$\Rightarrow 2z = -2$

$\Rightarrow z = -1$

so, Z-axis intersects the surface at the point (0, 0, –1).

Now, putting $y = z = 0$, we have

$x^2+0=2(0+1)$

$x^2 = 2$

$x = \pm 1.414$

so, X-axis intersects the surface at (± 1.414, 0, 0)

Now, putting $x = z = 0$, we get

$0+y^2=2(0+1)$

$y^2 = 2$

$y = \pm 1.414$

so, Y-axis intersects the surface at (0, ± 1.414, 0)

(b) Find the equation of the cylinder whose base is the circle $x^2 + y^2 = 4,\ z = 0$ and the axis is $x = \frac{y}{2} = z$.

Ans. Same as Chapter-5, Q.No.-7 (Pg. No.-126)

Q5. Find the new equation of the conicoid $4x^2 + 4y^2 - 8z^2 - xy + 5yz + 5zx = 0$ under the transformations given by the following table:

	x	y	z
x′	$\frac{4}{9}$	$\frac{4}{9}$	$\frac{7}{9}$
y′	$\frac{-8}{9}$	$\frac{1}{9}$	$\frac{4}{9}$
z′	$\frac{1}{9}$	$\frac{-8}{9}$	$\frac{4}{9}$

Ans. Same as Chapter-6, Q.No.-4 (Pg. No.-145).

MTE-5 : ANALYTICAL GEOMETRY
December, 2018

Note : Question no. 1 is **compulsory.** Do any **three** questions from questions no. 2 to 5. Use of calculators is not allowed.

Q1. Are the following statements true or false? Justify your answer with a short proof or a counter-example.

(a) There are more than one plane passing through the line $\frac{x}{2}=\frac{y}{4}=\frac{z-1}{3}$ and the point (2, 0, 1).

(b) Normal to the conic $x^2+4ay=0,\ a>0$ at the origin is the y-axis.

(c) The Cartesian form of the polar equation $r=\frac{2}{1-\cos\theta}$ is $y^2=4+2x$.

(d) $S=\{(x,\ y,\ z)\in R^3 \mid x^2+z^2=4\}$ represents a circle.

(e) The line x = y = z touches the conicoid $\frac{x^2}{2}+\frac{y^2}{4}+\frac{z^2}{6}=1$.

Q2. (a) Find the vertices, eccentricity, foci and directrices of the conic $4x^2-y^2=16$.

(b) Show that if the line ax + by = 1 touches the conic $x^2+y^2+2gx+2fy+c=0$, then $(a^2+b^2)(g^2+f^2-c)=(ag+bf+1)^2$.

Q3. (a) Find the equation of the plane passing through the points (a, 1, 1) (1, a, 1) and (1, 1, a), where a '" 1.

(b) To which point should the origin be shifted so that the curve $x^2+y^2+2x+2y+1=0$ transforms into $x^{1^2}+y^{1^2}=1$? Justify.

Q4. (a) Trace the conicoid represented by the equation $-x^2-y^2+\frac{z^2}{4}=1$.

(b) Find the reciprocal cone of the cone $x^2+y^2=2(xz+yz)$.

Q5. (a) Find the equations of the spheres that pass through the circle $x^2+y^2+z^2-x-y-z=1,\quad x+y+z=0$ and touch the place $2x-y-z=2\sqrt{2}$.

(b) Check whether the conicoid $2x^2+y^2-z^2+2zx+z=1$ has a centre or not.

MTE-5 : ANALYTICAL GEOMETRY
June, 2019

Note : Question no. 1 is **compulsory.** Do any **three** questions from questions no. 2 to 5. Use of calculators is not allowed.

Q1. (a) Find the equation of conic with focus (1, 0), eccentricity $\frac{3}{2}$ and $x + y = 0$ as its directrix.

(b) Find the equation of the plane passing through the lines $\frac{x+4}{3} = \frac{y}{2} = \frac{z-1}{3}$ and $\frac{x}{2} = y - 1 = z$.

Q2. (a) Check whether the plane $2x + y - z = 2$ cuts the sphere $x^2 + y^2 + z^2 + \frac{1}{2}x - \frac{3}{2}y + \frac{1}{2} = 0$ or not.

(b) Trace the conicoid $\frac{x^2}{4} + \frac{y^2}{9} + \frac{z^2}{4} = 1$.

Q3. (a) Find the equation of the cylinder passing through the curve:

$x^2 + y^2 + z^2 = 1,$

$x + y + z = 1$

(b) Check the symmetry of the curve:

$\frac{1}{x^2} + y^2 = a(x^3 + y^3)$, $a \in \mathbb{R}$ about the coordinate axes and the origin.

Q4. (a) Find the centre of the conicoid $3x^2 + y^2 + z^2 + 2xy + 2yz + x + 2z = 0$. What will be the new equation if the origin is shifted to the centre?

(b) Find the equation of the sphere which has (1, –1, 0) and (3, 3, 2) as the ends of its diameter.

Q5. Which of the following statements are true and which ones are false? Give reasons for your answer:

(a) the triple $-\frac{1}{2}, \frac{3}{4}, \frac{1}{2}$ represents the direction cosines of a line.

(b) The equation $x = z$ represents a line in three dimensional space.

(c) A tangent plane to a cone touches it at only one point.

(d) The normals at the points (4a, –4a) and (4a, 4a) are perpendicular to each other.

(e) The projection of the line segment joining (1, 1, 0) and (–1, 2, 3) on the line:

$\frac{x-1}{2} = \frac{Y-3}{3} = \frac{z-1}{4}$ is 9.

MTE-5 : ANALYTICAL GEOMETRY
December, 2019

Note: Question no. 5 is compulsory. Answer any three from the rest of the questions. Use of calculators is not allowed.

Q1. (a) Find the value of a so that the line $\frac{x}{a} = y = \frac{z-1}{2}$ lies in the plane $2x + 3y + z = 1$.

Ans. Since the line $\frac{x}{a} = \frac{y}{1} = \frac{z-1}{2}$

lies in the plane $2x + 3y + z = 1$

so

$2a + 3(1) + 1(2) = 0$

or $2a + 3 + 2 = 0$

$\Rightarrow 2a + 5 = 0$

$\Rightarrow 2a = -5$

$\Rightarrow a = \frac{-5}{2}$

(b) Find the foci, eccentricity, directrix and the asymptotes of the conic $3x^2 - 4y^2 = 5$.

Ans. Focus of a hyperbola = $(\pm ae, o)$ ...(i)

Directrix is $x = -\frac{a}{e}$ ...(ii)

and equation is $\frac{x^2}{a^2} - \frac{y^2}{b^2} = 1$ ...(iii)

where $b^2 = a^2(e^2 - 1)$ ...(iv)

Asymptotes of the hyperbola are given by the equations $y = \pm\frac{b}{a}x$ ...(v)

Now, Given equation of the conic is $3x^2 - 4y^2 = 5$ which is a hyperbola. It can be written in standard form as:

$$\frac{x^2}{20} - \frac{y^2}{15} = \frac{1}{12}$$

or $$\frac{x^2}{5/3} - \frac{y^2}{5/4} = 1$$

or $\dfrac{x^2}{\left(\sqrt{5/3}\right)^2}-\dfrac{y^2}{\left(\sqrt{5/4}\right)^2}=1$ ...(vi)

$\Rightarrow a=\sqrt{5/3},\ b=\sqrt{5/4},\ a^2=5/3,\quad b^2=5/4$

So, From (iv)

$\dfrac{5}{4}=\dfrac{5}{3}\left(e^2-1\right)$

$\Rightarrow \dfrac{1}{4}=\dfrac{1}{3}\left(e^2-1\right)$

$\Rightarrow \dfrac{3}{4}+1=e^2$

$\Rightarrow \dfrac{3+4}{4}=e^2$

$\Rightarrow \dfrac{7}{4}=e^2$

$\Rightarrow e=\dfrac{\sqrt{7}}{2}$

from (ii) $x=\dfrac{-\sqrt{5/3}}{\sqrt{7/2}}$

or $x=-\dfrac{\sqrt{5}}{\sqrt{3}}\times\dfrac{2}{\sqrt{7}}$

or $x=\dfrac{-2\sqrt{5}}{\sqrt{21}}$

(equation of directrix)

from (i) Focci = $\left(\pm\sqrt{5/3}\times\sqrt{7/2},0\right)$

$=\left(\pm\dfrac{1}{2}\sqrt{\dfrac{35}{3}},\ 0\right)$

and Asymptotes of the hyperbola are given by the equations

$y=\pm\dfrac{\sqrt{5/4}}{\sqrt{5/3}}x$

or $y=\pm\sqrt{\dfrac{3}{4}}x$

or $2y=\pm\sqrt{3}x$

Q2. (a) Find the equation of the circle $(x-1)^2+y^2=1$ when are axes are rotated by 45⁰.

Ans. Let origin is kept fixed and the x' and y' axes are obtained by rotating the x and y axes counter clockwise through an angle 45°.

A point P has coordinates (x, y) with respect to the original system and coordinates (x', y') with respect to the new system, then

$$x = x'\cos 45^\circ - y'\sin 45^\circ$$

$$y = x'\sin 45^\circ + y'\cos 45^\circ$$

substituting these values in the original (given) equation of the sphere

$$(x-1)^2+y^2=1$$

we obtain,

$$\left(x'\cos 45^\circ - y'\sin 45^\circ - 1\right)^2 + \left(x'\sin 45^\circ + y'\cos 45^\circ\right)^2 = 1$$

$$\Rightarrow \left(x'\cdot\frac{1}{\sqrt{2}} - y'\cdot\frac{1}{\sqrt{2}} - 1\right)^2 + \left(x'\cdot\frac{1}{\sqrt{2}} + y'\cdot\frac{1}{\sqrt{2}}\right)^2 = 1$$

$$\Rightarrow \left(\frac{x'}{\sqrt{2}} - \frac{y'}{\sqrt{2}} - 1\right)^2 + \left(\frac{x'}{\sqrt{2}} + \frac{y'}{\sqrt{2}}\right)^2 = 1$$

$$\Rightarrow \frac{x'^2}{2} + \frac{y'^2}{2} + 1 + \left(\frac{-2x'y'}{2}\right) + \left(-2\frac{x'}{\sqrt{2}}\right) + 2\frac{y'}{\sqrt{2}}\cdot 1 + \frac{x'^2}{2} + \frac{y'^2}{2} + \frac{2x'y'}{2} = 1$$

$$\Rightarrow \frac{2x'^2}{2} + \frac{2y'^2}{2} - x'y' - \frac{2x'}{\sqrt{2}} + \frac{2y'}{\sqrt{2}} + x'y' = 0$$

$$\Rightarrow x'^2 + y'^2 - \sqrt{2}x' + \sqrt{2}y' = 0$$

This is the required equation of the circle which is obtained by rotation the axes by 45°.

(b) Find the equation of the sphere passing through the points (1, 1, 0) (0, 0, 1) (1, 0, -1) and (1, 1, 1).

Ans. Same as Chapter-4, Q.No.-12 (Solved Examples)

Q3. (a) Check whether the cones $\frac{x^2}{2}+\frac{y^2}{3}+\frac{y^2}{4}=0$ and $2x^2+3y^2+4z^2=0$ are reciprocal or not.

Ans. Refer to Chapter-5, Q.No.-9 (Solved Examples)

(b) Find the section of the conicoid $y^2+2z^2=x$ by the plane x + y = 1. What object does it represent?

Ans. Refer to June-2007, Q.No.-1 (b)

Q4. (a) Find the direction cosines of the line which is perpendicular to both the lines with direction cosines $\frac{1}{\sqrt{6}}, \frac{2}{\sqrt{6}}, \frac{1}{\sqrt{6}}$ and $\frac{2}{\sqrt{21}}, \frac{1}{\sqrt{21}}, \frac{-4}{\sqrt{21}}$.

Ans. d.c's of first line are:

$$\frac{1}{\sqrt{6}}, \frac{2}{\sqrt{6}}, \frac{1}{\sqrt{6}}$$

so the d.r's of this line are:

1, 2, 1 ...(i)

and d.c's of second line are:

$$\frac{2}{\sqrt{21}}, \frac{1}{\sqrt{21}}, \frac{-4}{\sqrt{21}}$$

so the d.r's of this line are:

2, 1, –4 ...(ii)

Let the d.r's of the perpendiculars to both lines are a, b, c, ...(iii)

from (i) and (iii) & (ii) and (iii)

from $a + 2b + c = 0$ ...(iv) [lines are ⊥]

$2a + b - 4c = 0$ ...(v)

[lines are ⊥]

from (iv) & (v)

$$\frac{a}{-8-1} = \frac{b}{2+4} = \frac{c}{1-4} = k$$

$$\Rightarrow \frac{a}{-9} = \frac{b}{6} = \frac{c}{-3} = k$$

$$\Rightarrow \frac{a}{-3} = \frac{b}{2} = \frac{c}{-1} = k$$

$$\Rightarrow -\frac{a}{3} = \frac{b}{2} = -\frac{c}{1} = k$$

$$\Rightarrow a = -3k, b = 2k, c = -k$$

∴ d.r's are –3k, 2k, –k

or –3, 2, –1

Hence a.c's are: $\frac{-3}{\sqrt{9+4+1}}, \frac{2}{\sqrt{9+4+1}}, \frac{-1}{\sqrt{9+4+1}}$

$$= \frac{-3}{\sqrt{14}}, \frac{2}{\sqrt{14}}, \frac{-1}{\sqrt{14}}$$

(b) Identify the type of the conicoid $2x^2 - y^2 - z^2 - 8x - 2y - 2z + 7 = 0$. Give a rough sketch of it.

Ans. Same as Chapter-6, Q.No.-7

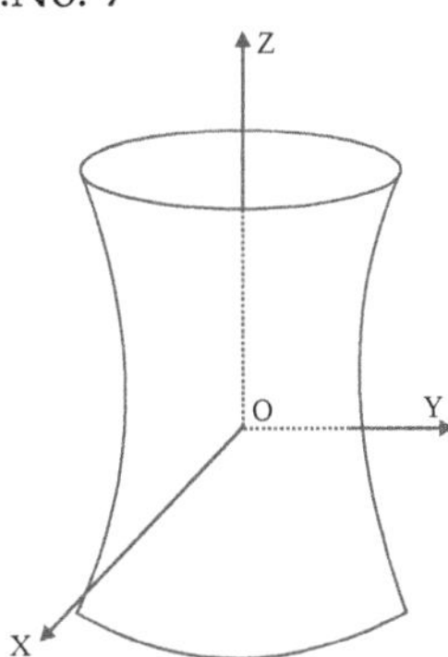

The hyperboloid of one sheet $\frac{x^2}{a^2}+\frac{y^2}{b^2}-\frac{z^2}{c^2}=1.$

Q5. Which of the following statements are true and which ones are false? Give reasons for your answers.

(a) The tangents at the points (a, 2a) and (a, -2a) on the parabola $y^2 = 4ax$ are perpendicular to each other.

Ans. False. Because the parabola is symmetric about x axis and these two points are symmetric about the point (a, 0) and so the given condition is impossible.

(b) The equation $ax^2 + by^2 + cz^2 + 2ux + 2vy + 2wz + d = 0, \quad abc \neq 0$, always represents a central conicoid.

Ans. True. $\begin{vmatrix} a & h & g \\ h & b & f \\ g & f & c \end{vmatrix} \neq 0$

(c) The equation $x^2 + y^2 = 1$ represents a cylinder in three dimensional space.

Ans. True. This is the equation of a cylinder with infinite length and with radius '1' (axis of the cylinder is z-axis)

(d) If a curve is symmetrical about the origin, it is symmetrical about the x-axis.

Ans. False. Because it is not necessary.

(e) The equation $4x^2 + 9y^2 + 12xy - 8x - 12y + 4 = 0$ represents a pair of coincident lines.

Ans. True. Same as Chapter-2, Q.No.-35

www.ingramcontent.com/pod-product-compliance
Ingram Content Group UK Ltd.
Pitfield, Milton Keynes, MK11 3LW, UK
UKHW021706190726
13853UKWH00001B/434